W. N. M. Geary

The Law of Theatres and Music-Halls

W. N. M. Geary
The Law of Theatres and Music-Halls
ISBN/EAN: 9783743393240
Manufactured in Europe, USA, Canada, Australia, Japa
Cover: Foto ©Suzi / pixelio.de

Manufactured and distributed by brebook publishing software (www.brebook.com)

W. N. M. Geary

The Law of Theatres and Music-Halls

THE LAW

OF

THEATRES AND MUSIC-HALLS

INCLUDING

CONTRACTS AND PRECEDENTS OF CONTRACTS.

BY

W. N. M. GEARY,

OF CHRIST CHURCH, OXFORD, AND OF THE INNER TEMPLE, BARRISTER-AT-LAW,
J. P. FOR THE COUNTY OF KENT.

WITH

HISTORICAL INTRODUCTION

By JAMES WILLIAMS, B.C.L., M.A.,

OF LINCOLN COLLEGE, OXFORD, AND OF LINCOLN'S INN, BARRISTER-AT-LAW.

Σκηνὴ πᾶς ὁ βίος καὶ παίγνιον· ἢ μάθε παίζειν,
Τὴν σπουδὴν μεταθεὶς, ἢ φέρε τὰς ὀδύνας.

PALLADAS.

LONDON:

STEVENS AND SONS, 119, CHANCERY LANE,
Law Publishers and Booksellers.

1885

TO

The Right Honourable LORD BRAMWELL

This Work

IS

BY HIS LORDSHIP'S PERMISSION

RESPECTFULLY DEDICATED.

PREFACE.

This is an attempt to throw together, for the use of laymen as well as of the profession, the law governing the most usual kinds of public amusement in London and the Provinces. As far as I am aware, there is no work dealing with the subject in a separate form. I had at first proposed to include a Chapter on Copyright, but that branch of the subject has been so amply treated in works specially devoted to Copyright, that I felt that in dealing with such a matter I should only be going over ground which had been more worthily occupied before me. I wish to take this opportunity of thanking Mr. James Williams, of the Northern Circuit, for much trouble bestowed upon other parts of the Work besides the Introduction, for which he alone is responsible. In addition, I must acknowledge my obligations to Mr. E. F. S. Pigott, the Examiner of Stage Plays, to Mr. Wilson Barrett and Mr. Augustus Moore, and to the Town Clerks and Clerks to the Justices of numerous towns in Great Britain, for the courtesy and assistance which I have received from them. Where the name of a town of importance does not occur in the Appendix, it is to be presumed either that there are no local regulations or that no information has been received. Any suggestions, whether from members of the profession or others, will be welcomed in view of a second Edition.

W. N. M. G.

2, PUMP COURT, TEMPLE,
    25*th March*, 1885.

TABLE OF CONTENTS.

	PAGE
TABLE OF CASES .	ix

INTRODUCTION 1

CHAPTER I.
THE THEATRE.

SECT.
1. Building 15
2. Performance 16
3. Stage Play 18
4. Licensing of Stage Play 23
5. Licensing of Theatres 25
6. Appeal from Justices 33
7. Penalties 34
8. Structure 38
9. Police 42

CHAPTER II.
THE MUSIC-HALL.

1. What is a Music-Hall 47
2. Licensing 52
3. Penalties 56

CHAPTER III.

CONTRACTS.

SECT.	PAGE
1. Concerning the Building	59
2. Between Manager and Performer	78
Precedents	119

CHAPTER IV.

TORTS AND CRIMES . . . 125

APPENDIX 139

INDEX 213

TABLE OF CASES.

Arc—Duc.
	PAGE
ARCHER *v.* Willingrice, 4 Esp. 186	48
Ashley *v.* Harrison, 1 Esp. 48; Peake, 194	125, 129
BARTLETT *v.* Vinor, Carth. 252	82
Beatty *v.* Mellillo, 10 C. B. 282; 1 L. M. & P. 571; 19 L. J. N. S. C. P. 362	117
Bellis *v.* Beal, 2 Esp. 592	48
Bellis *v.* Burghall, 2 Esp. 722	47
Benwell, *Ex parte*, 14 Q. B. D. 301	119
Bottini *v.* Gye, 1 Q. B. D. 183; 45 L. J. N. S. Q. B. 209; 34 L. T. 246; 24 W. R. 551	86
Blake *v.* Layon, 6 T. R. 221	130
Bowen *v.* Hall, 6 Q. B. D. 333	131
Brown *v.* Nugent, L. R. 6 Q. B. 693; 7 Q. B. 588; 41 L. J. M. C. 166; 26 L. T. 880; 20 W. R. 989	53, 56
CLARK *v.* Bishop, 25 L. T. N. S. 908	20
Clarke *v.* Bradlaugh, 7 Q. B. D. 38; 8 App. Cas. 354	36, *Add.*
Clarke *v.* Searle, 1 Esp. 25	49 n. (*f*)
Clifford *v.* Brandon, 2 Camp. 358	132
Coleman *v.* Foster, 1 H. & N. 37	69
Crepps *v.* Durden, 1 Sm. L. C. 8th ed. 711	33 n. (*i*)
Croft *v.* Lumley, 5 El. & Bl. 648; 6 H. L. Cas. 672; 25 L. J. Q. B. 223; 27 L. J. Q. B. 321; 2 Jur. N. S. 279; 4 Jur. N. S. 903	59
DAUNEY *v.* Chatterton, 44 L. J. C. P. 53; 45 L. J. C. P. 293; 31 L. T. 514; 33 L. T. 628	73
Davys *v.* Douglas, 4 H. & N. 180; 28 L. J. N. S. M. C. 193	15, 17
Day *v.* Simpson, 18 C. B. N. S. 680; 34 L. J. M. C. 149; 11 Jur. N. S. 487; 12 L. T. N. S. 386; 13 W. R. 748	22
De Begnis *v.* Armistead, 10 Bing. 107; 3 Mo. & Sc. 511	81
Duck *v.* Bates, 12 Q. B. D. 79; 13 Q. B. D. 843	18

Ell—Kim.

	PAGE
ELLISON, *Ex parte*, 8 L. T. N. S. 407	117
Ellwood v. Bullock, 6 Q. B. 383	33 n.
Ewing v. Osbaldiston, 2 My. & Cr. 53	11, 62, 64
FECHTER v. Montgomery, 33 Beav. 22	102, 110
Flight v. Glossop, 2 Bing. N. C. 125; 2 Scott, 220; 1 Hodges, 263	68
Fores v. Wilson, 1 Peake, 55	127
Frailing v. Messenger, 16 L. T. N. S. 332, 494	49 n. (*g*)
Frazer v. Bunn, 8 C. & P. 704	115
Fredericks v. Howie, 1 H. & C. 381; 31 L. J. M. C. 249	15, 45
Fredericks v. Payne, 1 H. & C. 584; 32 L. J. M. C. 14; 8 Jur. N. S. 1109	16, 17, 35
GALLINI v. Laborie, 5 T. R. 242	26, 55, 79
Garrett v. Messenger, L. R. 2 C. P. 583; 36 L. J. C. P. 337; 16 L. T. 414; 15 W. R. 164	56
Graddon v. Price, 2 C. & P. 610	111
Grant v. Maddox, 15 M. & W. 737; 16 L. J. N. S. Ex. 227	109, 116
Graves v. Legg, 9 Ex. 716	89
Green v. Botheroyd, 3 C. & P. 471	49 n. (*g*), 56
Gregory v. Duke of Brunswick, 6 M. & G. 205; 1 D. & L. 518; 6 Scott, N. R. 809; 1 C. & K. 24	136
Gregory v. Tuffs, 6 C. & P. 271	50
Guaglieni v. Mathews, 34 L. J. M. C. 116 48 n. (*b*), 49 n. (*f*), 50	
HALL v. Green, 9 Ex. 247	48 n. (*c*)
Harley v. Henderson, The Times, Feb. 18, 19, 1884	114
Helling v. Lumley, 28 L. J. Ch. 249; 4 Jur. N. S. 868; 5 Jur. N. S. 301	69
Hewitt v. Isham, 7 Ex. 77	72 n. (*o*)
Hoffman v. Bond, 32 L. T. N. S. 775	54, 55
INCHBALD v. Robinson, L. R. 4 Ch. 388; 20 L. T. N. S. 259; 17 W. R. 459	38, 57
JACKSON v. Union Marine Insurance Co., L. R. 10 C. P. 141	95
Jelfs v. Ballard, 1 B. & P. 468	52
KEMBLE v. Kean, 6 Sim. 333	101
Kimberley v. Jenning, 6 Sim. 340	101

Lac—R.

	PAGE
LACY v. Osbaldiston, 8 C. & P. 80	113
Langton v. Hughes, 1 M. & S. 596	83
Lea v. Simpson, 4 Dowl. & L. 666; 11 Jur. 127	19, 105
Leader v. Moody, 20 Eq. 145; 23 W. R. 606	75
Leary v. Patrick, 15 Q. B. 266; 19 L. J. M. C. 211	35
Levy v. Yates, 3 N. & P. 249; W. W. & H. 219; 8 A. & E. 129	64
Lewis v. Arnold, 4 C. & P. 354	131
Lumley v. Gye, 2 Ell. & Bl. 216; 22 L. J. Q. B. 463; 17 Jur. 827	126, 127, 128
Lumley v. Wagner, 5 De G. & S. 485; 1 De G. M. & G. 604	97, 128
Lyon v. Knowles, 3 B. & S. 556; 5 B. & S. 751; 32 L. J. Q. B. 71; 9 Jur. N. S. 774; 7 L. T. N. S. 670; 10 L. T. N. S. 876; 11 W. R. 266; 12 W. R. 1083	35 n. (*l*)
MALONE v. Harris, 11 Ir. Ch. R. 33	71
Mapleson v. Bentham, 20 W. R. 176	106
Marks v. Benjamin, 5 M. & W. 565	49
Marsh v. Conquest, 17 C. B. N. S. 418; 33 L. J. C. P. 319; 10 Jur. N. S. 989; 10 L. T. N. S. 717; 12 W. R. 1006	35 n. (*l*)
Mitchel v. Cockburne, 2 H. Bl. 379	82
Montague v. Flockton, 16 Eq. 189; 42 L. J. Ch. 677; 28 L. T. 580; 21 W. R. 668	107
Morris v. Colman, 18 Ves. 437	97, 101
Morris v. Paton, 1 C. & P. 189	110
PARSONS v. Chapman, 5 C. & P. 33	34
Poussard v. Spiers, 1 Q. B. D. 410; 42 L. J Ch. 677; 28 L. T. 580; 21 W. R. 668	90
R. v. Curll, 2 Str. 790	45
R. v. Delaval, 1 W. Bl. 410, 438	138
R. v. Glossop, 4 B. & A. 616	35
R. v. Handy, 6 T. R. 286	19
R. v. Horndon-on-the-Hill, 4 M. & Selw. 562	66
R. v. Moore, 3 B. & Ad. 184	57
R. v. Neville, 1 B. & Ad. 489	11
R. v. St. Martin's-in-the-Fields, 3 Q. B. 204; 11 L. J. M. C. 112	78
R. v. Saunders, 1 Q. B. D. 15	138
R. v. Strugnell, L. R. 1 Q. B. 93; 35 L. J. M. C. 78	25, 26
R. v. Tucker, 2 Q. B. D. 417; 46 L. J. M. C. 197; 36 L. T. 478; 25 W. R. 697	50
R. v. Turner, 5 M. & S. 206	52

Rob—Wood. PAGE

Robertson *v.* Thorne, 47 J. P. 566 . . . . . 40 n. (*t*)
Robinson *v.* Davison, L. R. 6 Ex. 269 . . . 84, 85, 86
Rodwell *v.* Redge, 1 C. & P. 220 80
Russell *v.* Briant, 8 C. B. 836; 19 L. J. C. P. 33; 14 Jur. 201 . . . . 35 n. (*l*)
Russell *v.* Smith, 12 Q. B. 217; 17 L. J. Q. B. 225; 12 Jur. 723; 15 Sim. 181 . . . . 19, 20

SCOTT *v.* Howard, 6 App. Cas. 295 77
Shelley *v.* Bethel, 12 Q. B. D. 11 . . . . . 16, 37
Shutt *v.* Lewis, 5 Esp. 128 . . . . . 48 n. (*d*), 51
Spencer's case, 5 Rep. 16 b 69
Spieres *v.* Parker, 1 T. R. 144 52

TAPLIN *v.* Florence, 10 C. B. 744 73
Tarleton *v.* MacGawley, 1 Esp. 386; 1 Peake, N. P. C. 207 . . . . 126, 130
Tarling *v.* Fredericks, 28 L. T. N. S. 814; 21 W. R. 784 . 16
Taylor *v.* Caldwell, 3 B. & S. 826; 32 L. J. Q. B. 164; 8 L. T. N. S. 356; 11 W. R. 726 61
Taylor *v.* Neri, 1 Esp. 386 . . . . . . 126, 130
Taylor *v.* Waters, 7 Taunt. 374; 2 Marsh. 551 . . 66, 67, 72
Thorne *v.* Colson, 3 L. T. N. S. 697 20

WALKER *v.* Brewster, L. R. 5 Eq. 25 57
Wall *v.* Taylor, 9 Q. B. D. 727; 11 Q. B. D. 102 . . 20
Webster *v.* Dillon, 3 Jur. N. S. 432 . . . . 101, 110
Weldon *v.* Rivière, The Times, Dec. 13, 1884 . . 68
Wigan *v.* Strange, L. R. 1 C. P. 175 . . . . 22, 23
Wilson *v.* Stewart, 3 B. & S. 913; 32 L. J. M. C. 198; 8 L. T. N. S. 277 43
Wood *v.* Leadbitter, 13 M. & W. 538 66

ADDENDUM.

Page 32, note (*e*). It is worthy of remark, as an additional argument, that 28 Geo. III. c. 30, repealed by 6 & 7 Vict. c. 68, provides, that it shall be lawful for the justices, *at their discretion*, to grant a licence for occasional performances. In *Clarke* v. *Bradlaugh*, 8 App. Cas. at p. 368, Lord Selborne, L. C., said, with reference to the interpretation of a new statute by the aid of a statute *in pari materiâ* repealed by it, " the legislature . . . . . . must, I think, be taken to have had under its eyes the provisions and terms . . . . . of the former statutes, and to have deliberately departed from them."

THE LAW

OF

THEATRES AND MUSIC-HALLS.

INTRODUCTION.

THE earliest forms of drama were in England, as in other countries, wholly religious. The first mention of the drama in its religious period is an allusion by Fitzstephen in his life of Becket, written about 1180 (*a*). Miracle plays were acted at first by the clergy themselves, or by persons under their immediate control, such as the parish clerks of Clerkenwell. The existing miracle plays belong to a later period. It does not appear that they were directly acted by ecclesiastical persons, unless in exceptional cases, such as those mentioned by Dean Colet (*b*), though no doubt the authority of the Church was necessary for the performance. The miracle plays were usually acted on Corpus Christi Day, and in a church (*c*), even when the clergy had given place to the great

---

(*a*) *Lundonia pro spectaculis theatralibus, pro ludis scenicis ludos habet sanctiores,* &c.

(*b*) See p. 3.

(*c*) The use of churches for such purposes is illustrated by a mediæval French ordinance, *Statuimus ne choreæ fiant in ecclesiis— quod facientes aut cantilenas cantantes in iisdem excommunicamus, Statuta Synodalia Ecclesiæ Trecorensis*, 1320 (Tréguier in Brittany). A relic of dramatic representation in churches seems still to linger in the Easter service at Seville Cathedral: possibly in other places.

trading guilds as managers of the spectacle. The morals or moral plays (*d*) were a later development in a secular direction, and the "Vice" of the moral play, three times alluded to by Shakespeare (*e*), is an important link of connection between the ancient and modern drama. The discontinuance of religious, or quasi-religious, drama is almost coincident with the rise of the secular drama. The interludes (*f*) of John Heywood marked the transition. While the religious drama was dying out, the theatre was used as a vehicle for enforcing particular religious or political views, not always as orthodox as those of a miracle play. Thus the Act of 34 & 35 Hen. VIII. c. 1, made it criminal to play in an interlude contrary to the orthodox faith declared, or to be declared, by that monarch. Profanity in theatres seems to have been a crying evil of the time. The earliest act of the government of Edward VI. was to pass a statute reciting that the most holy and blessed Sacrament was named in plays by such vile and unseemly words as Christian ears did abhor to hear rehearsed, and inflicting fine and imprisonment upon any person advisedly contemning, despising or reviling the said most blessed Sacrament (*g*). A proclamation of the same king in 1549 forbade the acting of interludes in English, on account of their dealing with sacred subjects. In 1556 the Council called attention to certain lewd persons in the livery of Sir F. Leke representing plays and interludes reflecting upon the Queen and her consort and the formalities of the mass (*h*). By the Act of Uniformity of 1558, it was made

(*d*) The words "mystery" and "morality" seem not to have been used in England.

(*e*) In Twelfth Night, Hamlet and Henry IV. (Part 2).

(*f*) The word "interlude" is interesting as denoting an early development of the drama, the name of which was preserved in legislation after the thing itself had disappeared.

(*g*) 1 Edw. VI. c. 1, s. 1.

(*h*) Strype, Ecclesiastical Memorials, vol. iii., App. 185.

an offence punishable by a fine of a hundred marks to speak anything in the derogation, depraving, or despising of the Book of Common Prayer in any interludes or plays (*i*). In 1605 "An Act to restrain the Abuses of Players" made it an offence punishable by a fine of ten pounds to jestingly or profanely speak or use certain sacred names in any stage play, interlude, show, May-game, or pageant (*k*). The first statute passed in the reign of Charles I. forbade interludes or common plays on the Lord's Day under a penalty of three shillings and fourpence (*l*). In consequence of the appearance of players in the characters of the King of Spain and Gondomar, an ordinance of James I. forbade the representation on the stage of any living Christian king.

The last hold of the Church upon the drama is marked by a sermon of Dean Colet's in 1511, directed against the acting of plays by the clergy, and in the claim of the General Assembly in Scotland to license plays (*m*). The licensing of plays soon passed from the Church, like the licensing of the press, to become a part of the prerogative of the Crown, and through the Crown the franchise of the great nobles. The drama, however, never became a State institution, as in Germany. The king and others maintained companies of their own under various names. The first king who maintained a company of players was Richard III. Most of Shakespeare's plays were acted by "the King's servants" or "the Lord Chamberlain's servants." "Romeo and Juliet" was acted by "the Lord Hunsdon's servants," Massinger's "Virgin Martyr" by the "the servants of His Majesty's Revels," Jonson's "Cynthia's Revels" by "the children of the Queen's Chapel," Lilly's "Campaspe" by "Her

(*i*) 1 Eliz. c. 2, s. 9.
(*k*) 3 Jac. I. c. 21.
(*l*) 1 Car. I. c. 1.
(*m*) See p. 12.

Majesty's children" and "the children of Paul's." Licences to temporary theatres seem to have been granted as early as the reign of Henry VIII. There was no permanent theatre until about 1570 (*n*), before that time plays were acted on scaffolds in the streets or in the yards of inns. The earliest permanent theatre was "The Theatre" in Shoreditch. The earliest patent was that under which the Blackfriars Theatre was erected in 1576. It was granted by Queen Elizabeth in 1574 to Burbage and others, "servants of the Earl of Leicester," empowering them to "use, exercise and occupy the art and faculty of playing comedies, tragedies, interludes, stage-plays, and other such like," allowed by the Master of the Revels. The authority of this officer is traced as far back as 1545, and he seems to have exercised it till 1624, when he was superseded by his official superior, the Lord Chamberlain. The right of the Lord Chamberlain was not acknowledged by statute until 1737 (*o*). In some cases the supervision was delegated, as to Daniel the poet in a warrant of 1603—4. Enrolment in a fixed company, or a patent or licence from the Crown or justices, was necessary for the personal safety of the actors; for now that the protection of the Church was withdrawn, players of any other kind were liable to the severe penalties denounced by the Act of 1572 for the punishment of vagabonds (*p*). It was enacted by that Act, that "all fencers, bearwards, common players in interludes, and minstrels (not belonging to any baron of this realm, or to any other honourable personage of greater degree)" wandering abroad without the licence of two justices at the least, were subject "to be grievously whipped and burned through the gristle of the right ear with a hot

(*n*) It should be noticed that in this as in some of the other dates in this Introduction the authorities are not quite consistent.
(*o*) 10 Geo. II. c. 28.
(*p*) 14 Eliz. c. 5.

iron of the compass of an inch about." This statute was superseded by 39 Eliz. c. 4, under which the punishment of the strolling player is not so severe, and there is no mention of a licence by justices. The jurisdiction of justices over the theatre does not appear again in legislation until 1788 (*q*). In the 39 Eliz. c. 4, there is a remarkable exception in favour of persons licensed by Dutton of Dutton in Cheshire, in accordance with his claim to liberty and jurisdiction in Cheshire and Chester established by proceedings in *quo warranto* in the reign of Henry VII. The stricter wording of this Act as to the licence seems to show that the licence had been abused, perhaps that in some cases privileges had been assumed without authority. In 14 Eliz. the privileges of a player attached by service of a noble or licence from justices, in the later Act only by service of a noble, and this was to be attested under his hand and arms. The spirit of the Acts of Elizabeth frequently appears in later Acts, and occurs as lately as the Vagrant Act of 1744 (*r*), which was law till 1824. It does not appear in the Vagrant Act of 1824 (*s*). The Theatre Act of 1737 (*t*) narrowed the definition of a player of interludes for the purposes of punishment as a vagabond to mean a person acting interludes, &c., in a place where such person had no legal settlement. An alternative penalty of 50*l.* was also imposed by the Act; payment of the penalty exempted the person paying it from being proceeded against as a vagabond.

It is worthy of notice that the players were regarded in the Elizabethan age as transferable; thus John Heywood, a

(*q*) 28 Geo. III. c. 30.
(*r*) 17 Geo. II. c. 5. The social sanction was apparently as strong as the legal, if one may judge from the lines,
"The strolling tribe, a despicable race,
Like wandering Arabs, shift from place to place."
(*s*) 5 Geo. IV. c. 83.
(*t*) 10 Geo. II. c. 28.

servant of the Earl of Worcester, was bestowed upon the Queen at the accession of James I.

In addition to the penalties incurred by players, any theatre, whether properly licensed or not, might be proceeded against at common law as a nuisance. A playhouse was not a nuisance in itself, but became so if it disturbed the neighbourhood or admitted improper performances. In such a case the players, though they played by proper authority, and so were not subject to be treated as vagabonds, might be indicted for an unlawful assembly (*u*). A petition against the Blackfriars Theatre as a nuisance was presented by the inhabitants to the Privy Council in 1596, but not granted. In 1700 the Grand Jury of Middlesex presented the two playhouses and also the bear-garden as riotous and disorderly nuisances.

So far notice has been taken only of the professional player. There were at the same time certain persons and places regarded as privileged. A licence was not needed by members of the Royal or of the great noble families and their servants acting plays in their own houses. Thus a mask was acted at Whitehall in 1632, in which Queen Henrietta Maria herself appeared. It was this mask that called forth the ponderous "Histriomastix" of unfortunate John Prynne. In 1634 "Comus" was represented for the first time at Ludlow Castle before the Earl of Bridgwater. The Universities and Inns of Court were considered as privileged places. "Ferrex and Porrex" was acted in 1561 by members of the Inner Temple; the first representation of

---

(*u*) Examples of such proceedings will be found in 1 Roll. 109; 1 Vent. 169; 1 Mod. 96; 5 Mod. 142. The cases in Vent. and 1 Mod. are cases of rope-dancing, and are good illustrations of the debased taste of the theatrical public two centuries ago. In the case in 5 Mod. Betterton's theatre in Lincoln's Inn Fields, though duly licensed, was held to be a nuisance.

"Gordobuc" took place at the Inner Temple in 1562, and of "Twelfth Night" at the Middle Temple in 1601. "Gammer Gurton's Needle," the production of a bishop's pen, was acted at Cambridge in 1575. Acting at a private house, other than one of the privileged places, or even at such a place if the subject of the drama was distasteful to the authorities, brought with it serious consequences. Thus when Sir Thomas Pope gave a mask in honour of the Princess Elizabeth at Hatfield, Queen Mary forbade its recurrence, for she "misliked these follies." In 1614 a fine was imposed by the Star Chamber on Sir John Yorke for representing a Catholic drama in his house.

The secular drama had from the beginning to contend with a powerful foe in the Puritan party. In 1580 the Puritan influence led to the forbidding of all theatres in the City of London. Of the then existing theatres, the Theatre and the Curtain in Shoreditch, and the Globe, were all without the bounds of the city, and the Blackfriars was in a liberty. In 1600 appeared an Order in Council limiting the number of playhouses about London to two, one in Middlesex and one in Surrey (*x*). But this does not seem to have been very strictly carried out. The Puritan opposition culminated in Ordinances of the Long Parliament in 1642 and 1647, the first temporarily, the second permanently, suppressing stage-plays. In 1648 it was made criminal even to be present as a spectator at a play. At the same time performances took place during the Commonwealth at private houses (especially at Holland House), and entertainments not wholly dramatic were allowed. Davenant's opera "The Siege of Rhodes" was produced in 1657.

The Restoration introduced a different policy. In 1662

(*x*) This is probably what is alluded to in Hamlet, act ii. sc. 2: "I think their inhibition comes by reason of the late innovation."

patents were granted by Charles II. to two companies, "the King's servants" under Killigrew, and "the Duke of York's servants" under Davenant. It is remarkable that each patent prohibits the acting of parts offensive to piety and good manners. *Clodius accuset mœchos, Catilina Cethegum!* In 1682 the King's servants and the Duke of York's servants combined, and played under a double patent, now represented by Drury Lane. Drury Lane, however, was closed by the Lord Chamberlain in 1709, its patent revoked in 1719, and it was afterwards only licensed. A third patent was granted to the theatre in Lincoln's Inn Fields in 1714, now represented by Covent Garden, first opened in 1732. A fourth patent was refused after the burning of Drury Lane in 1809. The Theatre Royal, Haymarket, had no patent, but only a licence. It was opened by Sir John Vanbrugh in 1705, under the Lincoln's Inn Fields' licence. In 1708 the Lord Chamberlain asserted his authority by uniting the Haymarket and Drury Lane companies. In 1733 the Haymarket company called themselves "the Comedians of His Majesty's Revels." It appears from what has been said that there was at the time of the passing of the Act of 1843 only one patent theatre—Covent Garden—and only one company strictly entitled to the designation of " Her Majesty's servants " (*y*), although Drury Lane was popularly regarded as a patent theatre. There was nothing in the patents of Charles II. to prevent the Lord Chamberlain granting a licence for the performance of regular drama in the City of Westminster; but, as a matter of fact, this was never done, except to Drury Lane, no doubt because it had been originally a patent theatre. For all practical purposes it remained a patent theatre. The Music Hall Act of 1752 (*z*) specially

(*y*) Baddeley, who died in 1794, is said to have been the last actor who wore Court uniform as one of "His Majesty's servants."

(*z*) 25 Geo. II. c. 36.

exempts from the operation of the Act "the Theatres Royal in Drury Lane and Covent Garden, and the King's Theatre in the Haymarket." In 1737 there were six theatres in London. That in Goodman's Fields was the earliest of the non-privileged theatres. In consequence of the increase in the number of theatres, the Act of 1737 (*a*) was introduced and carried by Sir Robert Walpole. The immediate cause of this legislation is said to have been the production of a political extravaganza of Fielding's, "The Golden Rump." The title of the Act is remarkable as illustrating the English tendency to indirect legislation. It is "An Act to repeal so much of an Act made in the Twelfth Year of the Reign of Queen Anne, entitled *An Act for reducing the Laws relating to Rogues, Vagabonds, Sturdy Beggars, and Vagrants into one Act, &c.* as relates to Common Players of Interludes." The effect of the Act was to make it impossible to establish any theatre except in the City of Westminster, and in places where the King should in person reside, and during his residence only. In spite of this provision, the regular drama was performed at Richmond, Windsor, and Brighton, when the King was not in residence. The Act did not confine the prerogative within the City of Westminster; but, as a matter of policy, it was not exercised in favour of the non-privileged theatres, except those where the "legitimate drama" was not performed. The legitimate drama was thus confined to Covent Garden, Drury Lane, and the Haymarket for more than a century (1735—1843). In 1832 there were five theatres licensed by the Lord Chamberlain for the performance of Italian and English opera, ballets d'action, music, dancing, burlettas, spectacle, pantomime, and horsemanship (*b*). In

---

(*a*) 10 Geo. II. c. 28.

(*b*) These words are taken from the licences to these theatres, which are set out in the Appendix to the Report of the Select Committee on Dramatic Literature (1832).

the case of Drury Lane, no doubt because it filled the place of one of the patent theatres, the licence was for twenty-one years; in the other cases, and in the case of the theatres at Richmond, Windsor, and Brighton, the licence was for one year. Covent Garden was protected by its patent, and needed no licence. In the provinces patent theatres were established at Bath by 8 Geo. III. c. 10, at Liverpool by 11 Geo. III. c. 16 (*c*), at Bristol by 18 Geo. III. c. 8. Each of these Acts repealed *pro tanto* the Act of 1737. Besides limiting the number of theatres, the Act of 1737 increased the powers of the Lord Chamberlain. Before the Act he could prohibit the continuance of an existing play, but could not exercise a preventive censorship and forbid its appearance at all. The Act gave him authority to do so, and, for the first time, enforced the sending of plays for examination before appearance. The acting of plays at the Universities was forbidden by an enactment of the same year (*d*). The restrictions upon the drama were found very inconvenient in the large towns, especially in those which did not possess patent theatres. To remedy this an Act was passed in 1788 (*e*), under which licences for occasional performances might be granted in general or quarter sessions for a period of not more than sixty days. The rights of patent theatres were preserved by the prohibition to grant such a licence to any theatre within eight miles of a patent theatre. In the period between 1737 and 1843 there were several Acts passed dealing with Covent Garden and Drury Lane, and regulating the rights of parties, the application of charitable funds,

---

(*c*) The Liverpool patent is set out in the Appendix to the Report of 1832.

(*d*) 10 Geo. II. c. 19. It is not a little remarkable that the Universities, once possessing unusual dramatic privileges, should not only have lost those privileges, but become subject to special disabilities.

(*e*) 28 Geo. III. c. 30.

&c. (*f*). In the same period there were several decisions of the Courts which practically went to confirm the operation of the Act of 1737 as creating a monopoly (*g*).

The results of theatrical monopoly were beneficial neither to the public nor to the monopolists themselves. In 1832 a Select Committee of the House of Commons was appointed to report upon the condition of dramatic literature. Their report recommended the legal recognition of stage-right and the abolition of theatrical monopoly. It is curious to notice in the evidence as annexed to the Report of the Committee something of the old Puritan hostility to the theatre. Some of the witnesses regarded as one of the causes of the diminished profits of theatres in the years immediately preceding 1832 the spread of "evangelical principles." The recommendations of the report as to stage-right were carried out immediately by Bulwer Lytton's Act (*h*). But it was not till 1843 that the present Theatre Act (*i*) was passed, a previous Bill upon the same lines having been rejected by the House of Lords. The Act of 1843 inaugurated a more liberal policy, and there is now complete "free trade" in theatres, subject to the conditions imposed by the Act. The convenience of the public was further considered by the clause enacting that a licence might be granted at a special session, so that application for a licence to hold an occasional performance can now be made at any time on twenty-one days' notice. Under the Act of 1788 such a licence could only have been granted at general or quarter sessions. The jurisdiction of

(*f*) See 16 Geo. III. cc. 13, 31; 50 Geo. III. c. ccxiv; 52 Geo. III. c. xix; 1 Geo. IV. c. lx.

(*g*) See *R.* v. *Neville*, 1 B. & Ad. 489; *Levy* v. *Yates*, 8 A. & E. 129; *Ewing* v. *Osbaldiston*, 2 My. & Cr. 53 (where it was held that an agreement for a partnership violating the provisions of the Act of 1737 could not be enforced in Chancery).

(*h*) 3 & 4 Will. IV. c. 15.

(*i*) 6 & 7 Vict. c. 68.

the Lord Chamberlain is not affected by the Act of 1843. Jurisdiction is for the first time conferred on justices to license buildings for regular as distinguished from occasional performances. Their jurisdiction practically extends to all places in which dramas could not have been represented before the passing of the Act. This is not the place to dwell upon the social effects of more liberal theatrical legislation. But it must at least be conceded that no injury to public morality has been the result; much of the reproach levelled at the stage by Prynne and Collier, and appearing in the Report of 1832, however just it might have been in another state of society, would now be pointless.

Music was at no time the object of such severe restrictions as those imposed upon the drama. Wandering musicians, however, were liable to be treated as rogues and vagabonds under the Vagrant Act of 1744 as well as under previous Acts. The present Music Hall Act was passed in 1752 (*k*), probably in consequence of the publication, in 1750, of Fielding's "Inquiry into the Causes of the late Increase of Robbers." The full title of the Act is "An Act for the better preventing Thefts and Robberies, and for regulating Places of Publick Entertainment, and punishing Persons keeping Disorderly Houses." It is remarkable that two works of the same writer should from opposite causes have led to both theatre and music-hall legislation of lasting importance.

In Scotland the theatre has always exercised less influence than in England. But the history of the theatre in the two countries proceeds on very much the same lines. In 1574 the General Assembly claimed to license players, and forbade exhibitions on Sunday. As in England, the licensing then seems to have passed from the Church to the Crown, for in 1599 James VI. licensed a company at Edinburgh.

(*k*) 25 Geo. II. c. 36.

The Restoration gave the theatre in Scotland a liberty which it had not enjoyed before. By the Act 1672, c. 21, comedians (*l*) while upon the stage were exempt from the sumptuary provisions of the Act respecting apparel. No permanent theatre existed in Scotland till the erection of the Canongate Theatre at Edinburgh in 1746. The Chamberlain of Scotland (an official long extinct) appears to have exercised a certain police jurisdiction over theatres. The Theatre Acts of 1737 and 1843 included Scotland, the Music Hall Act was confined to England.

Ireland was never regarded as falling within the Lord Chamberlain's jurisdiction. Theatrical legislation, so far as it went, was based upon English models. Thus ridicule of the liturgy was forbidden by 2 Eliz. c. 2 (Ir.); common players of interludes and wandering minstrels were deemed vagabonds, 10 & 11 Car. I. c. 4 (Ir.) The drama in Dublin was regulated by special legislation, 26. Geo. III. c. 57 (Ir.). No play could be exhibited in Dublin without a patent from the Crown. The existing Theatre and Music Hall Acts do not apply to Ireland.

In the United States public entertainments, dramatic and otherwise, are usually under the control of the municipal authorities. There is no Act of Congress upon the subject. In some States, such as New York and Massachusetts, there is State legislation, requiring places of public entertainment to be licensed by the proper authority. It is in many States a condition of the licence that intoxicating liquors shall not be sold in such places.

(The authorities upon which this chapter is mainly founded are Collier, History of English Dramatic Poetry and Annals

---

(*l*) It is remarkable that in this Act and in Scotch law books the term "comedian" is generally the only one found. Yet the success of "Douglas" proves that tragedies were appreciated as well as comedies.

of the Stage; Doran, Their Majesties' Servants; Genest, History of the Stage; Gifford, Introduction to Ben Jonson's Works; Halliwell, Life of Shakespeare; Hawkins, Origin of the English Drama; Penny Cyclopædia, *Drama, Theatre;* Encyclopædia Britannica, *Drama;* Report of the Select Committee on Dramatic Literature, 1832).

J. W.

1, NEW SQUARE, LINCOLN'S INN,
    March, 1885.

CHAPTER I.

THE THEATRE.

THE law by which theatres are governed is mainly statutory. The present Act in force is 6 & 7 Vict. c. 68, which applies to Great Britain. For the purposes of this Act, a theatre is a building into which the public is admitted on payment as spectators of a stage-play.

§ 1.—*Building.*

It must be a building of a permanent character (*a*); a booth theatre, called Douglas' Theatre, which was taken to pieces and carried from place to place, was held not to be such a house of public entertainment as to be capable of being licensed (*b*).

A portable or temporary booth, consisting of two caravans or waggons drawn from place to place, but containing the ordinary arrangements of a theatre, and accommodation for about 300 persons, is neither a theatre under 6 & 7 Vict. c. 68, s. 2, nor a tenement within 2 & 3 Vict. c. 47, s. 46 (*c*).

It must not, however, be assumed that persons acting in such booths are not punishable: for this very same Fredericks, who owned the caravans above referred to, was a few months

---

(*a*) In the Metropolis a temporary erection of wood or corrugated iron would not be licensed, as it would not conform to the necessary structural conditions. See p. 39.

(*b*) *Davys* v. *Douglas*, 4 H. & N. 180.

(*c*) *Fredericks* v. *Howie*, 1 H. & C. 381.

later fined under sect. 11 of 6 & 7 Vict. c. 68 (*d*). In fact, it appears that all performances of stage-plays in a temporary theatre, except at a fair, are against the statute, and all taking part in such performances are liable to come under the penalty of 10*l.* imposed by sect. 11.

So if a person acts in an open field he will be liable, except when licensed at a lawful fair. Even if the theatre is only opened occasionally, it will come within the prohibition of the statute.

The owner of a private theatre adjacent to his own dwelling-house, who lent it gratuitously to persons who gave three performances for which money was received, was held liable for having or keeping a theatre (*e*).

§ 2.—*Performance.*

It is the performance only that need be for hire to bring it within the statute. Sect. 16 of 6 & 7 Vict. c. 68, declares what shall be evidence of acting for hire, as follows:—

"That in every case in which any money or other reward shall be taken or charged directly or indirectly, or in which the purchase of any article is made a condition for the admission of any person into any theatre to see any stage-play, and also in every case in which any stage-play shall be acted or presented in any house, room, or place in which distilled or fermented exciseable liquor shall be sold, every actor therein shall be deemed to be acting for hire."

The acting for hire must be strictly proved. Where a proprietor issued printed bills announcing that Shakespeare's tragedy of "Hamlet" would be performed, with other entertainments, in such theatre, and that the prices of admission to

---

(*d*) *Fredericks* v. *Payne*, 1 H. & C. 584; *Tarling* v. *Fredericks*, 28 L. T., N. S. 814.

(*e*) *Shelley* v. *Bethell*, 12 Q. B. D. 11.

boxes, pit and gallery would be 1s., 6d., and 3d. "Hamlet" was performed as announced, but it was not proved that 1s., 6d., or 3d., or any other sum of money or reward was taken or charged, directly or indirectly, on the night of the 7th of July (being the opening night), or the purchase of any article made a condition for the admission of any one into the theatre, or that any distilled or fermented exciseable liquor was sold within it.

The justices did not feel justified in convicting under sect. 11, because they had no evidence before them of an acting for hire on the said 7th of July beyond the mere play-bill. The Court unanimously affirmed the decision of the justices (*f*).

Further, Bramwell, B., doubted whether this would apply to actors engaged for pay at private theatricals, or to amateurs assisting for charitable purposes at a private house (*g*).

But the latter proposition has since been affirmed by *Shelley* v. *Bethell* (*h*), already referred to. In this case a person having in his own private house a theatre of the ordinary kind, but without any box-office or place for paying money, lent the use of the theatre gratuitously, and without reserving any right of entry was actually present and helped in placing the spectators. Mr. Hamilton Aidé, to whom the owner had lent the theatre, advertised a performance of a play, under his own personal supervision, in aid of the funds of the School of Dramatic Art, and that tickets—price 1*l*. 1*s*.—were to be procured of the secretary at the School of Dramatic Art. Over 300 tickets were sold by the secretary, but the tickets were not sold within or outside the theatre. The owner never parted with the possession of the theatre, but only allowed its use for these three performances. It

(*f*) *Davys* v. *Douglas*, 4 Hurl. & N. 180.
(*g*) *Fredericks* v. *Payne*, 1 Hurl. & C. 381.
(*h*) 12 Q. B. D. 11.

was not alleged that the owner had received any money or other reward on account of or for the use of the theatre.

The magistrate was of opinion that the appellant had contravened the provisions of 6 & 7 Vict. c. 68, s. 2; and, on a case stated, Lord Coleridge, C. J., and Mathew, J., upheld the conviction.

It seems doubtful whether, if a private person in his own house engaged actors for pay, and gave a performance to which he admitted his friends gratuitously, he might not be liable under sect. 2, as above explained. In a case of copyright under 3 & 4 Will. IV. c. 15, where a copyright piece was performed by amateurs, who acted without pay, in the board-room of a theatre, to which students and their friends were admitted by tickets distributed gratuitously; in considering whether the board-room was "a place of dramatic entertainment," Lord Coleridge, C. J., and Stephen, J., declined to adopt as a conclusive test of a public entertainment, that "no charge was made for admission" (*i*). It seems to follow from this, that the recent Homeric dramas and performances of Æschylus in London, where tickets were issued on payment to select persons known personally or through report to the distributor of tickets, would come within the statute.

§ 3.—*Stage-Play.*

By sect. 23, "the word 'stage-play' shall be taken to include every tragedy, comedy, farce, opera, burletta, interlude, melodrama, pantomime, or other entertainment of the stage, or any part thereof."

The two tests of a stage-play appear to be—(1) The excitement of emotion; (2) The representation of action. This is a question of degree and a matter of fact for a jury, and

---

(*i*) *Duck* v. *Bates*, 12 Q. B. D. 79; affirmed 13 Q. B. D. 843.

may be best understood by reading the cases subjoined. It will be noticed that some of the decisions which follow are upon the Copyright Acts. It is important to distinguish between the generic terms used in those Acts and in 6 & 7 Vict. c. 68. The generic term in that statute is "stage-play," whereas in 5 & 6 Vict. c. 45, it is "dramatic piece"; and there is some difference in the interpretation given of these terms in the respective statutes, owing to the difference of their purview. In an indictment in 1795, under the repealed Act 10 Geo. II. c. 28, where the performance in question was tumbling, Russell, for the defence, pointed out that tumbling is an entertainment, not of, but on the stage; and Kenyon, C. J., said, "I do not think that tumbling is an entertainment of the stage within the meaning of that Act of Parliament; it might equally be said that fencing on a public stage is" (*k*).

An introduction to a pantomime was held, in an action for penalties under 3 & 4 Will. IV. c. 15, to be a dramatic piece or entertainment (*l*).

In a subsequent case under the 3 & 4 Will. IV. c. 15, the plaintiff was owner of a song called the "Ship on Fire," describing a ship taking fire at sea, the distress, and finally the escape of the persons on board, and their words and actions during the several incidents.

It was sung at a piano without characteristic dress or scenery, but dramatic effect was given to the various passages by tone of voice and otherwise.

An expert witness said that he considered the song *descriptive and dramatic*.

The song was described on the hand-bill as a "dramatic scena." Lord Denman, C. J., in delivering judgment, after saying that he thought the song dramatic, gave as a reason,

---

(*k*) *R.* v. *Handy*, 6 T R. 286.
(*l*) *Lea* v. *Simpson*, 4 Dowl. & L. 666.

that it moved terror and pity and sympathy by representing danger and despair and joy and maternal and conjugal affection. Referring to the expert's evidence, he said that there was no evidence that anyone considered it not dramatic.

Thus the nature of the piece placed it rather in the representative than in the narrative class of poetry, according to Lord Bacon's division (Adv. of Learning, Bk. II., Poesy).

The words in the interpretation clause, sect. 2 of 5 & 6 Vict. c. 45, comprehend any piece which, on being presented by any performer to an audience, would produce the emotions which are the purpose of the regular drama, and which constitute the entertainment of the audience (*m*).

That the plaintiff was in the habit of singing a song, "Come to Peckham Rye," with actions, in a Quaker's dress at a music-hall, was held to constitute the song "a dramatic piece or entertainment" within 3 & 4 Will. IV. c. 15 (*n*). In *Wall* v. *Taylor* (*o*), Brett, M. R., used as a test of coming within the Copyright Act, "where, to give effect to the song, it is necessary that the singing should be made to represent something."

A dramatic performance (a duologue) by two persons, who went out and reappeared in various costumes, sometimes speaking in soliloquy and sometimes holding a dialogue with each other, was held a stage-play within 6 & 7 Vict. c. 68, s. 23 (*p*).

In the case of a ballet at a music-hall the question was whether it was an entertainment of the stage. Owing to the use of the technical term *ballet divertissement* in the statement the conviction was quashed. The facts are as follows:—A great number of females, dressed in theatrical costume,

(*m*) *Russell* v. *Smith*, 12 Q. B. 217.
(*n*) *Clark* v. *Bishop*, 25 L. T. N. S. 908.
(*o*) 11 Q. B. D. 107.
(*p*) *Thorne* v. *Colson*, 3 L. T. N. S. 697.

descended upon a stage and performed a sort of warlike dance; then came a *danseuse* of a superior order, who performed a *pas seul*. When all the dancers were down they defiled to the right and left. Four were placed on each side in front of the proscenium with property, viz. sham, musical instruments, in their hands, supposed to be played by them to the dancers. The dancers began to dance the *pas des poignards*, each lady, armed with two daggers, charging through each other's ranks, striking right and left with the daggers in mimic warfare, then in front as far as the footlights. The performance of the dagger dance ended in several of the females standing over the others as if in triumph, and retiring when others came forward holding property, viz. sham, palm leaves, in their hands, and danced waving them, and formed an avenue as if expecting an arrival. Then the *première danseuse* entered, and the other dancers went through evolutions with palm leaves and baskets of flowers.

The opinion of the majority of the Court was that these facts constituted an entertainment of the stage.

Erle, C. J., said : " It appears to me that the question presented to us is one of degree, and is more a question of fact than of law. It is difficult to appreciate the scene described without having witnessed it. I am utterly unable to determine at what point public dancing in a place unlicensed by the Lord Chamberlain ceases to be lawful and becomes a stage-play or an entertainment of the stage. The thing so described certainly approaches very nearly to a dramatic performance, and it is extremely difficult to say where the line is to be drawn. The magistrate uses two terms of art, viz., *ballet d'action* and *ballet divertissement*. The former, it is said, has a story, the latter has none. I rather incline to think that the line must be drawn between the two. The *ballet divertissement* involves *no consecutive train of ideas*, but consists merely of poses and evolutions by a number of persons elegant in shape and graceful in action. On the other hand, the *ballet d'action* has a regular dramatic story, which may give rise to all manner of emotions incident to tragedy, comedy or farce, accompanied by elegance of form and grace of motion. But I do not think that a *ballet divertissement* comes within the meaning and definition of a stage-play in the statute" (*q*).

In a case stated by the stipendiary magistrate of Birmingham, the defendant was licensed proprietor of a music-hall, and a licensed victualler. The only peculiarity of the entertainment was that, with the exception of two persons, the dialogue between whom was wholly subordinate to the plot of the piece, none of the characters were at any time on the stage, but being placed in a chamber below were reflected by lenses and mirrors. There was dancing, music and singing, but no change of dress or scenery.

The conviction was affirmed; and in the course of his judgment Byles, J., said: "Brother Hayes" (counsel for the defendant) "asks whether a public lecture delivered on a stage with scenery and footlights would be a dramatic entertainment or stage-play within the Act. I am by no means clear that it would not. I do not say that the reflection of figures in mirrors on a stage, without the accessories of actors, dialogue, scenery, lights or music, would constitute an infringement of the statute, but I am clearly of opinion that this is within the prohibition."

He also said, commenting on sect. 23 of 6 & 7 Vict. c. 68: "I observe two words in this Act which were not in the former Act of 10 Geo. II. c. 28, viz., burletta and pantomime, which may well have been introduced still further to enlarge the meaning of stage-play" (*r*).

(*q*) *Wigan* v. *Strange*, L. R. 1 C. P. 175.
(*r*) *Day* v. *Simpson*, 18 C. B. N. S. 680.

A performance called "Robin Hood" was given at the Canterbury Theatre of Varieties, and F. Hall was prosecuted as actor and author and manager for performing a stage-play without licence. The dialogue was to a certain degree impromptu, and the matter forming the sketch was written from time to time on slips of paper, passed from one to the other, and destroyed after the parties engaged had learned it. The plot was not very connected, and extraneous matter, popular songs and allusions to passing events, were introduced.

Mr. Chance refused to convict (s).

How far the learned magistrate was right is open to question, having regard to the two tests already stated as decisive of the question. See p. 18.

The absence of an existing written part is not in itself sufficient to take a piece out of the category of a stage-play.

It seems obvious that Mr. and Mrs. German Reed's entertainment and Mr. Brandram's recitals are entertainments of the stage.

A *ballet divertissement* pure and simple requires no licence, unless it either forms an essential part or occurs in the course of a play or opera, though by the report in *Wigan* v. *Strange* the Lord Chamberlain apparently makes orders concerning ballets of this kind.

§ 4.—*Licensing of Stage-Play.*

A stage-play must be duly licensed.

Sects. 12 and 13 of 6 & 7 Vict. c. 68, prescribe that a copy of every new play, and of every addition to every old one, and of every new prologue or epilogue or addition thereto (such copy to be signed by the master or manager), shall be sent to the Lord Chamberlain, and if the Lord Chamberlain

---

(s) See The Saturday Review, October 18, 1884.

does not forbid within seven days after sending the play and fee, it may be represented.

Sect. 13 gives power to the Lord Chamberlain to fix a scale of fees, not exceeding two guineas, for the examination of such plays, and such fee shall be paid at the time when such play, &c. shall be sent to the Lord Chamberlain; and such period of seven days shall not begin to run in any case until the said fee shall have been paid to the Lord Chamberlain or his deputy.

In accordance with sect. 13 the Lord Chamberlain has fixed, as a scale, a charge of two guineas for every stage-play of three or more acts, and one guinea for every stage-play of less than three acts.

All stage-plays that have been represented previous to the 6 & 7 Vict. c. 68, are held to be licensed.

There is a register of all new stage-plays that have been licensed by the Lord Chamberlain for representation under 6 & 7 Vict. c. 68.

A new stage-play thus licensed is licensed once for all for representation at any theatre in Great Britain, unless or until the licence is revoked under sect. 14 (*t*).

Sect. 14 empowers the Lord Chamberlain, whenever he shall be of opinion that it is fitting for the preservation of good manners, decorum, or the public peace so to do, to forbid the acting or presenting any stage-play, &c., or any part thereof, anywhere in Great Britain, or in such theatres as he shall specify, and either absolutely or for such time as he shall think fit. It would seem to be under the authority conferred by this section that the Lord Chamberlain might regulate the dress of performers.

It does not appear that there is any appeal from the Lord

(*t*) This information was kindly communicated to the author by Mr. E. F. S. Pigott, the Examiner of Stage Plays.

Chamberlain's decision, and it would seem that his discretion is unfettered.

It will be noticed that the only ground alleged in the Act for forbidding a play is "the preservation of good manners, decorum, or of the public peace." Perhaps, if it could be shown that the Lord Chamberlain based his decision upon a ground other than one of these, the Court might possibly interfere (*u*).

Sect. 15 imposes a penalty of 50*l.* on anyone who for hire acts or presents, or causes to be acted or presented, any play, or part of a play, until the same shall have been allowed by the Lord Chamberlain, or which shall have been disallowed by him, and further, the licence of the theatre becomes absolutely void.

This appears to include author, manager, actor, and perhaps all engaged in the theatre.

§ 5.—*Licensing of Theatres.*

By sect. 2 of 6 & 7 Vict. c. 68, all theatres must be licensed.

By sect. 7 no licence is to be granted to any person except to the actual and responsible manager for the time being of the theatre in respect of which the licence is granted.

Thus, where strolling players hired the Exchange Hall, Grantham, for six nights, paying 7*l.* to the secretary, and they were convicted under sect. 2 by the justices, and it was argued that the owners of the Exchange Hall were the real keepers and owners under sect. 2, the Court quashed the conviction, on the ground that the defendants were only

---

(*u*) For the method in which the Examiner of Plays exercises his discretion, see the evidence of Mr. J. Payne Collier and Mr. George Colman before the Select Committee on Dramatic Literature (1832).

performing by the permission of the secretary, and did not come within sect. 2, which refers to one who has a permanent interest in a theatre or who is the responsible manager of it. In this case Lush, J., said: "When the responsible manager has procured a licence he may allow other persons to perform within the building. But any such person who has the use of this building for a few entertainments by night is not required by the statute to take out a licence" (*x*). They could, however, have been fined under sect. 11.

After the actual and responsible manager, as above defined, has obtained his licence, whether in the metropolis or provinces, by sect. 7 the name and place of abode of such manager shall be printed on every play-bill announcing any representation at such theatre.

Theatres may be divided into Metropolitan (*y*) and Provincial.

Metropolitan are again to be divided into patent theatres, those subject to the Lord Chamberlain, and those not subject.

It is believed that the only patent theatre now existing in the metropolis is Covent Garden (*z*).

There are also three patent theatres in the provinces, at Liverpool, Bristol and Bath.

But in an early case of *Gallini* v. *Laborie* (*a*), Lord Kenyon said that these theatres were only excepted on the supposition that they could be licensed by letters patent from the Crown or the Lord Chamberlain. But the Legislature did not mean to except these places unless they were licensed.

Apparently if either of these theatres had a patent or

(*x*) *Reg.* v. *Strugnell*, L. R. 1 Q. B. 93.

(*y*) For the extent of the metropolis see 18 & 19 Vict. c. 120, s. 250.

(*z*) See 25 Geo. II. c. 36, s. 4. These patent theatres, though not licensed by the Lord Chamberlain, are still to a certain extent under his jurisdiction. See below. See, too, the Historical Introduction.

(*a*) 5 T. R. 242.

licence for performing stage plays, and they performed without authority something that was not a stage play, e. g. the Promenade Concerts at Covent Garden, they would be liable under 25 Geo. II. c. 36, though apparently the promenade concerts do take place without any licence under 25 Geo. II. c. 36.

Under the Lord Chamberlain's jurisdiction are all theatres, except patent theatres, within the Parliamentary boundaries of the cities of London and Westminster, and of the boroughs of Finsbury, Marylebone, the Tower Hamlets, Lambeth, and Southwark (b); and further, all those places where her Majesty, her heirs and successors, shall in their royal persons occasionally reside.

The latter part of the section as quoted is slightly obscure. Does "place" mean parish? If so, in whatever parish of London her Majesty might choose to reside, the theatres, unless they were patent theatres, would immediately become subject to the Lord Chamberlain's jurisdiction during the time in which she or her heirs or successors were so therein resident, lapsing back to the magistrates on her leaving such parish. As it happens, the three Royal palaces in London, Buckingham, St. James's, and Kensington, are all within the Parliamentary boundaries of the old City of Westminster, and so are at once under the jurisdiction of the Lord Chamberlain.

By sect. 4, the fee to be charged by the Lord Chamberlain on licensing is not to exceed 10s. for each calendar month during which the theatre is licensed to be kept open, according to a scale of fees to be fixed by the Lord Chamberlain and paid to him.

By sect. 7, the manager shall become bound himself in such penal sum as the Lord Chamberlain requires, being in no

---

(b) For these divisions, as existing in 1843, others have since been substituted.

case more than 500*l*., and two sufficient sureties to be approved by the Lord Chamberlain, each in such penal sum as the Lord Chamberlain shall require, being in no case more than 100*l*., for the due observance of the rules which shall be in force at any time during the currency of the licence for the regulation of such theatre, and for securing payment of the penalties which such manager may be adjudged to pay for breach of such rules or any of the provisions of the Act.

It does not appear that the Lord Chamberlain has any discretion in granting the licence. His act, it would seem, is purely ministerial. Once it is proved to his satisfaction that the applicant is the actual and responsible manager, and that he and his two sureties are of sufficient substance to give bonds for 500*l*. and 100*l*. respectively, it would seem that he must grant the licence. Neither has the Lord Chamberlain any power to make suitable rules for enforcing order and decency at the theatres licensed by him.

However, by sect. 8, if there has been a riot or misbehaviour in any theatre licensed by him, or in any patent theatre, the Lord Chamberlain may suspend such licence or order such patent theatre to be closed for such time as shall seem fit to him, and during such suspension or order any such theatre is to be deemed unlicensed.

Every other theatre within Great Britain beyond the limits of the authority of the Lord Chamberlain, is to be licensed by the justices having jurisdiction over the place in which the applicant's theatre is situated.

Provincial Theatres

may be divided into—(1) Lord Chamberlain's theatres; (2) theatres at Oxford and Cambridge; and (3) all other or justices' theatres.

(1) Lord Chamberlain's theatres are—

(a) Theatres in the boroughs of New Windsor, in the county of Berks, and at Brighthelmstone (Brighton), in the county of Sussex.

(b) Theatres situated in the places where her Majesty occasionally resides, but only during the time of such occasional residence, *e.g.*, in the parishes in which Osborne and Balmoral are respectively situated.

As to place and parish, see above, p. 27.

(2) Theatres at Oxford and Cambridge, or within fourteen miles thereof, are licensed by the justices having jurisdiction therein, but before such licence can come into force the consent of the respective chancellors or vice-chancellors must be given.

Further, the rules to be made by the justices for the management of the theatre are to be subject to the approval of the respective chancellors or vice-chancellors.

The chancellor or vice-chancellor may also impose any condition which may seem good to his discretion before giving his consent to the said licence.

In case of the breach of any such condition imposed as above, or any of the rules approved as above, it is lawful for the chancellor or vice-chancellor to annul the licence, which thereupon becomes void.

All other theatres are to be licensed by four justices at a special session, see p. 31.

Various municipal corporations have obtained Acts of Parliament conferring on them special powers with regard to public buildings; see Appendix. By the Towns Improvement Act, 1847 (10 & 11 Vict. c. 34), which may be incorporated by any municipal corporation, it is enacted, by sect. 110, that any person intending to build any place of public amusement or entertainment, or for holding large numbers of people for any purpose whatsoever, is to give fourteen days' notice to the commissioners (*c*) under the Act, and send a plan of the means of supplying fresh air; that no person shall begin to build such building until the means for supplying fresh air have been approved by the commissioners; and that in default of sending the notice, or in case the building be erected without approval, the commissioners may cause the building or any part of it to be pulled down or altered at the expense of the owner.

By sect. 111, if the commissioners fail to signify their approval of the plan within fourteen days, the party may proceed to build, provided that the building be otherwise in accordance with the provisions of this and any special Act.

By sect. 112 an appeal lies against the determination of the commissioners.

By the Public Health Act, 1875 (38 & 39 Vict. c. 55), s. 110, these powers appear to be conferred on an urban sanitary authority under the Act.

The Towns Police Clauses Act, 1847 (10 & 11 Vict. c. 89), which may be incorporated in special Acts, and which is further, by sect. 171 of the Public Health Act, 1875, rendered applicable to all urban sanitary districts, empowers, by sect. 21, commissioners to give directions to constables for keeping order and preventing any obstruction of the streets in the neighbourhood of theatres and other places of public resort; and a wilful breach of such order is to be an offence, and is subject to a penalty not exceeding 40*s*.

Sect. 28 makes it an offence to—

(1) Exhibit in a caravan or otherwise any show or public entertainment, except in a market or lawful fair;

(*c*) For the meaning of commissioners, see sect. 2.

(2) Exhibit to public view any profane, indecent or obscene representation, or sing any profane or obscene song or ballad.

Sects. 34 and 35 make it an offence for the keeper of a place of public resort to harbour a constable on duty, except for purposes of restoring order, under a penalty not exceeding 20*s*., or to knowingly suffer common prostitutes or reputed thieves to assemble and continue on his premises, under a penalty not exceeding 5*l*.

The way in which the licence is to be granted is prescribed by 6 & 7 Vict. c. 68, s. 5: The justices, after application shall have been made to them for a licence, shall, within twenty-one days next after such application (*d*) shall have been made to them in writing, signed by the party making the same, and countersigned by at least two justices acting in and for the division within which the property proposed to be licensed shall be situate, and delivered to the clerk to the said justices, hold a special session, of the holding of which session seven days' notice shall be given by their clerk to each of the justices acting within such division; and every such licence shall be given under the hands and seals of four or more of the justices assembled at such session, and shall be signed and sealed in open Court, and afterwards shall be publicly read by the clerk with the names of the justices subscribing the same.

Sect. 7 enacts that the manager shall become bound himself in such penal sum as the justices shall require, being in no case more than 500*l*., and two sufficient sureties, to be approved by the justices, each in such penal sum as the justice shall require, being in no case more than 100*l*., for the due observance of the rules which shall be in force at any

---

(*d*) A form of an application is given in the Appendix, under " Norwich," p. 192.

time during the currency of the licence for the regulation of such theatre, and for securing payment of the penalties which such manager may be adjudged to pay for breach of such rules or any of the provisions of this Act.

It does not appear that the justices have any discretion in granting the licence. Their act and signature is purely ministerial. Once it is proved to their satisfaction that the applicant is the actual and responsible manager, and that he and his sureties are of sufficient substance to give their respective bonds for 500*l.* and 100*l.*, it would seem that the special session must grant the licence (*e*).

By sect. 9, the justices have (what the Lord Chamberlain has not) authority to make at the special session suitable rules for enforcing order and decency at the theatres licensed by them, and for regulating the times during which they may be open; and from time to time at another special session, of which notice is to be given as before, to rescind or alter such rules. A Secretary of State has also power to rescind or alter such rules, and to make such other rules at his discretion. A copy of all rules in force are to be annexed to every licence. In case of riot or breach of the rules being proved on oath before any two justices usually acting in the jurisdiction where the theatre is situated, they may order the

---

(*e*) In the Music and Dancing Act, 25 Geo. II. c. 36, it is expressly enacted, that the justices are to grant such licences as they *in their discretion* shall think proper; and in 9 Geo. IV. c. 61, it is enacted that the justices shall grant such licences as they shall *in the exercise of their discretion* think fit and proper. The insertion of these words in the other Licensing Acts and the omission in the Theatre Act, clearly implies that the justices have no discretion to consider whether the applicant is a fit person or whether the neighbourhood requires a theatre. It seems further very doubtful whether the owners of existing theatres have any *locus standi* to oppose the grant of a licence to a new theatre. The purpose of 6 & 7 Vict. c. 68, was to abolish the existing monopoly and introduce free trade in theatres.

closing of the theatre for such time as they may think fit, and while such order is in force the theatre ordered to be closed is to be deemed an unlicensed house (*f*).

It does not appear that there is any limit to the authority to make rules under sect. 9; but no doubt the general principle as to bye-laws would apply, viz., that they must be reasonable (*g*) and not inconsistent with any statute or the general principles of the law of the land (*h*).

Rules are often made by justices forbidding the sale of intoxicating liquors in theatres. It appears doubtful how far such rules are in accordance with the principle.

§ 6.—*Appeal from Justices.*

(1) Refusal of justices to grant licence.

There is no appeal in the proper sense of the word in this case, but the decision of the justices may be reviewed by applying to the Queen's Bench Division for a rule for a mandamus, or a rule to show cause under 11 & 12 Vict. c. 44, s. 2.

(2) Order for closing theatre.

An appeal lies to the general or quarter sessions, whose order is to be final. Nevertheless, in spite of this provision, certiorari will lie in some cases (*i*).

(*f*) It is under this power of making rules that the justices can enforce such structural conditions and alterations as they think necessary for the safety of the public, especially where there is no local Act requiring structural inspection for places of public entertainment.

(*g*) In *Elwood* v. *Bullock*, 6 Q. B. 383, a bye-law "that no person should erect any booth or place any caravan for the purpose of a show or public entertainment within the borough without the licence of the mayor, and that any such licence given at any other time than fair time should be revoked by the mayor if 300 inhabitants residing within 100 yards of the place for which it was granted should memorialise the mayor," was held to be unreasonable and void.

(*h*) See Grant on Corporations, p. 70.

(*i*) See notes to *Crepps* v. *Durden*, 1 Sm. L. C. 8th ed. p. 711.

As regards the licence of a theatre in the metropolis, it is subject to conditions as to structural efficiency. See p. 38.

§ 7.—*Penalties.*

By sect. 2 of 6 & 7 Vict. c. 68, if a building which has been licensed as a theatre is used as a theatre without a licence, the person who has and keeps it, *i.e.* the actual and responsible manager (see p. 25), is liable by the Act to a penalty not exceeding 20*l.* for every day the theatre is open without a licence. And again, by sect. 11, there is a penalty not exceeding 10*l.* for every day on which the offence is committed, imposed upon every person who for hire (see p. 16) shall act or present, cause, permit, or suffer to be acted or presented, any part in any stage-play in any place not being a patent theatre or duly licensed as a theatre.

In a case of *Parsons* v. *Chapman* (*i*), which was an action for penalties under 10 Geo. II. c. 28, s. 2 (almost identical with sect. 11 of 6 & 7 Vict. c. 68), against a manager for performing a play without licence, it was proved by Mr. Gattie that he had been an actor in the theatre in question, and that the defendant was the acting manager, and generally paid him his salary, and that he also dismissed him from the theatre, Lord Tenterden, C. J., said: "It is proved that the defendant was the acting manager, and paid Mr. Gattie his salary, and finally dismissed him; and I do not know that there can be any stronger evidence that a person causes the pieces to be performed. If the defendant causes the performance, that is sufficient; it makes no difference that he did so as an agent for others."

Slight evidence will be sufficient to establish that a person

---

(*i*) 5 C. & P. 33.

has caused a performance (*k*). See also the cases of "causing a representation" under the Copyright Acts (*l*).

Further, by sect. 11, the proprietor and all performers are liable if they act in a caravan which does not require, and indeed could not have, a licence under sect. 2, or in an open field, unless they are performing at a lawful fair, and have been for that purpose licensed by justices, sect. 23 (*m*). As to a lawful fair, see p. 42.

By *Leary* v. *Patrick* (*n*) it does not seem quite certain that the justices have jurisdiction to give costs in addition to the penalty; indeed, it would be difficult to ascertain their amount, as by sect. 21 the prosecutor's expenses are paid out of the penalty.

It was argued that if there was jurisdiction to give costs, they could only be given if the penalty imposed was under 5*l*., but if the penalty was 5*l*. or over the costs were included. But it was agreed by all the Court that even if there is jurisdiction to adjudicate costs, the justices must actually adjudicate that costs should be levied, for costs do not follow *ipso facto* from conviction and imposition of a penalty.

The pecuniary penalties imposed by the Act can, by sect. 19, be recovered either before the Courts of Record at Westminster—now the High Court of Justice (Queen's Bench Division)—or in Scotland before the Court of Session or of Justiciary, or in Great Britain before two justices having jurisdiction in the place where the offence was committed.

If the theatre is proved to have been used for play, it lies on the defendant to prove that it was licensed.

(*k*) *R.* v. *Glossop*, 4 B. & A. 616.
(*l*) *Russell* v. *Briant*, 8 C. B. 836; *Lyon* v. *Knowles*, 3 B. & S. 556; *Marsh* v. *Conquest*, 17 C. B. N. S. 418.
(*m*) *Fredericks* v. *Payne*, 32 L. J. (N. S.) M. C. 14.
(*n*) 15 Q. B. 266.

In all the cases reported, the Commissioner or Superintendent of Police has sued on behalf of the Crown.

But it is not certain whether a common informer can sue or not.

The law on the subject of a common informer is laid down very fully in *Clarke* v. *Bradlaugh* (o).

Lord Selborne recognized as law, " That where a penalty is created by statute and nothing is said as to who may recover it, and it is not created for the benefit of a party grieved, and the offence is not against an individual, it belongs to the Crown, and the Crown alone can maintain a suit for it." . . . . "The onus is upon a common informer to show that the statute has conferred upon him a right of action to recover the particular penalty he claims." . . . . " I do not agree with the argument of the appellant, that for such a purpose express words are necessary, silence as to the person who is to recover the penalty creates no more difficulty or uncertainty than if the statute had simply imposed the penalty and had said nothing at all about the manner of recovering it. It must be recovered by him to whom it is due, and it is due to the Crown, and not to the informer, unless there is enough in the statute to show affirmatively by words pointing to the informer, or negatively by words exclusive of the Crown, that the informer was meant to have it."

The old Act, 10 Geo. III. c. 28, inflicting a penalty of 50*l*. for acting without licence, expressly provides, by sect. 6, after speaking of all the pecuniary penalties thereby imposed, that half the penalty should go to the informer or person suing or prosecuting for the same, and the other moiety to the poor of the parish where such offence shall be committed.

There are no corresponding words in 6 & 7 Vict. c. 68.

(o) 8 App. Cas. 354.

Sect. 21 provides for the prosecutor's costs being paid first out of the penalty, the residue (if any) going to the Crown.

In *Shelley* v. *Bethell* (*p*) the point does not seem to have been raised.

On the whole, considering that sect. 21 separates the Crown from the prosecutor, and looking at *Shelley* v. *Bethell*, the weight of argument seems to be in favour of the common informer.

It only remains to add, that for all offences under the Act, by sect. 22 the prosecution must be commenced within six calendar months after the offence is committed.

Further, there is a sanction, apart from the statute, in that contracts relating to an unlicensed theatre cannot be enforced. See pp. 62, 79.

By 1 Car. I. c. 1, every person using interludes or common plays within his own parish on the Lord's Day shall forfeit 3*s*. 4*d*. to the poor of the parish.

By 21 Geo. III. c. 49, it is forbidden to open on Sunday any house, room, or other place for public entertainment or amusement to which persons are admitted by payment.

(This will include not only theatres and music-halls, but lectures, wax-work shows, circuses and other places not required to be licensed by 25 Geo. II. c. 36, more than twenty miles from London or Westminster, and in particular the Brighton Aquarium, and apparently the Fisheries or Health Exhibition.)

Any such house or place is to be deemed a disorderly house, and a penalty of 100*l*. is imposed on the owner or keeper, and 50*l*. on the man who sells the tickets; the said penalties to be sued for by a common informer within six months after the offence is committed.

(*p*) 12 Q. B. D. 11,

But the penalties incurred under this Act may, by 38 & 39 Vict. c. 80, be remitted by the Crown.

This was passed for the purpose of relieving the Brighton Aquarium from the penalties incurred under 21 Geo. III. c. 49.

Further, the Chancery Division might restrain a theatre being so used to be a nuisance, if the performance of the orchestra and the clapping of the audience is so clearly heard in the neighbouring houses as to interfere with the ordinary occupations of life (*q*).

By 42 & 43 Vict. c. 34 (which applies to Ireland as well as Great Britain), it is made an offence on the parent, guardian or employer, to cause, or aid in causing, a child of either sex, under the age of fourteen years, to take part in any public exhibition or performance, whereby, in the opinion of a court of summary jurisdiction, the life and limbs of such child shall be endangered, and imposes a penalty of 10*l.* for each offence.

And in case bodily harm occurs to such child in the course of such dangerous performance, the court of summary jurisdiction can order the employer to pay a sum not exceeding 20*l.* to the child, or some person named by the Court on behalf of the child.

§ 8.—*Structure.*

By an Act passed in the year 1878 (41 & 42 Vict. c. 32), theatres, music-halls, and other places of public entertainment in the metropolis became subject to new regulations for protection of the public from fire.

(*q*) *Inchbald* v. *Robinson,* L. R. 4 Ch. 388.

As to New Theatres or Music-halls.

By sect. 13 of the Act a new procedure for obtaining a licence is introduced. Instead of speaking of the actual and responsible manager the Act allows a person interested in any premises about to be constructed to be used for a theatre or other public entertainment, to apply to the licensing authority for a provisional licence.

The grant of the provisional licence is subject to the same conditions as those applicable to a licence not provisional (*r*).

The holder of a provisional licence for a new theatre, &c., who has been granted his certificate of structural fitness from the Board, can apply at once to the licensing authority, and can demand a confirmation of his provisional licence, which it must give if no objection can be made to his character. Is this objection to character a new enactment, or is it supposed to carry out the provisions of 6 & 7 Vict. c. 68, in which nothing is found with regard to character, and under which it would appear that, except as to the conditions (*s*) above mentioned, the licensing authority have no discretion?

The structural certificate of the Board is, by sect. 12, required for all theatres and for all music or public dancing-halls, containing a superficial area of not less than 500 square feet, which are licensed for the first time after the passing of the Act, the 22nd of July, 1878.

The Board is, by sect. 12, empowered to make such regulations as in their opinion are necessary for the protection of all persons who may frequent the same (*i.e.*, both public and performers) against dangers from fires which may arise therein or in the neighbourhood thereof.

(*r*) It has been proposed by the Metropolitan Board of Works that a Bill should be introduced into Parliament making it compulsory for places of amusement to have a structural certificate from the Board before applications are made for licences. See The Times, October 18, 1884.

(*s*) Viz., that the person applying for a licence should be the actual and responsible manager, and that he should find sufficient security.

A copy of the present regulations will be found in the Appendix, p. 157.

The certificate is only granted on completion, and if there is an opening without a certificate a penalty of 50*l.* is imposed.

As to Theatres and Music-halls existing at the time of the passing of the Act.

The Board is, by sect. 11, empowered, if in its opinion any theatre, of whatever size, or any music-hall, containing an area of more than 500 superficial feet for the accommodation of the public, authorized to be kept open and kept open at the time of the passing of the Act, is so defective in its structure that special danger from fire may result to the public, and if, in its opinion, the said structural defects can be remedied at a moderate expenditure, after obtaining the consent of the Lord Chamberlain or Secretary of State, by notice in writing to require the owner to remedy the defects within a reasonable time; and in case of default imposes a penalty of 50*l.*, and 5*l.* for every day during which default continues. The owner can appeal to an arbitrator, to be appointed by the First Commissioner of Works, whose decision is to be final (*t*).

For the purpose of the more effectual carrying out of these regulations, and that the Board may be satisfied before giving its certificate, sect. 21 gives power to architects of

(*t*) The owner of the Vaudeville Theatre, in pursuance of a notice from the Metropolitan Board of Works, incurred certain expenses in executing the works required. In an action against the lessee to recover these expenses, under a covenant to bear, pay and discharge, *inter alia*, every other rate, tax, charge, assessment, burthen, duty and imposition whatsoever, parliamentary, parochial or otherwise, to which the lessor then was or should or might be hereafter liable, the lessor was held entitled to recover. *Robertson* v. *Thorne*, 47 J. P. 566. For the meaning of "owner," see 18 & 19 Vict. c. 120, s. 250, and c. 122, s. 3, both of which Acts are to be construed with the Act of 1878.

the Board, or those authorized in writing under seal by the Board, to enter such theatres and music-halls at all reasonable times after completion or during construction. The district surveyor may also at all reasonable times during the progress, and the three months next after the completion of such theatres, &c., enter and inspect the same. In case admittance or reasonable assistance is refused a penalty of 20*l*. is incurred.

Sect. 23 provides for the mode in which penalties may be recovered. Theatres and music-halls in the metropolis are liable to all the general provisions as to foundations, &c., prescribed by the Metropolitan Building Act, 1855, and the Acts amending the same. They are further liable to the special regulations prescribed for a *public building*, which is defined by 18 & 19 Vict. c. 122, s. 3, to include, *inter alia*, every building used as a theatre, public concert-room, public ball-room, public lecture-room, public exhibition-room, or for any other public purpose. By sect. 22, in every public building the floors of the lobbies, corridors, passages and landings, and also the flights of stairs, shall be of stone or other fireproof material, and carried by supports of a fireproof material. By sect. 30 every public building, including the walls, roof, floors, galleries and staircases, shall be constructed in such a manner as may be approved by the district surveyor, or, in the event of disagreement, may be determined by the Metropolitan Board of Works; and the section further goes on to say, that all public buildings are subject to the same rules of construction as other buildings (*t*).

(*t*) See Woolrych, Metropolitan Building Acts, 3rd ed. pp. 40, 41. In the case of a concert-room forming part of the Albert Exhibition Palace in Battersea Park, the Board of Works, in October, 1884, refused to grant a structural certificate, on the ground that the building was of unusual construction and did not conform to the Board's regulations. Among other objections the staircases were constructed of wood. See The Times, October 18, 1884.

The Metropolitan Building Act of 1882 (45 Vict. c. 14), by sect. 15, subjects to and includes under the previous rules and regulations as to public buildings and their staircases, &c., all buildings originally built for other purposes and then proposed to be converted into public buildings.

§ 9.—*Police.*

2 & 3 Vict. c. 47, by sect. 38, provides that the business and amusements of all metropolitan fairs shall cease at 11 p.m., and not begin earlier than 6 a.m., and if a house, room, booth, standing, tent, caravan, waggon or other place is open for business or amusement between these hours, a constable may take into custody the person having the care or management thereof, and also every person therein who shall not quit the same on being bidden; and the person having the care or management of any such house, &c., is liable to a penalty of not more than 5*l.*, and the persons who were therein, after having been bidden, to a penalty of not more than 40*s.*

Sect. 39 provides for an inquiry if such metropolitan fairs are lawful, and if such fair is declared unlawful the Metropolitan Board may order constables to remove booths placed or being placed there, and to arrest the persons erecting or frequenting them, who are made liable to a penalty not exceeding 10*l.* The powers under this section are extended by 31 & 32 Vict. c. 106, which deals with unlawful fairs, and provides for removal of booths, &c., and the arrest of persons erecting the same, and imposes 10*l.* penalty.

Sect. 44 inflicts a penalty of not more than 5*l.* on any person having a place of public resort, where provisions, liquors or refreshments are consumed, who permits drunkenness or other disorderly conduct, or knowingly suffers unlawful games or gaming therein, or permits prostitutes or persons of a notoriously bad character to meet together or remain therein. In a case of *Wilson* v. *Stewart* (*u*), it was laid down that if the keeper of such a place of public resort instructs his servant to manage it in such a way as to offend against the above section, and the servant does so, the master is guilty of an offence within the Act, and the servant is guilty of aiding and abetting him.

Sect. 45 prohibits any internal communication between any place of public resort not licensed for the sale of wine, spirits, beer or exciseable articles, and any house, room or place so licensed, and imposes a penalty of not more than 10*l*. for every day such communication is open.

It is the general view that this section forbids any internal communication between a theatre and music-hall and a refreshment room, *e. g.* at the Criterion and Gaiety Theatres, London; but from a consideration of the enactments bearing on the question, this seems at least doubtful.

5 & 6 Will. IV. c. 39, s. 7, directs the Excise Commissioners to grant licences for the sale of intoxicating liquors to any theatre or other place of public entertainment, when licensed by their proper authority, without producing an inn or alehouse licence (*x*).

Supposing the theatre or music-hall has no excise licence, sect. 45 of 2 & 3 Vict. c. 47, will of course come into operation, and a communication will be unlawful. But if a theatre or music-hall has the excise licence, how can it come under the head of "a place of public resort not licensed for the sale of wine, &c. within the said district?"

(*u*) 3 B. & S. 913; Giffard's Jurisdiction of Magistrates, 2nd ed. p. 21.

(*x*) Query. In consideration of this provision, might it not follow that rules forbidding the sale of intoxicating liquors in a theatre are invalid, as contrary to the general law of the land? See p. 33.

The Licensing Act of 1872 (35 & 36 Vict. c. 94), s. 72, preserves 5 & 6 Will. IV. c. 39, s. 7.

The Licensing Act of 1874 (37 & 38 Vict. c. 69), s. 7, recites 5 & 6 Will. IV. c. 39, s. 7, and provides that the sale of intoxicating liquors under the recited Act shall be restricted to such parts of the theatre as are specified in the licence, and the liquor is only to be supplied to persons *bonâ fide* employed in or attending the performance. It further says, that no part of such theatre or other place of public entertainment which shall during the performances in the same be accessible to persons other than those employed or attending the performances therein, shall be included in such licence. That is to say, where a hall of a theatre is open to servants and footmen from carriages on the look-out for their masters, it could not be licensed for the sale of liquors. Nor could you have an internal communication between such hall and a neighbouring public-house. But the whole of that part of the theatre, to enter which you must show your ticket or return pass, can be licensed for the sale of liquors. Nor does there seem to be, either from the words or intention of the Act (and there is no judicial interpretation), any objection to an internal communication between the interior of a theatre and a restaurant, so that persons attending the performance might pass from the inside of the theatre to the restaurant, or, on showing their tickets or return passes, enter from the restaurant by the internal communication to the interior of the theatre.

The Licensing Act of 1880 (43 & 44 Vict. c. 20), s. 43 (5), says that the amount payable for an excise licence to a theatre shall be not more than 20*l*.

Sect. 46 of 2 & 3 Vict. c. 47, authorises the Commissioners of Police, by order in writing, to authorise a superintendent to enter into any house or room kept or used within the metropolitan district for stage-plays or dramatic entertainments into which admission is obtained by payment of money, and which is not a licensed theatre, at any time when the same shall be open for the reception of persons resorting thereto, and to take into custody all persons found therein without lawful excuse; and every person keeping, using, or knowingly letting any house or other tenement (*y*) for the purpose of being used as an unlicensed theatre, is liable to a penalty of not more than 20*l*., or, at the discretion of the magistrate, two calendar months imprisonment; and every person performing, or being therein without lawful excuse, is liable to a penalty of not more than 40*s*.; and a conviction for this offence does not exempt from the penal consequences of keeping a disorderly house or of the nuisance thereby occasioned. Apparently this section does not touch music-halls.

Sect. 52 gives power to the Commissioners of Police to give directions to constables for keeping order and preventing obstructions of the thoroughfares in the immediate neighbourhood of a theatre or other place of public resort.

Sect. 54 makes it an offence—

(1) To show any caravan containing an animal or any other show or public entertainment to the annoyance of the inhabitants or passengers;

(9) To knowingly disregard the traffic regulations of the police;

(12) To exhibit any profane, indecent, or obscene representation, or to sing any profane, indecent, or obscene song or ballad, to the annoyance of the inhabitants or passengers;

Further, it seems that players may be prosecuted as guilty of a nuisance at common law in acting obscene plays (*z*).

(*y*) *Fredericks* v. *Howie*, 1 H. & C. 381. See p. 15.
(*z*) *R.* v. *Curll*, 2 Str. 790.

(14) To blow a horn or noisy instrument for the purpose of announcing any show or entertainment;

and the constable may, without warrant, take into custody any person committing these offences within view of the constable.

CHAPTER II.

THE MUSIC-HALL.

THERE is a distinction between the music-halls within twenty miles of London and Westminster and those in the provinces.

§ 1.—*What is a Music-Hall.*

A music-hall within twenty miles of London or Westminster is any place to which the public are habitually admitted by the proprietor for the purpose of either hearing music or seeing or taking part in dancing or any like entertainment. Every such music-hall must be licensed under 25 Geo. II. c. 36 (originally passed for a term of three years, but made perpetual by 28 Geo. II. c. 19, s. 1).

Any place where music is performed, whether "a house, room, garden or other place," requires to be licensed; and further, if it is an actual building and situate within the metropolitan area, it must conform to the structural conditions prescribed by the Metropolitan Board of Works. See p. 38.

If the public are not admitted indiscriminately, it will not be within the statute.

Thus in *Bellis* v. *Burghall*(a), the defendant was a dancing-master and proprietor of a large room, not part of his

---

(a) 2 Esp. 722.

dwelling-house, where a considerable number of persons met every Wednesday night for the purpose of dancing. Tickets were issued to subscribers only for a given number of nights. The gentlemen having tickets were permitted to introduce a lady. No money was taken at the door, nor were persons admitted indiscriminately—nor, in fact, any person but subscribers, persons introduced by subscribers, or persons who came there by the permission of the defendant as his friends. Lord Kenyon ruled that it was not a meeting within the prohibition of the statute.

As regards music or dancing being the purpose for which the house is had or kept, it need not be the main or principal purpose; even if it is a collateral or subsidiary purpose (*b*) it will come within the prohibition of the statute (*c*).

The majority of cases under this head have arisen in the case of public-houses and refreshment-rooms at which the proprietor gave music gratis to his customers, or at which the customers danced. In all these cases the main purpose of the opening and keeping of the house was not music or dancing, but the sale of liquors or refreshments, and the proprietor supplied the music as a means of attracting customers. The verdicts of the juries have been varying and contradictory, but the law is settled and plain.

That where the public (*d*) are habitually (*e*) admitted to a house or place for the purpose of hearing music or taking

---

(*b*) The mere fact of music being played, if merely incidental to the performances, as in a circus, would not bring the performance within the statute. *Guaglieni* v. *Matthews*, 34 L. J. M. C. 116.

(*c*) *Hall* v. *Green*, 9 Ex. 24.

(*d*) The admission must be indiscriminate and not restricted to a specified class of persons. *Archer* v. *Willingrice*, 4 Esp. 186; *Shutt* v. *Lewis*, 5 Esp. 128.

(*e*) In *Bellis* v. *Beal*, 2 Esp. 592, the fact that the room was open from Easter to Michaelmas was regarded by Lord Kenyon as important to show the habitual keeping.

part in dancing (*f*), this is an offence within the statute. Whether the house is kept with such purpose is a question for the jury. As regards the habitual admission, a distinction is drawn between the premises of licensed victuallers and private houses, for in the former case a much smaller number of times will fulfil the condition " habitually."

The fact that no payment is made will not of itself exempt, but if there is payment it is strong *primâ facie* evidence that the proprietor " keeps the house for the purpose "(*g*).

The whole law is well summarised by Parke, B., in *Marks v. Benjamin* (*h*) : " In the first place, the house or room must be kept with the defendant's knowledge; secondly, it must be kept *for the purpose* prohibited by the statute; there must be something like a habitual keeping of it which, however, need not be at stated intervals; thirdly, it must be public, to which all persons have a right to go, whether gratuitously or on payment of money, no matter whether paid to the defendant or not, if he knows of the payment. All these are questions to be left to the jury. There would be a difficulty in making the owner of a private house liable, because that is kept for the purpose of occupation, whereas a public-house is kept for entertainment, and a much less number of instances may be sufficient to render the owner liable for keeping it for the purposes mentioned in the statute."

(*f*) In *Guaglieni* v. *Mathews*, 34 L. J., M. C. 116, Cockburn, C. J., said, "To bring a case within the statute, I do not think it necessary that the public should actually participate in the dancing." See, too, *Clarke* v. *Searle*, 1 Esp. 25.

(*g*) It is immaterial that payment is not made to the proprietor, and that he derives no benefit from it. *Green* v. *Botheroyd*, 3 C. & P. 471; or even that payment is optional. *Frailing* v. *Messenger*, 16 L. T., N. S. 332, 494.

(*h*) 5 M. & W. 565.

T. E

The words "other public entertainment of the like kind" have been judicially interpreted in *Reg.* v. *Tucker* (*g*), where the defendant was found guilty of keeping a place of public entertainment (a skating rink) of a like kind to music and dancing, without licence. After argument before the Court for the consideration of Crown Cases Reserved, Cockburn, C. J., said: "I am not prepared to overrule the decision in *Guaylieni* v. *Mathews*. It is not necessary either to affirm or question it. The decision only applies where the music is merely subsidiary to something else which forms the real substance of the performance. It does not apply where the music forms an independent attraction and an integral part of the entertainment. The third count charges the defendant with keeping a place for an entertainment of a like kind with music and dancing. Rinking may or may not be similar to dancing, but when it takes place to the accompaniment of music it becomes of a like kind with dancing to music. It is sufficient to decide that, where rinking is combined with music, it is within the statute."

Gregory v. *Tuffs* (*h*) is important as showing upon whom the burden of proof falls. It was proved by the plaintiff that on more than twelve different nights between the 1st of July and the 21st of September, there was, in a tap-room at the defendant's house, a man playing the violin and persons dancing, and that on each occasion the dancing continued as long as the witness stayed. It was also proved that no money was taken for admission, and that the words "licensed dealer in foreign wines and spirits" were painted on the defendant's house, but no words importing that the defendant had a licence for music under 25 Geo. II. c. 36.

It was submitted that this was not the proper way of

(*g*) 2 Q. B. D. 417.
(*h*) 6 C. & P. 271.

proving that the house was not licensed. Whether it was licensed or not would appear by the record of the sessions.

Lord Lyndhurst, C. B.: "By this Act of Parliament persons having licensed houses for music are to have it painted on the outside of the house that they are so, and it is proved that that is not so here." Counsel for defendant: "This not being painted in front of the house may make the party liable to a penalty, but still he may be licensed." Lord Lyndhurst, C. B.: "The Act has directed it to be done; but if it is not so, it is *primâ facie* evidence that this is an unlicensed house. But you may rebut it if you can do so." Counsel for defendant submitted that, as no money was taken for admittance, it might be merely the act of persons who had come to defendant's house and danced without his knowledge, and this would not be within the statute. He cited *Shutt* v. *Lewis*, 5 Esp. 128. Lord Lyndhurst, C. B., in summing-up: "I agree entirely with the learned counsel for the defendant, that the mere occasional or accidental use of a room for the purpose of music and dancing is not within this Act of Parliament, but the case he cited does not apply, as the room was hired by a Jew, and it therefore was for the time his private room. I am of opinion that, to bring this case within the Act of Parliament, it is not essential that the room should be used exclusively for this purpose, nor is it necessary that money should be taken for admission. One can easily understand that a person keeping a public-house would find it his interest to have an attraction to draw persons in great numbers to his house, as it would remunerate him without his receiving money specifically for admission into the room. It seems to me to be difficult to say that this could have gone on in the defendant's house from July to September without his knowledge unless he was absent from home during the whole time, which, if the fact were so, he might easily have proved. The case therefore comes to this—are you satisfied that this room was kept by the defendant for the purpose of public dancing?"

As to the proof of want of licence, Lord Ellenborough laid down, in *R.* v. *Turner* (i) (action *qui tam* against a carrier for being in possession of game without a licence), "The question is upon whom the *onus probandi* lies—whether it lies upon the person who affirms a qualification to prove the affirmative, or upon the informer, who denies any qualification, to prove the negative; but in *Spieres* v. *Parker* (1 T. R. 144), I find Lord Mansfield laying down the rule—that in actions on the game laws (and I see no good reason why the rules should not be applied to informations as well as actions) the plaintiff must negative the exceptions in the enacting clause though he throw the burden of proof on the other side. The same was said by Heath, J., in *Jelfs* v. *Ballard* (1 B. & P. 468), and such has been, I believe, the prevailing opinion of the profession and the practice. I am therefore of opinion that this conviction, which specifies negatively in the information the several qualifications mentioned in the statute, is sufficient without going on to negative by the evidence those qualifications."

§ 2.—*Licensing.*

The licence of any music-hall within twenty miles of London or Westminster is to be granted at Michaelmas Quarter Sessions for the county, city, riding, liberty, or division in which such music-hall is situated. It must be applied for annually, and the justices have an absolute

(i) 5 M. & S. 206.

discretion to refuse either a new application, a transfer, or a renewal, however proper may be the character of the applicant or the house.

The justices must actually hear each case on its merits before refusing it. They must not act on one general rule, e. g., that all music-halls, as to the conduct of which the superintendent of police complains, shall be refused a licence.

The licence is to be signified under the hands and seals of four or more of the justices there assembled. An unlicensed music-hall is to be deemed a disorderly house. Every licence is to be signed and sealed by the justices in open Court, and afterwards publicly read by the clerk of the peace, together with the names of the justices subscribing the same. No such licence shall be granted at an adjourned session, and no fee or reward is to be charged for it (*k*).

Further, a licence may be granted for either music or dancing, or for both.

In *Brown* v. *Nugent* (*l*), the defendant, owner of Cambridge Music-Hall, having a licence for music only, produced a ballet divertissement. The jury found that dancing was a substantial part of the entertainment, and the music only ancillary thereto.

Kelly, C. B., said: "It seems to me clear that the intention of the legislature was, that it should be in the discretion of the magistrates, according to the place and the position of the house, the nature of the neighbourhood, the kind of persons who would be likely to assemble in such a house, and also in regard to the recommendation and expressed opinions of the inhabitants in the neighbourhood in which the house is to be licensed—to grant a licence for public entertainment only or for the purpose of public dancing."

(*k*) 25 Geo. II. c. 36, s. 2.
(*l*) L. R., 6 Q. B. 693; 7 Q. B. 588.

The duration of a licence under 25 Geo. II. c. 36, seems to be without doubt for a year.

By a Local Act (25 & 26 Vict. c. 123) for Cardiff, it was provided that the house, &c. was to be licensed by justices on their general annual licensing day, and further, in case of breach of conditions of licence, the licence might be forfeited and revoked by the justices at any subsequent licensing day.

The appellant was convicted by the justices under the Local Act for having, on the 24th of September, 1873, unlawfully rented a room called Victoria-rooms for public music and stage dancing without licence.

It appeared from the case that the Victoria-rooms were held by the appellant under a lease from N. Laurence. They were first licensed at the adjourned general annual licensing meeting held in September, 1870. A licence was then granted to N. Laurence, and was renewed to him annually until 1873, when at the adjourned licensing meeting on the 24th of September a further renewal was refused, on the ground that Laurence had transferred his licence without the permission of the magistrates, that he had recently been convicted of selling wine there without a licence, and that some of the performances had been indecent. On the 25th of September, 1871, Laurence entered into an agreement with the appellant to transfer the then existing licence to him, and since that time the appellant had the management in his own hands and received the profits. The sanction of the magistrates to this transfer was not had or asked for. Subsequent to, and notwithstanding this agreement, the licence was applied for and taken out by Laurence and not by the appellant.

The licence granted to Laurence on the 11th of September, 1872, expired on the 10th of September, 1873. But on the 24th of that month, the date charged in the summons, the rooms were kept open by the appellant for the usual entertainment.

Cockburn, C. J., said: "The magistrates have unconditional power to grant a licence, and may limit it for the time they think proper. I think that if a man takes a licence on general terms, and understanding it to be a licence for a year, comes and takes another licence, which is a licence for a year, he must be taken to surrender the first. That is the state of things here. There is a licence in 1871 that does not prescribe the period for which a licence was granted, and then in 1872 Laurence comes and takes out a licence for a year, and when he obtained that licence I think he surrendered the other. The new licence of 1872 was terminated, and the renewal refused, before the entertainment for which the appellant is charged. I think he was rightly convicted" (*m*).

Sect. 3 of 25 Geo. II. c. 36, provides that, in order to give public notice what places are licensed pursuant to the Act, there is to be affixed and kept up in some notorious place over the door or entrance an inscription in large capital letters in the words following, namely, "Licensed pursuant to Act of Parliament of the twenty-fifth of King George the Second."

The same section, as amended by 38 & 39 Vict. c. 21, provides that no such house or place shall be open before the hour of noon, and that the affixing and keeping up of such inscription, and the said limitation in point of time, shall be inserted in and made conditions of every such licence. Breach of the conditions leads to forfeiture. See below, p. 57.

Sect. 4 exempts from the operation of the Act the theatres of Drury Lane, Covent Garden, and Haymarket. On this section see *Gallini* v. *Laborie* (p. 26), especially the judgment

(*m*) *Hoffman* v. *Bond*, 32 L. T., N. S. 775.

of Ashurst, J.: "The legislature did not mean, by the statute 25 Geo. IV. c. 36, to give any magic virtue to the walls of the Opera House in the Haymarket, but merely that that place, which was supposed to be licensed by the Lord Chamberlain, need not have any licence from any other magistrates. But that clause cannot extend to the Opera House unless it has been so licensed."

§ 3.—*Penalties.*

For keeping an unlicensed house or place a penalty of 100*l.* is incurred, recoverable by a common informer. In addition the keeper is punishable as for a disorderly house. Further, any constable or other person authorized by warrant may enter such house or place, and seize every person found therein, to be dealt with according to law, 25 Geo. II. c. 36, s. 2.

As to the common informer, see also sect. 13, and *Green* v. *Botheroyd*, 3 C. & P. 471.

As to arrest, see *Brown* v. *Nugent*, L. R., 7 Q. B. 588.

As to the proceedings against disorderly houses, see sects. 5—10.

Only one penalty is recoverable under sect. 2. In a case of *Garrett* v. *Messenger* (*m*), two actions were brought by common informers to recover in each case the penalty of 100*l.* imposed by 25 Geo. II. c. 36; the second being for an offence committed on a different day from that alleged in the first action. Willes, J., directed a verdict for the defendant in the second action, and gave him leave to add a plea that the penalty was recovered in the first action, and leave to plaintiff to move to enter verdict for him. On motion

(*m*) 16 L. T., N. S. 332 (at Nisi Prius); L. R., 2 C. P. 583.

made, the Court held that only one penalty could be recovered, as it was all one keeping, at all events during one year.

By sect. 14 the penalty must be sued for within six calendar months after the commission of the offence.

The penalty imposed by sect. 3 for breach of the conditions contained in that section is forfeiture of the licence, which is revocable by the next general or quarter sessions, and not renewable, and no new licence is to be granted to the same person, or any person on his behalf, for any such house or place.

In addition to the statutory penalties, in certain cases the common law remedies for nuisance will be available. The nuisance may be caused by proceedings either in or out of doors.

An open-air garden with a brass band, where fireworks were discharged, and crowds assembled and remained, is a nuisance: *Walker* v. *Brewster* (n). In this case Wood, V.-C., following *R.* v. *Moore* (3 B. & Ad. 184), granted an injunction against the continuance of the nuisance on the ground that the defendant made a profit by giving entertainments which were carried on so as to induce a crowd of idle people to collect and remain in large numbers to the annoyance of the plaintiff.

In *Inchbald* v. *Robinson*, and *Inchbald* v. *Barrington* (o), proceedings were taken against two circuses. In one case the plaintiff complained of drawing crowds together. As to this the Court said, after drawing a distinction between outdoor and indoor performances, that the plaintiff cannot complain of the temporary crowding occasioned by people going to the circus or leaving it, and no such continuous crowding is shown as to justify the interference of the Court.

(n) L. R., 5 Eq. 25.   (o) L. R., 4 Ch. 388.

If an injunction in such a case were to be granted and upheld it would prevent the setting up near a dwelling-house of any exhibition likely to be attended by a large number of people.

In the second case, after deciding that the noise of the performances was heard inside the houses to such a degree as materially to interfere with the comfort of the inhabitants, according to the ordinary habits of life, the Court granted an injunction.

CHAPTER III.

CONTRACTS.

§ 1.—*Concerning the Building.*

A CONTRACT, the subject-matter of which is a theatre or place of entertainment, or the relations between manager and performers, falls of course under the same rules as any other kind of contract. It may be useful, however, to deal with a few cases of theatrical contract which have come before the Court.

These may be divided into—
 (1) Contracts concerning the building.
 (2) Contracts between manager and performers.

This arrangement does not, of course, profess to be a scientific one, but it will serve to introduce some of the more usual difficulties which may arise under the construction of theatrical contracts.

A precedent of an agreement between a manager and a performer will be found at the end of this chapter. It attempts to meet some of the difficulties which are illustrated by decided cases.

CONTRACTS CONCERNING THE BUILDING.

Covenants between lessor and lessee with regard to the use of the building have received judicial interpretation in *Croft* v. *Lumley* (a), an action of ejectment to recover the

(a) 5 E. & B. 648; 6 H. L. Cas. 672.

Queen's Theatre in the Haymarket on a forfeiture. The defendant became tenant under a lease from the plaintiff, dated the 10th of July, 1845, for terms commencing on different days, both of which would by efflux of time expire on the 29th of September, 1891. The lease contained, among others, the following covenant by Lumley :—" That the said B. L., his executors, &c., shall not nor will at any time hereafter, during the said respective terms hereby granted, convert the said theatre or opera house, or any part thereof, to any other use than for acting or performing operas, plays, concerts, balls, masquerades, assemblies, and such theatrical and other public diversions and entertainments as have been usually given therein, but shall and will during all the said terms use his and their utmost endeavours to improve the same for that use and purpose." There was a power of re-entry by lessor on default of performance of any of the covenants. The defendant entered under the lease and used the premises as an opera house. Since the season of 1852 the house had not been opened for entertainments of any sort, but it had not been converted to any other uses than those contemplated by the lease to the defendant. It was given in evidence at the trial by Mr. Martelli, on the part of the plaintiff, that the fact of the house not having been opened since 1852 was, in his judgment, injurious to the property.

Lord Campbell, C. J., after stating the facts and the evidence, said :—" We are of opinion that the plaintiff has not substantiated any breach of this covenant. The negative part of it most certainly has not been broken. The positive part is only that the lessee would use his best endeavours to improve the theatre for the use and purpose to which it was destined, which seems to refer to the condition of the theatre as to repair and fitness for theatrical purposes, not to its being opened for such performances every season ; at any rate, there is no evidence that Mr. Lumley has not used his best endeavours to keep it open every season, although, unfortunately, it has been closed since 1852. We should have no difficulty in drawing the inference that this has been injurious to the property by bringing rival establishments into fashion, but the covenant relied upon is not framed to meet such a contingency."

On error in the Exchequer Chamber, the point was abandoned. In the House of Lords Lord Cranworth said: "With regard to this covenant, your lordships at the time of argument intimated a very strong and decided opinion that the facts warranted no such conclusion; that there was no pretence for saying that there had been any breach of the covenant on that ground; that the meaning of the covenant was, that he should, by having proper scenes, and by having the house properly painted and kept in order, improve the house, but not if he found that there would be no benefit in opening the house at all; if it would not pay the expenses of having theatrical representation at all that he should, at his own loss, with no benefit to the landlord, keep it open without any corresponding advantage."

There was a further covenant in the lease not to grant away, assign, or dispose of, &c. the stalls and boxes "for any longer period than one year or season." On the 21st of December, 1851, the lessee leased certain boxes for one year, to commence from March, 1852. On the 1st of August, 1852, he made another lease of the same boxes to another person with this habendum, "from the 1st of February now next ensuing, or from such subsequent day during the year upon which the theatre shall be opened, and thenceforth for the full term of one year to be computed from that day."

It was held that this was not a breach of the covenant.

In *Taylor* v. *Caldwell* (b) the defendants contracted to

(b) 3 B. & S. 826.

supply the plaintiff with a room in a music-hall on a particular occasion. Before that occasion arrived the hall was burnt down, and the defendant was held not to be liable on his contract. The existence of the room was the foundation on which both parties proceeded, and the fire, which had happened through the default of neither, excused both. Blackburn, J., in delivering judgment, said: "There are authorities which we think establish the principle that where from the nature of the contract it appears that the parties must from the beginning have known that it could not be fulfilled unless when the time for the fulfilment of the contract arrived some particular specified thing continued to exist, so that when entering into the contract they must have contemplated such continuing existence as the foundation of what was to be done; there, in the absence of any express or implied warranty that the thing shall exist, the contract is not to be construed as a positive contract, but as subject to an implied condition that the parties shall be excused in case, before breach, performance becomes impossible from the perishing of the thing without default of the contractor."

It would appear to follow from this decision that if a manager engaged performers to play at a particular theatre and it was burnt down, the manager would be held not liable to the performers for salaries.

Where parties have knowingly entered into a contract for the use of a building for illegal purposes, the contract cannot be enforced, nor can money paid in pursuance of it be recovered. Thus, in *Ewing* v. *Osbaldiston* (c), plaintiff and defendant were partners in a speculation for hiring the Surrey Theatre to act plays there. The theatre had a music licence under 25 Geo. II. c. 36, but it had not, nor could it

(c) 2 My. & Cr. 53.

have, a theatrical licence. The bill was to establish a partnership, and that accounts might be taken, or that it should be dissolved and accounts wound up.

Lord Cottenham, L. C., after deciding on the facts that there was a partnership, and that by the then existing law the dramatic representations at the theatre were contrary to law, and that it was clear that the contract of partnership was formed for the unlawful purpose of representing there prohibited performances—*i. e.*, stage-plays—then alluded to the music licence, and the argument that it might lawfully have been used for musical entertainments, adding: "The question is, not whether the premises might not have been used for a legal purpose, but whether the contract between the parties, and their partnership and their intentions, were not altogether to use them for an illegal purpose, and undoubtedly such was the case. It is therefore impossible that the plaintiff can be entitled to any decree which shall be founded upon or growing out of this contract, and in this case every part of the joint transaction, such as the purchase of the lease and of other articles about the theatre, was auxiliary to, and in execution and furtherance of, the illegal object.

"It was then urged that the plaintiff ought at least to recover the money he had advanced, and it was said that he had a lien for it upon the property purchased. If the plaintiff be entitled to recover back the money paid, and that right be a personal demand against the defendant, this is not the Court in which such a demand can be enforced; and as to the alleged lien, it is sufficient to observe that no such case is made out by the bill. If it had been, it is difficult to imagine how such a case could have been supported consistently with the ground upon which the Court declines to give the plaintiff the benefit of his contract; for such undoubtedly would, to a certain extent, be giving him the benefit of it. The mere payment of money can give no lien. You must therefore look to the contract to raise the question of lien, and if the plaintiff be entitled to any lien, it must be upon or in consequence of the illegal contract; but I do not consider this question before me. It is undoubtedly a case of great hardship upon the plaintiff to have parted with his money and now to be denied the fruits of it, but this hardship is common to all cases of contract which cannot be enforced from their illegality."

In *Levy* v. *Yates* (d), an action of assumpsit, the declaration stated that plaintiff was proprietor of the Victoria Theatre, and that the defendant had agreed to open at that theatre, with certain performers and a new piece, for a month certain, with a power of renewal for another month, the defendant to have one clear half of each night's clear profits; that the defendant had refused to open.

Plea: That the said theatre was not licensed, and could not be licensed under 10 Geo. II. c. 28, and neither plaintiff nor defendant could or would have procured a licence if they had applied.

On the trial, Lord Denman, C. J., was of opinion that the plea was made out, and a verdict was found for the defendant.

On motion to enter judgment for plaintiff, *non obstante veredicto*, the opinion of Lord Denman, C. J., was sustained, chiefly on the authority of *Ewing* v. *Osbaldiston*.

Coleridge, J.: "The plea is good. It discloses facts which bring this theatre within the restrictions of 10 Geo. II. c. 28. It is immaterial to consider whether it was the duty of plaintiff or defendant to procure the licence, as it could not legally have been procured by either of them with a view to licensing the performances in question."

(d) 8 A. & E. 129.

It will be noticed that both these cases arose before 6 & 7 Vict. c. 68.

In order to give a right of admission to any part of a theatre, or to a specific part, there must be a deed under seal. Any demise short of this is a mere parol licence, and may be revoked at will by the grantor (subject to an action on the contract if given for valuable consideration); but even if for valuable consideration, it is a mere personal covenant, and will not bind the assignee of the grantor.

If, however, there is a grant by deed under seal of a certain specified box, this vests in the grantee such an interest in the box as to give him a right to prevent the grantor using or converting it for or to non-theatrical purposes. But if the theatre is burnt down, unless the right is, in express words, charged upon the land, it will determine, and not revive because a new theatre is erected on the same ground. Such a grantee of a box is liable to be rated to the poor as the occupier of a tenement.

The case comes to this:—If a manager hires a theatre, and is not told by the lessor that there are some persons who have a grant by deed of the right of entry to the theatre, he may disregard all claims made to him or the door-keeper for admission, however threatened by legal proceedings.

If the lessor of the manager has granted a licence not by deed, and even informed the manager of it, and, perhaps even if the manager assents, still the licensee cannot sue the manager.

If there are grantees by deed, and the manager was not informed of them by his lessor, and they sue him, he will have a right of indemnity from his lessor.

The proper course for him to adopt in regard to any persons who present themselves at the door, and of whose right he is ignorant, is to say that his lessor told him nothing of them; and if that does not satisfy them, say, that unless they

T. F

have right of entry by deed under seal they have no right against him. If they then assert they have a deed under seal, he should inquire if they have it with them. If they say no, let him call on them to pay the price of the place to which their deed admits them, and he will hold the money; and if they either produce the deed to him, or if he receives a letter from the lessor to say that the applicants have a right under deed, the money shall be returned.

The law thus laid down is derived from and exemplified by the cases which follow:—

It was held in 1817, in *Taylor* v. *Waters* (*f*), that a licence for valuable consideration, giving admission to a theatre for twenty-one years, but not by deed, was irrevocable. But this case can no longer be considered as law.

In *Wood* v. *Leadbitter* (*g*), in 1845, Alderson, B., delivering the judgment of the Court, made the following observations on *Taylor* v. *Waters*:—

"The judgment is stated by the learned reporter to have contained the substance of the arguments on both sides, and which, therefore, he does not give in his report. We must infer from this that the attention of the Court was not called in the argument to the principles and earlier authorities to which we have adverted.

"Brooke in his Abridgment, Dodderidge in the case of *Webb* v. *Paternoster*, and Lord Ellenborough in the case of *R.* v. *Horndon-on-the-Hill* (4 M. & Sel. 562), all state in the most distinct manner that every licence is, and must be, in its nature revocable so long as it is a mere licence. Where, indeed, it is connected with a grant, there it may, by ceasing to be a naked licence, become irrevocable. But then it is obvious that the grant must exist independently of the licence, unless it be a grant capable of being made by parol, or by

(*f*) 7 Taunt. 374. (*g*) 13 M. & W. 838.

the instrument giving the licence. Now, in *Taylor* v. *Waters* there was no grant of any right at all, unless such right was conferred by the licence itself. Gibbs, C. J., gives no reason for saying that the licence was a licence irrevocable; and we cannot but think that he would have paused before he sanctioned a doctrine so repugnant to principle and to the earlier authorities if they had been fully brought before the Court. Again, the Chief Justice is represented as saying that the interest of the plaintiff was not an interest in land within the Statute of Frauds, and *consequently* it might be granted without deed. How the circumstance that the interest was not an interest in land within the Statute of Frauds showed it to be grantable without deed, we cannot discover. The precise point decided in *Webb* v. *Paternoster* is not adverted to, and it is assumed, without discussion, that the licence there must have been a parol licence, and a naked licence, unconnected with an interest, capable of being created by parol. The action was not, as it may have been in *Wood* v. *Lake,* an action founded on the contract. It was an action on the case for the obstruction, and was founded on the supposition that an actual right to enter and remain in the theatre had vested in the plaintiff, under the licence conferred by the silver ticket. With all deference to the high authority from which the judgment in *Taylor* v. *Waters* proceeded, we feel warranted in saying that it is to the highest degree unsatisfactory; an observation which we have the less hesitation in making, in consequence of its soundness having obviously been doubted by the Court of King's Bench and Mr. Justice Bayley in the case of *Hewlins* v. *Shippam.*"

This case plainly shows that the ordinary stall or box ticket handed to persons paying for admission is a mere parol licence, revocable at will, and that the person in possession of the theatre may, after requesting a spectator to depart, remove him, without using undue violence. The manager, of course, will be liable to an action on the contract.

In *Weldon* v. *Rivière* (h), an action for assault, Wills, J., said, in summing-up:—"The law was, that when a person had a licence to enter upon another person's premises, and that licence had been revoked, and notice was given of the revocation, he or she could no longer claim to remain on those premises. And where reasonable notice had been given, and he or she refused to depart, and so long as no unreasonable force was used, that person could be removed." In this case the verdict was for the plaintiff, as the jury found the defendant had never been in possession of the theatre.

Flight v. *Glossop* (i) was an action brought on account of the plaintiff's exclusion from the defendant's theatre. The defendant was the assignee of Abbott & Egerton, who had covenanted for valuable consideration to admit the plaintiff. Tindal, C. J., in his judgment, said: "It is sufficient to say that this is a mere personal covenant. In consideration of 313*l.* paid by the plaintiff on the 26th of April, 1834, to Abbott & Egerton, they agreed to pay the plaintiff 360*l.* on the 31st of December, 1834, if Abbott & Egerton, the plaintiff and Flight should be living on that day; and that till that day, if they should all live so long, the plaintiff should have the use of two private boxes in the theatre without paying anything for them; but if either of the parties should die, the plaintiff should pay a reasonable compensation for the use of the boxes. The use of the boxes is only thrown in as a sort of bonus. Why then are we to split the covenant, and say that part of it applies to land and part to personalty, when we see that it is no more than a covenant to pay money on a given day, the lender having the use of the boxes in the

(h) The Times, Dec. 13, 1884.
(i) 2 Bing. N. C. 125.

meantime. If it were necessary to go further, we might observe that this deed does not pass an interest in any specific part of the theatre, or a licence to enter and continue on any specific part: and it would be carrying the doctrine of covenants running with the land far indeed, to say that so general an agreement is binding on the assignee. It is a covenant on which the plaintiff might sue Abbott & Egerton, nothing more." He then referred to *Spencer's case*, 5 Rep. 16 b.

In *Coleman* v. *Foster* (*k*), the declaration was for breaking and entering the plaintiff's theatre. Third plea, that Rix and Cooper, being trustees for themselves and the other proprietors, demised the theatre for three years to Sydney upon the terms, among others, that Rix, Cooper, and the other proprietors should have free liberty and licence of admission to the theatre; that Sydney entered and became tenant subject to those terms; and it was afterwards agreed between the plaintiff and Sydney that the plaintiff should have the use of the theatre for two nights; that the plaintiff knew at the time of the agreement the terms under which Sydney held; that the plaintiff became possessed under the agreement; and that defendant was one of the proprietors, and as such proprietor entered. Plaintiff denied knowledge at the time of his agreement with Sydney, and it further appeared that the demise to Sydney was not under seal.

The Court held that the permission was determined by the demise, Pollock, C. B., adding, "If a man gives a licence and then parts with the property over which the privilege is to be exercised, the licence is gone."

Helling v. *Lumley* (*l*) was a bill to establish right of possession to a box numbered 124, or at any rate to compensation.

(*k*) 1 H. & N. 37.
(*l*) 28 L. J. Ch. 249.

In 1792 the Opera House was demised to a Mr. Taylor, and under the lease Mr. Waters, and subsequently the plaintiff, became entitled. Certain specified boxes, including 124, were prohibited from being leased for any term exceeding from season to season or from year to year. The lessee was to be entitled to let forty-one specified boxes, in which No. 124 was not included, without any such restriction. That lease having become vested in Mr. Waters, and there being also covenants for renewal contained in the original lease, Mr. Waters on the 25th of August, 1821, contracted to sell to Mr. Chambers the interest in the lease and also the renewed terms, subject to the right of possession of Mr. Waters, his executors, administrators, and assigns, to the box numbered 124, hitherto usually occupied by him, on the east side of the theatre, or his or their nominees, not exceeding six persons nightly, during the remainder of the several terms granted by the lease, and the terms covenanted by the lease to be granted. Accordingly box 124 was reserved to Waters on the purchase by Chambers; and he was also to have the right of possession of that box to him, his executors, administrators and assigns, during the remainder of the term thereby assigned, and during any renewed term to be granted under the covenant for renewal contained in the original lease. Waters by a deed dated the 15th of March, 1823, assigned all his interest in the Opera House. The plaintiff afterwards was appointed a trustee of the deed of the 15th of March, 1823. In 1845 the assignees of Chambers sold their interest to Lumley for the then residue of the terms of years subsisting therein in equity; by virtue of the covenants for renewal contained in the lease mentioned in the contract of the 25th of August, 1821 (the terms of years granted by the lease having then expired), and by the contract for such sale, it was provided, that the sale was subject to such rights to boxes as the premises were then subject to as against the assignees of Chambers. That contract was completed by means of a renewed lease dated the 10th of July, 1845, and granted to Lumley by direction of the assignees of Chambers, and by virtue of the covenant for renewal contained in the expired lease of the Opera House for the term of years mentioned in the lease; and Lumley was thereby restrained on the same terms in which the lessee in the original lease had been, from disposing of boxes for more than one year, except forty-one boxes to be selected by him within five years, which he was to be at liberty to dispose of at pleasure.

Stuart, V.-C., made an order establishing the plaintiff's rights and restraining the defendants from interfering with them.

On appeal the decree was substantially affirmed.

In an Irish case of *Malone* v. *Harris* (*m*) the facts were these:—H. Harris had erected a theatre in Dublin under letters patent. He afterwards raised a sum of 10,000*l*. on the security of the theatre and of the letters patent by granting debentures. In 1839, in consequence of difficulties which had arisen concerning the debenture holders, their rights and privileges, a deed was executed, in which the debenture holders, including the petitioner, released all claims for interest on their debentures; and in consideration of this it was provided that the holders of debentures should have a right to free admission to the theatre for themselves, and should also have a right to issue certain tickets for free admission for others.

The respondent, John Harris, obtained a lease of the theatre from the assignee of H. Harris, with full knowledge of the deed of 1839, and on the 24th of September, 1854, he issued a circular by which he required the debenture holders

(*m*) 11 Ir. Ch. R. 33.

to produce their debentures for inspection, in order that the names of the holders might be registered.

The petitioner alleged that he had lost his debentures, and was consequently unable to register them. The respondent then refused to permit the petitioner to exercise any of the privileges of a debenture holder, and the petitioner brought an action at common law against the respondent for such refusal, which terminated in a verdict and judgment for the respondent. The petitioner prayed for a declaration that he was entitled to two debentures and the privileges flowing from them, and that the respondent might be restrained from obstructing the exercise of the rights conferred by the deed of the 31st of May, 1839, as a debenture holder. In the course of his judgment dismissing the petition, Brady, L. C., said:—

"It could not be said that there is to be found in this deed any covenant running with the land on which the theatre had been built. Has any equity been fastened on the premises by the lessors of the lease under which the respondent derives? In my opinion there has not; the privilege conferred, and the provisions by which such privilege is secured, are simply personal, and the respondent ought not to be bound by obligations which he has not contracted to fulfil. The debentures originally issued were founded on a twofold right. There was the repayment of the sum advanced; there was the right of free admission to the theatre by tickets. The latter claim is what is now sought to be enforced. It originated in what was supposed to be the law in *Taylor* v. *Waters* (n), a case often questioned, but at last deliberately overruled by the Court of Exchequer in England in *Wood* v. *Leadbitter* (o). The right of admis-

(n) 7 Taunt. 374.
(o) 13 M. & W. 838; see also *Hewitt* v. *Isham*, 7 Ex. 77.

sion is but a licence to enter on the premises of the licenser; there is not any grant of an interest in the subject of the licence. If this be a licence to enter upon the premises, in which it grants nothing by way of interest, but is simply a licence for pleasure, there is nothing to attach an equity to the premises in the occupation of the respondent. It is simply a right of free entry for pleasure, granted for pecuniary consideration; and so the case is governed by *Wood* v. *Leadbitter*, and especially as that case is explained in *Taplin* v. *Florence* (*p*). The distinction should always be noted between a mere licence and a licence either expressly or impliedly coupled with an interest."

Dauncy v. *Chatterton* (*q*) was a case interpreting the private Act regulating Drury Lane Theatre, 1 Geo. IV. c. lx. By sect. 3 a life renter is entitled to admission into the usual audience part of the theatre, subject to the regulations of the sub-committee.

The plaintiff, being a life renter, on applying to the freelist clerk, was given a card marked "Renter," and shown into a seat in the dress-circle. He then wished to change for a stall, gave up his card "Renter," and was given a ticket "Dress-circle cross," and went to the stall registrar, who gave him a stall ticket, but asked him to pay 2s. He refused, and tried to force his way into the stalls. The officials prevented him, and he was ejected, but without violence. He brought an action of trespass, and, on a case stated, the Divisional Court decided, and in this they were affirmed by the Court of Appeal, that the plaintiff as a new renter had a right of admission to the stalls of the theatre.

The second question was, since he had thus the right to enter the stalls, whether, having gone to the dress-circle and

(*p*) 10 C. B. 744.
(*q*) 44 L. J. C. P. 53; 45 L. J. C. P. 293.

there obtained admission to a seat in the first instance, he had the right to change his mind and obtain admission to the stalls without making any payment? The third question, assuming both of these to be answered affirmatively, was, whether there was anything in the conduct of the plaintiff, or in the mode in which he tried to enforce his right, to afford an excuse to the defendant for keeping him out of the stalls on that particular occasion?

The Court of Appeal, reversing the Divisional Court, decided against the plaintiff on the second question, and so did not assume to decide the third.

The Court decided on the ground of what was the usage at the time the private Act was passed, delivering judgment as follows:—"It appears to us to be the usage now and at the time of the passing of the Act, and we think it a reasonable usage, that every free renter is entitled to elect to which part of the theatre he will go, to the boxes, pit, or gallery; but when he has made his election, then, on entering the public boxes, pit, or gallery, he gives up his ticket marked 'Renter,' and from thenceforth he is entitled to the same privileges (neither less nor greater) as the person who has paid for admission into that part of the theatre into which he has elected to go. It was expressly found that it has not been the practice for the renter to get back the card, or to go down to the vestibule again and have a second interview with the free-list clerk, and write his name in the book and get another card. If that was so when the Act was passed, has anything happened to alter that? It is said this has happened to alter the right: that now the lessees or proprietors have by usage given to the person who pays for admission to the dress-circle a right to go into the stalls on payment of 2s.; and it is said that every free renter has the right to do, without payment, everything that an ordinary man may do with payment, and if one of the public, who pays for admission into the dress-circle, by payment is entitled to go into the stalls, that, therefore, the free renter is entitled to do so without any payment at all. We cannot readily suppose that. We should rather doubt whether a person who has paid for entrance into the dress-circle has a right, by virtue of his having paid his fee for entrance into the dress-circle, to go into the stalls by payment of 2s. We should rather draw the inference that that is in the nature of a fresh bargain, which they may or may not make, but which, it seems, people generally do not object to make. But we rest our decision simply on this, that it appears to us, according to the usage, that the new renter is entitled, having elected to go to the dress-circle and having given up his ticket marked 'Renter,' to all the rights that the person who has paid to go into the dress-circle has, neither less nor more."

In *Leader* v. *Moody* (r), Lord Dudley, under whom the defendant claimed, had demised to the plaintiff for valuable consideration certain stalls by deed dated 28th July, 1862. In March, 1875, Lord Dudley, in consideration of 1,200*l.*, agreed with S. & P. to let the theatre to them for three months from the 20th of March, 1875, to be used for religious services conducted by Messrs. Moody & Sankey.

In order to convert the theatre into a place convenient for the holding of the services, the divisions, consisting of boards sliding in grooves between all the boxes, were removed, and the entire pit of the theatre (including the site of the pit-stalls allotted to the plaintiff) was boarded over, so as to make a new floor of the same level as the stage. This boarding was of a temporary nature, and could be easily removed in a few days.

Plaintiff's counsel said his only object was to try the question of right.

(r) L. R. 20 Eq. 145.

Jessel, M. R.: "In my opinion the plaintiff is entirely right, though I do not grant an injunction. As I understand, the meaning of the disputed instrument is this: Earl Dudley represents that he has a lease of the theatre containing covenants that it shall not be used for any other purpose except as a theatre, with the exception of balls and masquerades. Having a lease of the theatre, he takes money from the plaintiff or his predecessors in title for leases or subdemises of boxes and stalls, and I have no doubt that it is a lease of the boxes and stalls for all theatrical purposes, if I may say so; and, in addition, it is a legal demise of the boxes and stalls themselves. Now, what is the meaning of such a demise? It surely never could be intended that the man who had taken money for boxes and stalls in a theatre could, the day after, destroy the theatre, and turn it, for example, into a stable, if he got a licence from his superior landlord. It seems to me it would be altogether extravagant. When the lessor covenants for quiet enjoyment of the thing demised as against his own acts, he must mean that he will keep it as a theatre, ready to be used at all times for theatrical purposes, and so as to enable the person who has taken the sub-demise from him to have the benefit of that sub-demise by using the boxes and stalls during theatrical performances. Therefore, I am of opinion that any permanent alteration of the theatre, so as to convert it to purposes which are not theatrical and do not allow of its being used as a theatre, is a breach of the covenant on the part of the lessor, which I find clearly implied throughout the lease. Neither has the lessor, except for the purposes reserved, any right to enter upon the boxes and stalls at all; and I think that his doing so, without the leave, permission, or licence, as it might be called, of the owner of the boxes and stalls under the sub-demise, is a trespass utterly unwarrantable at law."

But his lordship went on to say, because the alterations

were only temporary, and there was no reasonable prospect of letting the theatre for theatrical purposes during the six weeks which had then to elapse under the agreement with S. & P., he did not grant the injunction.

Scott v. *Howard* (s) was a case in which the plaintiff, as trustee for the rentallers of the Theatre Royal, Edinburgh, claimed to insist on a right of free admission. The theatre, and the ground on which it stood, had been sold in 1858, to Brown, the defendant's predecessor in title, in consideration of the said Brown paying certain debts for which vendors and himself were jointly liable, and in consideration of certain annuities payable to the vendors, which were charges on the land. Since 1858 the theatre had been twice burnt down and rebuilt. Had the rentallers a right of admission to the new theatre?

Lord Blackburn in his judgment said:—" What was it the parties meant by the deed of 1858, and what is the effect of the instrument as far as regards this privilege of admission to the theatre? It seems quite clear that it was agreed first of all, that there should be an annuity of 2*l.* a year secured upon the land as a real burden, and it was intended that that annuity should be transmitted with each share. There was added, that, besides the annuity passing with the share, there should also pass the privilege of free admission, after-mentioned in these words, ' be entitled to free admission to the audience department of the said theatre, other than the present private boxes.' I come, therefore, to the conclusion that under the deed of 1858 the shareholders would have a right of free admission to the theatre so long as that theatre continues to exist, and yet, when that theatre was destroyed by fire, that right of free admission was gone—had perished with the theatre—and was not revived when the new theatre

(s) 6 App. Cas. 295.

was built in its place." The House therefore decided against the right of the rentallers to admission to the new theatre.

In *Reg.* v. *St. Martin's-in-the-Fields* (*t*), Lord Denman, C. J., delivered the judgment of the Court as follows:—

"The question is, whether Miss Burdett-Coutts is liable to be rated under an Act 10 Geo. III. c. 75, in respect of a private box at the Theatre Royal, Drury Lane.

"The box was demised to the late Mr. Coutts, under an Act for rebuilding the theatre, for a long term of years. The lease grants an exclusive right to occupy the box, and a small room adjoining, whenever any performances take place, and a private entrance to the same in common with other private boxes.

"The words of the statute 10 Geo. III. c. 75, s. 13, are that the persons there mentioned shall make one or more rate or rates, &c. upon all and every person or persons who do or shall inhabit, hold, occupy, possess or enjoy any land, house, shop, wharf, warehouse, or any other building, tenement or hereditament.

"We are of opinion that the box in question is a tenement within the meaning of the Act, and that it is held and occupied by the appellant so as to make her liable to be rated."

CONTRACTS BETWEEN MANAGER AND PERFORMERS.

If the theatre at which a performer has contracted to perform is unlicensed, the manager cannot enforce his contract by injunction or sue for damages for breach of contract.

The performer must prove on his part that the theatre was unlicensed during the time for which he had contracted to perform. But the performer can sue the manager for

(*t*) 3 Q. B. 204.

arrears of salary or for work and labour even if the theatre was unlicensed, unless, perhaps, if the performer knew it was unlicensed.

In *Gallini* v. *Laborie* (*u*) the plaintiff sued upon a contract by which the defendant, a foreigner, undertook to come over to England in order to dance ballets at the Italian opera in the Haymarket, or at such other places as the plaintiff should appoint. The defendant never came at all. But it appeared that during the time for which the defendant had engaged there had been no licence from the Lord Chamberlain for the Opera House, though the plaintiff's company had exhibited dancing entertainments there; but the plaintiff had a licence for performing musical entertainments at a house in Hanover Square. No request, however, was made to the defendant to perform there; nor did it appear that he had any notice that the plaintiff had such a licence. A verdict was found for the plaintiff.

On motion to set aside the verdict, on the ground that the plaintiff had not obtained a licence from the Lord Chamberlain to perform entertainments of the stage, Lord Kenyon, C. J., said: "I think 10 Geo. II. does extend to this and every other entertainment of the stage. Under that Act no entertainment of the stage, of which dancing is one, can be exhibited without the Lord Chamberlain's licence, and none having been obtained in this case the plaintiff cannot call upon the defendant for the breach of an agreement which, without such licence, it was unlawful for him to execute. As to the circumstances of other performers having recovered in similar agreements against the plaintiff for their salaries, those verdicts are right, for being engaged to the plaintiff and ready to execute the agreement on their part,

(*u*) 5 T. R. 242.

they ought not to suffer because he did not obtain a licence which it was his business to have procured."

In *Rodwell* v. *Redge* (*x*) the plaintiffs were the owners of the Adelphi Theatre, and the defendant an actor known as Signor Paulo. The action was for a breach of the following agreement:—

"June 6th, 1823.

"I, Paul Redge, do hereby agree to perform at the "Adelphi Theatre for the two ensuing seasons" (stating the respective commencements and terminations) "at 3*l*. a week, "subject to the usual terms.

"(Signed)   PAUL REDGE.

"The said Paul Redge to be entitled to introduce 25*l*. "worth of benefit tickets one night in each season, to be "named by the manager.

"(Signed)   J. T. RODWELL."

It was proved that the defendant had notice to attend at the commencement of the season and refused, and that there were performances in which he was very much wanted, being a favourite with the public.

On behalf of the defendant it was objected, firstly, that the plaintiffs were stated in the declaration to be the proprietors of a licensed theatre, and the licence had not been proved.

Abbott, C. J.: "I shall presume the licence from the fact that the performance went on. If it were not so they would all be rogues and vagabonds" (*y*).

(*x*) 1 C. & P. 220.

(*y*) It seems to be no part of the case to be made out on the part of the plaintiff that the theatre was licensed, the whole the plaintiff had to prove was the contract and the breach of it. If the theatre was not licensed that was a matter of defence to excuse the breach of the agreement, and therefore, if it had been a licensed theatre, it lay on the defendant to show it in his defence.

CONTRACTS.

De Begnis v. *Armistead* (z) w[...] by an opera singer against the [...] atre at Liverpool to reco[...] hange accepted by the [...] count. The declaration [...]

In September, [...] ement to bring out Ita[...] eks at the defendant's [...] ement the defendant [...] enery, orchestra, an[...] or the dancers; and [...] opera singers, and [...] d that the parti[...] qually betwee[...] enefit night [...] specu- latio[...] of the acco[...] red to be d[...] ed the bill [...] oid, as give[...] ity for money [...] ich it appeared [...] The plaintiff, [...] espect of money [...] t, viz. 120*l.* for dre[...] se of carrying down [...] aster, and 30*l.* for def[...]

Gaselee, J., b[...] hat if the bill was give[...] t the doors of an unli[...] d the plaintiff could no[...] er, to say whether it wa[...] n the

T.

80   THE LAW OF THEATRES AND MUSIC-HALLS.

they   because he did not obtain a licence
which   procured."

De Begnis v. *Armistead* (z) was an action brought by an opera singer against the proprietor of the Amphitheatre at Liverpool to recover 167*l*., the amount of a bill of exchange accepted by the latter in payment of a balance of account. The declaration contained also the usual money counts.

In September, 1831, the parties entered into an agreement to bring out Italian operas and dancing for a few weeks at the defendant's theatre. By the terms of that agreement the defendant bound himself to furnish the lights, scenery, orchestra, an efficient corps de ballet, and dresses for the dancers; and the plaintiff contracted to provide the opera singers, and also their dresses. It was further stipulated that the parties were to divide the receipts on each night equally between them, and they were each to have one clear benefit night. That agreement was acted upon, but the speculation turned out a losing one. On the winding-up of the accounts between the parties, a balance for 167*l*. appeared to be due to the plaintiff, for which he ultimately obtained the bill in question. The defence was, that the bill was void, as given for an illegal consideration, namely, as a security for money received for performances at a theatre which it appeared that the plaintiff knew was unlicensed. The plaintiff, however, proved that the bill was given in respect of money which he had paid at the defendant's request, viz. 120*l*. for dresses for the dancers, 78*l*. to pay the expense of carrying down the ballet corps and Venafra, the ballet-master, and 30*l*. for defendant's expenses in London.

Gaselee, J., before whom the cause was tried, held that if the bill was given to secure payment of money taken at the doors of an unlicensed theatre, it was void in law, and the plaintiff could not recover; he left it to the jury, however, to say whether it was given for that purpose, or, as stated on the

(z) 10 Bing. 107.

part of the plaintiff, for money paid by the plaintiff on account of the defendant. The jury were of the latter opinion, and returned a verdict for the plaintiff for the amount of the bill.

After argument *in banco*, the following judgment was delivered. Tindal, C. J. : " We can entertain no doubt that the agreement between the plaintiff and defendant of the 21st of September, 1831, was an illegal agreement. It was an agreement to become equal sharers in the profits to be derived from acting operas and ballets at a theatre not licensed according to the provisions of 10 Geo. II. and 28 Geo. III., and, from the language of part of the agreement, we can feel no doubt but that it was known to both parties at the time of entering into it, that exhibition in such unlicensed theatre was a breach of the law.

" If, therefore, the bill of exchange had been given for the sake of profits claimed by the plaintiff, or for the excess of advance made by the plaintiff on account of such illegal partnership, it is clear, upon the authority of *Mitchel* v. *Cockburne*, 2 H. Bl. 379, that the plaintiff could recover no part of his demand. But it is contended by the plaintiff that the jury, having expressly found that the bill of exchange was given in respect of three distinct payments made by the plaintiff, the bill of exchange may be left out of view altogether, and that the sums so paid may be recovered under the money counts. The principle by which the present case is to be decided is that which is very clearly expressed by Holt, C. J., in *Bartlett* v. *Vinor*, Carth. 252 : 'Every contract made for or about any matter or thing which is prohibited and made unlawful by statute is a void contract, though the statute does not mention that it shall be so, but only inflicts a penalty on the offender; because a penalty implies a prohibition, though there are no prohibitory words in the statute.' The same principle was more briefly expressed by Lord Ellenborough in the case of *Langton* v. *Hughes*, 1 M. & S. 596. What is done in contravention of the provisions of an Act of Parliament cannot be made the subject of an action. Now, as to one of these sums, viz. the sum of 78*l*., it appeared in evidence that the ballet-master, when in London, applied to the plaintiff, at the request of the defendant, to advance a sum of money on the credit of the defendant, to pay the expense of carrying down the ballet-master and the company which he had hired from London to Liverpool. This sum the plaintiff accordingly advanced to the ballet-master, as the defendant had by the terms of the agreement engaged to furnish every evening of the performance, after the opera, a ballet of good and efficient dancers at his expense; this sum of money, paid for the express purpose of conveying them down to the place where the illegal exhibition was to be made, appear to us to fall within the principle above laid down.

"Again, as to the sum of 120*l*.; the plaintiff, at the request of the defendant, paid that sum to Nathan for dresses purchased of him for the very purpose of being used by the dancers in the unlicensed theatre. It is true that the defendant has also a licensed theatre at Manchester, and that the dresses would in all probability be, and, in fact, were, used in both theatres. But we cannot, upon the evidence, doubt that the object and purpose of the plaintiff in paying for the dresses was not to assist the defendant in preparing for his own theatre at Manchester, in which the plaintiff had no interest, but to assist in carrying into effect the illegal contract between himself and the defendant, of sharing in the profits of the unlicensed theatre at Liverpool. This sum, therefore, appears to fall within the same rule as the former. But as to the remaining sum of 30*l*., the only evidence is, that the defendant had borrowed that sum of the plaintiff to pay his expenses at an hotel in London, where the defendant was residing in the month after the agreement was made. It seems, therefore, to us that there is no ground for holding this money to have been advanced for the necessary purpose of carrying the agreement into execution; and, therefore, as to this sum, we think the verdict ought to stand."

Rule absolute to reduce the verdict to 30*l*.

If a performer is so ill that at the time of performance it would be either impossible or unreasonable that he or she should perform, he is excused from performing, and will not be liable in damages for non-performance; and further, even if he offers to perform the manager may refuse to allow him, if the illness is such that he will be palpably unable to perform efficiently.

If the illness precedes for some time the performance, the performer should send notice to the manager.

It should be noticed that the Court, in saying that illness excused the party, spoke of it as brought on by the act of God, and not by the default of the party; it might be argued thence that illness arising from the act of the party, *e. g.* drunkenness, would not excuse.

However, if the non-performance caused by illness is so important (*e. g.* non-attendance on the opening-night of a play) that it goes to the root of the matter, the manager is at liberty, though he cannot sue the performer for damages, to rescind the contract.

The law seems established by the following cases:—

In *Robinson* v. *Davison* (*a*) the plaintiff was a professor of music and defendant the husband of an eminent pianist, known professionally as Miss Arabella Goddard. In December, 1870, the plaintiff entered into an agreement with

(*a*) L. R. 6 Ex. 269.

Mrs. Davison that she should perform on the piano at a concert at Brigg, on the evening of the 14th of January, 1871, for an agreed fee; Mrs. Davison to provide a piano and a vocalist for the occasion. Nothing was expressly said as what was to be done in case Mrs. Davison should be ill on the day in question, or in any way incapacitated from performing. The defendant's responsibility in respect of his wife's contract was not disputed. On the morning of the 14th of January the plaintiff received a letter from Mrs. Davison stating that she was too ill to attend at the concert. A medical certificate was enclosed. Upon receipt of this communication the plaintiff despatched messengers to the people in the neighbourhood who had taken tickets to prevent their coming, and took all other steps he could to give notice to the public that the concert was unavoidably postponed. All the money he had taken was of course returned. If Mrs. Davison had telegraphed the fact of her illness on the 13th of January, instead of writing, the plaintiff could have put off the concert at a less expense than that which was actually incurred.

The jury found a verdict for the defendant on the main issue, and for the plaintiff for the $2l.\ 13s.\ 9d.$, the expenses of special messengers to give notice of postponement. A rule was obtained on the ground of misdirection in the judge telling the jury that the contract was subject to the implied condition that the defendant should be excused if Mrs. Davison was so ill as to make it unreasonable on the ground of illness that she should perform.

After argument, the rule was discharged on the grounds well stated by Bramwell, B. :—" It is admitted that the lady was not fit to play, that it would have been dangerous to her life to go to the concert, and, if she had gone, that she could not have played efficiently. I think that, under such circumstances, we may well hold that it was part of the bargain, not merely that she should be excused from playing, but that she should not be at liberty to play. It cannot be, surely, that she would have had a right to insist on performing her engagement as best she could, however ineffectually that might be, and then demand payment of her fee from Mr. Robinson.

"It is contended, however, that to say that illness incapacitating from performance excuses, is to engraft a new term on an express contract. But this is a fallacy—first, in supposing that there is in the first instance an absolute contract; and secondly, that the new term is a condition added to its express terms; whereas the whole question is what the original contract was, and whether it was a contract with or without a condition. This is a contract to perform a service which no deputy could perform, and which, in case of death, could not be performed by the executors of the deceased; and I am of opinion that, by virtue of the terms of the original bargain, incapacity either of body or mind in the performer, without default on his or her part, is an excuse for non-performance. Of course, the parties might expressly contract that incapacity should not excuse, and thus preclude the condition of health from being annexed to their agreement. Here they have not done so; and as they have been silent on that point, the contract must, in my judgment, be taken to have been conditional, and not absolute. This is the conclusion I come to upon principle, and the cases cited seem to me in accordance with it."

In *Bettini* v. *Gye* (b), the defendant was director of the Royal Italian Opera, and plaintiff was a dramatic artist and professional singer. An agreement was entered into at Milan to the following effect:—

(b) 1 Q. B. D. 183.

"Royal Italian Opera,
"Covent Garden, London.
"Year 1875.

"The undersigned—Mr. F. Gye of the one part, and Mr. "Bettini of the other part—have agreed as follows:—

"1. Mr. Bettini undertakes to fulfil the part of *primo tenore* "*assoluto* in the theatres, halls, and drawing-rooms, both "public and private, in Great Britain and in Ireland, during "the period of his engagement with Mr. Gye.

"2. This engagement shall begin on the 30th of March, "1875, and shall terminate on the 13th of July, 1875.

"3. The salary of Mr. Bettini shall be 150*l.* per month, to "be paid monthly.

"4. Mr. Bettini shall sing in concerts as well as operas, "but he shall not sing anywhere out of the theatre in the "United Kingdom of Great Britain and Ireland from the "1st of January to the 31st of December, 1875, without the "written permission of Mr. Gye, except at a distance of "more than fifty miles from London, and out of the season "of the theatre.

"5. Mr. Gye shall furnish the costumes to Mr. Bettini for "his characters, according to the ordinary usage of theatres.

"6. Mr. Bettini will conform to the ordinary rules of the "theatre in case of sickness, fire, rehearsals, &c.

"7. Mr. Bettini agrees to be at London, without fail, at "least six days before the commencement of his engagement, "for the purpose of rehearsals.

"8. In case Mr. Gye shall require the services of Mr. Bet-"tini at a distance of more than ten miles from London, he "shall pay his travelling expenses.

"9. Mr. Bettini shall not be obliged to sing more than "four times a week in opera. Mr. Bettini, in order to assist "the direction of Mr. Gye, will sing, upon the request of Mr. "Gye, in the same characters in which he has already sung, "and in other characters of equal position. In case of the sickness of other artists, Mr. Bettini agrees to replace them in the character of first tenor assoluto.

"10. Mr. Gye shall have the right to prolong the period limited upon the same conditions, provided that the period does not go beyond the end of the month of April.

"*Milan, Dec.* 14th, 1874. "F. GYE."

The plaintiff owned that he was unable, from temporary illness, to arrive before March 28 in London, but he was otherwise ready to perform his part, but defendant refused to receive plaintiff into his service.

Defendant pleaded that plaintiff was not in London six days previous to the 30th of March, and that he, the defendant, had no notice of the illness, and that the plaintiff did not attend rehearsals, which it was necessary he should do. Plaintiff demurred.

The judgment of the Court was delivered by Blackburn, J.:—". . . . The question raised by the demurrer is not whether the plaintiff has any excuse for failing to fulfil this part of his contract, which may prevent his being liable in damages for not doing so, but whether his failure to do so justified the defendant in refusing to proceed with the engagement, and fulfil his, the defendant's, part. And the answer to that question depends on whether this part of the contract is a condition precedent to the defendant's liability, or only an independent agreement, a breach of which will not justify a repudiation of the contract, but will only be a cause of action for compensation in damages. We think the answer to this question depends on the true construction of the contract taken as a whole. Parties may think a thing apparently of very little importance essential; and if they sufficiently express an intention to make the fulfilment of such a thing a condition precedent, it will be one; or they may think that the performance of some matter, apparently of essential importance, and *primâ facie* a condition precedent, is not really vital, and may be compensated for in damages, and if they sufficiently expressed such an intention, it will not be a condition precedent. In this case, if to the seventh paragraph of the agreement there had been added words to this effect:— 'But if Mr. Bettini is not there at the stipulated time Mr. Gye may refuse to proceed further with the agreement.' Or if, on the other hand, it had been said, 'And if not there, Mr. Gye may postpone the commencement of Mr. Bettini's engagement for as many days as Mr. Bettini makes default, and he shall forfeit twice his salary for that time,' there could have been no question raised in the case. But there is no such declaration of the intention of the parties either way. And in the absence of such an express declaration, we think that we are to look at the whole contract, and applying the rule stated by Parke, B. (*c*), to be acknowledged, see whether the particular stipulation goes to the root of the matter, so that a failure to perform it would render the performance of the rest of the contract a thing different in substance from what the defendant has stipulated for; or whether it merely partially affects it, and may be compensated for in damages. Accordingly as it is one or the other, we think it must be taken to be, or not to be, intended to be a condition precedent.

"If the plaintiff's engagement had been only to sing in operas at the theatre, it might very well be that previous attendance at rehearsals with the actors in company with whom he was to perform was essential. And if the engagement had been only for a few performances, or for a short time, it would afford a strong argument that attendance for the purpose of rehearsals during the six days immediately before the commencement of the engagement was a vital part of the agreement. But we find, in looking at the agreement, that the

---

(*c*) In *Graves* v. *Legg*, 9 Ex. 716.

plaintiff was to sing in theatres, halls and drawing-rooms, both public and private, from the 30th of March to the 13th of July, 1875, and that he was to sing in concerts as well as in operas, and was not to sing anywhere out of the theatre in Great Britain or Ireland from the 1st of January to the 31st of December, 1875, without the written permission of the defendant, except at a distance of more than fifty miles from London. The plaintiff, therefore, has in consequence of this agreement been deprived of the power of earning anything in London from the 1st of January to the 30th of March; and though the defendant has, perhaps, not received any benefit from this, so as to preclude him from any longer treating as a condition precedent what had originally been one, we think this at least affords a strong argument for saying that subsequent stipulations are not intended to be conditions precedent, unless the nature of the thing strongly shows they must be so. And, as far as we can see, the failure to attend at rehearsals during the six days immediately before the 30th of March could only affect the theatrical performances, and perhaps the singing in duets or concerted pieces during the first week or fortnight of this engagement, which is to sing in theatres, halls and drawing-rooms and concerts for fifteen weeks. We think, therefore, it does not go to the root of the matter so as to require us to consider it a condition precedent. Judgment must be given for the plaintiff."

In *Poussard* v. *Spiers & Pond* (d) the declaration was on an agreement by the defendants to employ plaintiff's wife to sing and play in an opera at the defendants' theatre. Breach that the defendants refused to allow the plaintiff's wife to perform according to the agreement.

Pleas: (1) That the defendants did not agree as alleged; (2) that the plaintiff's wife was not ready and willing to

(d) 1 Q. B. D. 410.

perform; (3) that the plaintiff rescinded the contract before breach. Issue joined.

At the trial before Field, J., judgment was entered for defendants, with leave to move to enter judgment for the plaintiff for 83*l*.

The judgment of the Court was delivered by Blackburn, J.: "This is an action for the dismissal of the plaintiff's wife from a theatrical engagement. On the trial before my brother Field it appeared that the defendants, Messrs. Spiers & Pond, had taken the Criterion Theatre, and were about to bring out a French opera, which was to be produced simultaneously in Paris and London. Their manager, Mr. Hingston, by their authority, made a contract with the plaintiff's wife, which was reduced to writing in the following letter:—

'Criterion Theatre, Oct. 16, 1874.

'To Madame Poussard.

'On behalf of Messrs. Spiers & Pond I engage you to sing and play at the Criterion Theatre on the following terms:—

'You to play the part of Friquette in Lecocq's opera of "Les Prés St. Gervais," commencing on or about the 14th of November next, at a weekly salary of 11*l*., and to continue on at that sum for a period of three months, providing the opera shall run for that period. Then at the expiration of the said three months I shall be at liberty to re-engage you at my option, on terms then to be arranged, and not to exceed 14*l*. per week, for another period of three months. Dresses and tights requisite for the part to be provided by the management, and the engagement to be subject to the ordinary rules of the theatre.

"E. P. HINGSTON, *Manager*.

'(Ratified) SPIERS & POND.'

"The first performance of the piece was announced for Saturday, the 28th of November. No objection was raised on either side to this delay, and Madame Poussard attended rehearsals, and such attendance, though not expressed in the written engagement, was an implied part of it. Owing to delays on the part of the composer, the music of the latter part of the piece was not in the hands of the defendants till a few days before that announced for the production of the piece, and the latter and final rehearsals did not take place till the week on the Saturday of which the performance was announced. Madame Poussard was taken ill, and though she struggled to attend the rehearsals, she was obliged, on the 23rd of November, to leave the rehearsal and call in medical attendance. In the course of the next day or two an interview took place between the plaintiff and Mr. Leonard (Madame Poussard's medical attendant) and Mrs. Liston, who was the defendant's stage manager, in reference to Madame Poussard's ability to attend and undertake her part, and there was a conflict of testimony as to what took place. According to the defendants' version, Mrs. Liston requested to know as soon as possible what was the prospect of Madame Poussard's recovery, as it would be very difficult on such short notice to obtain a substitute; and that in the result the plaintiff wrote, stating that his wife's health was such that she could not play on the Saturday night, and that Mrs. Liston had better therefore engage a young lady to play the part; and this, if believed to be accurate, amounted to a rescission of the contract. According to the evidence of the plaintiff and the doctor, Mrs. Liston told them that Madame Poussard was to take care of herself, and not come out till quite well, as she (Mrs. Liston) had procured, or would procure, a temporary substitute; and Madame Poussard could resume her place as soon as she was well. This, it was contended by the plaintiff, amounted to a waiver by the defendants of a breach of the condition precedent, if there was one.

"The jury found that the plaintiff did not rescind the contract, and that Mrs. Liston, if she did waive the condition precedent (as to which they were not agreed), had no authority from the defendants.

"These findings, if they stand, dispose of those two questions.

"There was no substantial conflict as to what was in fact done by Mrs. Liston. Upon hearing, on the Wednesday (the 25th of November), the possibility that Madame Poussard might be prevented from illness from fulfilling her engagement, she sent to a theatrical agent to inquire what artists of position were disengaged, and learning that Miss Lewis had no engagement till the 25th of December, she made a provisional arrangement with her, by which Miss Lewis undertook to study the part, and be ready by Saturday to take the part in case Madame Poussard was not then recovered so far as to be ready to perform. If it should turn out that this labour was thrown away, Miss Lewis was to have a douceur for her trouble. If Miss Lewis was called on to perform she was to be engaged at 15*l.* a week up to the 25th of December, if the piece ran so long. Madame Poussard continued in bed and ill, and unable to attend either the subsequent rehearsals or the first night, and Miss Lewis's engagement became absolute, and she performed her part on Saturday, Monday, Tuesday, and up to the close of the engagement, the 25th of December. The piece proved a success, and in fact ran for more than three months. On Thursday, the 4th of December, Madame Poussard, having recovered, offered to take her place, but was refused, and for this refusal the action was brought. On the 2nd of January, Madame Poussard left England. My brother Field, at the trial, expressed his opinion that the failure of Madame Poussard to be ready to perform, under the circumstances, went so much to the root of the consideration as to discharge the defendants, and that he should therefore enter judgment for the defendants; but he asked the jury five questions.

"The first three related to the supposed rescission and waiver. The other two questions were in writing, and were: (4) Whether the non-attendance on the night of the opening was of such material consequence to the defendants as to entitle them to rescind the contract? to which the jury said 'No.' And (5) Was it of such consequence as to render it reasonable for the defendants to employ another artiste, and whether the engagement of Miss Lewis, as made, was reasonable? to which the jury said 'Yes.' Lastly, he left the question of damages, which the jury assessed at 83*l*.

"On these questions he reserved leave to the plaintiff to move to enter judgment for 83*l*. A cross rule was obtained, on the ground that the verdict was against evidence, and that the damages were excessive.

"We think that from the nature of the engagement to take a leading, and, indeed, the principal, female part (for the *prima donna* sung her part in male costume as the Prince de Conti) in a new opera, which (as appears from the terms of the engagement) it was known might run for a longer or shorter time, and be a profitable or losing concern to the defendants, we can without the aid of a jury see that it must have been of great importance to the defendants that the piece should start well; and, consequently, that the failure of the plaintiff's wife to be able to perform on the opening and early performances was a very serious detriment to them.

"This inability having been caused by sickness, was not any breach of contract by the plaintiff, and no action can lie against him for the failure thus occasioned. But the damage to the defendants, and the consequent failure of consideration, is just as great as if it had been occasioned by the plaintiff's fault instead of by his wife's misfortune. The analogy is complete between this case and that of the charter-party in the ordinary terms, where the ship is to proceed in ballast (the act of God, &c. excepted) to a port and there load a cargo. If the delay is caused by the excepted perils, the shipowner is excused. But if it is so great as to go to the root of the matter, it frees the charterer from his obligation to furnish a cargo: see per Bramwell, B., delivering the judgment of the majority of the Court of Exchequer Chamber in *Jackson* v. *Union Marine Insurance Co.*, L. R. 10 C. P. 141.

"And we think that the question, whether the failure of a skilled and capable artiste to perform in a new piece through serious illness is so important as to go to the root of the consideration, must to some extent depend on the evidence; and is a mixed question of law and fact. Theoretically the facts should be left to, and found separately by, the jury, it being for the judge or the Court to say whether they, being so found, show a breach of the condition precedent or not. But this course is often (if not generally) impracticable; and if we can see that the proper facts have been found, we should act on these without regard to the form of the questions. Now, in the present case, we must consider what were the courses open to the defendants under the circumstances. They might, it was said on the argument before us (though not on the trial), have postponed the bringing out of the piece till the recovery of Madame Poussard, and if her illness had been a temporary hoarseness incapacitating her from singing on the Saturday, but sure to have been removed by the Monday, that might have been a proper course to pursue. But the illness here was a serious one of uncertain duration, and if the plaintiff had at the trial suggested that this was the proper course, it would no doubt have been shown that it would have been a ruinous course; and that it would have been much better to have abandoned the piece altogether than to have postponed it from day to day for an uncertain time, during which the theatre would have been a heavy loss.

"The remaining alternatives were to employ a temporary substitute until such time as the plaintiff's wife should recover; and if a temporary substitute capable of performing the part adequately could have been obtained upon such a precarious engagement on any reasonable terms, that would have been a right course to pursue; but if no substitute capable of performing the part adequately could be obtained, except on the terms that she should be permanently engaged at higher pay than the plaintiff's wife, in our opinion it follows, as a matter of law, that the failure on the plaintiff's part went to the root of the matter, and discharged the defendants.

"We think, therefore, that the fifth question put to the jury, and answered by them in favour of the defendants, does find all the facts necessary to enable us to decide as a matter of law that the defendants are discharged.

"The fourth question is, no doubt, found by the jury for the plaintiff; but we think, in finding it, they must have made a mistake in law as to what was sufficient failure of consideration to set the defendants at liberty, which was not a question for them.

"This view taken by us renders it unnecessary to decide anything as to the cross rule for a new trial.

"The motion must be refused with costs."

If the performer has covenanted with the manager not to perform elsewhere during his engagement, the Court will enforce this covenant by injunction.

It has also been held that a covenant not to perform elsewhere during the continuance of the engagement is an implied condition of the contract, and such performance will be restrained, even although the other performance is on a different hour or day, or even if the performer's services were not at the period in question required at the theatre.

It should be observed that the Court will not, as a rule, interfere by injunction unless the other party has performed his part of the contract. Thus, where it was part of the contract that the performer should appear on the London stage at the theatre of the party engaging his services, and, in consequence of the benefit to his reputation which he expected to derive thereby, the performer had accepted a smaller salary than that which he had in the provinces, and the other party did not let the performer appear on the London stage, though he paid him his salary, the Court refused to restrain the performer from appearing elsewhere. Also, where the terms of the contract are ambiguous and the injury is insignificant and the time nearly expired, the Court has refused to grant an injunction on an interlocutory application.

In *Morris* v. *Colman* (e), it was held by Lord Eldon, L. C., that there was nothing contrary to public policy in a covenant by a dramatist not to write plays except for a particular theatre.

In *Lumley* v. *Wagner* (f), a bill was filed by the plaintiff, as lessee of Her Majesty's Theatre, against Johanna Wagner, Albert Wagner, her father, and Frederick Gye, the lessee of Covent Garden Theatre.

In November, 1851, Joseph Bucher, as agent of the defendants A. Wagner and J. Wagner, entered into an agreement that J. Wagner should sing at the plaintiff's theatre. At a later date there was added to the agreement an article,

(e) 18 Ves. 437.
(f) 5 De G. & Sm. 485; 1 De G. M. & G. 604.

in writing, which, being translated into English, was as follows:—

"Mdlle. Wagner engages herself not to use her talents at any other theatre, nor in any concert or reunion, public or private, without the written authorization of Mr. Lumley.

"Dr. JOSEPH BUCHER,
"For Mdlle. Johanna Wagner, and
"authorized by her."

The bill then stated that the defendants J. and A. Wagner subsequently made another engagement with the defendant F. Gye, by which it was agreed that the defendant J. Wagner should, for a larger sum than that stipulated by the agreement with the plaintiff, sing at the Royal Italian Opera, Covent Garden, and abandon the agreement with the plaintiff. The bill then stated that the defendant F. Gye had full knowledge of the previous agreement with the plaintiff, and that the plaintiff had received a protest from the defendants J. and A. Wagner repudiating the agreement on the allegation that the plaintiff had failed to fulfil the pecuniary portion of the agreement. The bill prayed that the defendants J. and A. Wagner might be restrained from violating or committing any breach of the last article of the agreement; that the defendant J. Wagner might be restrained from singing and performing or singing at the Royal Italian Opera, Covent Garden, or any other theatre or place, without the sanction or permission in writing of the plaintiff during the existence of the agreement with the plaintiff; and that the defendant Albert Wagner might be restrained from permitting or sanctioning the defendant Johanna Wagner singing and performing or singing as aforesaid; that the defendant F. Gye might be restrained from accepting the professional services of the defendant J. Wagner as a singer and performer or singer at the said Royal Italian Opera,

Covent Garden, during the existence of the agreement with the plaintiff, without the permission or sanction of the plaintiff.

The answer of the defendants A. and J. Wagner attempted to show that J. Bucher was not their authorized agent, at least for the purpose of adding the restrictive clause, and that the plaintiff had failed to make the stipulated payment by the time mentioned in the agreement. The plaintiff having obtained an injunction from Parker, V.-C., the defendants appealed to the Lord Chancellor to dissolve the injunction.

Lord St. Leonards, L. C., in the course of his judgment affirming the decision of Parker, V.-C., said:—" The question which I have to decide in the present case arises out of a very simple contract, the effect of which is, that the defendant, Johanna Wagner, should sing at Her Majesty's Theatre for a certain number of nights, and that she should not sing elsewhere—for that is the true construction—during that period. As I understand the points taken by the defendant's counsel in support of this appeal, they in effect come to this,—that a Court of Equity ought not to grant an injunction except in cases connected with specific performance, or where the injunction being to compel a party to forbear from committing an act (and not to perform an act), that injunction will complete the whole of the agreement remaining unexecuted . . . . . The present is a mixed case, consisting, not of two correlative acts to be done, one by the plaintiff and the other by the defendants, which state of facts may have, and in some cases has, introduced a very important difference, but of an act to be done by J. Wagner alone, to which is superadded a negative stipulation on her part to abstain from the commission of any act which will break in upon her affirmative covenant—the one being ancillary to, concurrent, and operating with, the other. The agreement to sing for the plaintiff during three months at his theatre, and during that time not to sing for anyone else, is not a correlative contract, it is in effect one contract, and though, beyond all doubt, this Court could not interfere to enforce the specific performance of the whole of this contract, yet in all sound construction, and according to the true spirit of the agreement, the engagement to perform for three months at one theatre must necessarily exclude the right to perform at the same time at another theatre. It was clearly intended that J. Wagner was to use her vocal abilities to the utmost to aid the theatre to which she agreed to attach herself. I am of opinion that if she had attempted, even in the absence of any negative stipulation, to perform at another theatre, she would have broken the spirit and true meaning of the contract, as much as she would now do with reference to the contract into which she has actually entered.

"It was objected that the operation of the injunction in this case was mischievous, excluding the defendant, J. Wagner, from performing at any other theatre, while this Court had no power to compel her to perform at Her Majesty's Theatre. It is true that I have not the means of compelling her to sing, but she has no cause of complaint if I compel her to abstain from the commission of an act which she has bound herself not to do, and thus possibly cause her to fulfil her engagement. The jurisdiction which I now exercise is wholly within the power of the Court, and being of opinion that it is a proper case for interfering, I shall leave nothing unsatisfied by the judgment I pronounce. The effect, too, of the injunction, in restraining J. Wagner from singing elsewhere, may, in the event of an action being brought against her by the plaintiff, prevent any such amount of vindictive damages being given against her as a jury might probably be inclined to give if she had carried her talents and exercised them at the rival theatre: the injunction may also, as I have said, tend to the fulfilment of her engagement; though, in continuing the injunction, I disclaim doing indirectly what I cannot do directly."

His lordship then again referred to the authorities. He mentioned and approved of *Morris* v. *Colman*, 18 Vesey, 437, above mentioned; and overruled *Kemble* v. *Kean*, 6 Sim. 333 and *Kimberley* v. *Jenning*, 6 Sim. 340 (*g*).

In *Webster* v. *Dillon* (*h*) the bill was filed for the purpose of obtaining an injunction to restrain the defendant from violating or committing any breach of an agreement whereby he had stipulated with the plaintiff, the lessee of Sadler's Wells Theatre, to play for twelve nights at Sadler's Wells Theatre, and from acting or playing at Drury Lane Theatre, or any other theatre or place, without the sanction or permission of the plaintiff. The agreement was contained in a letter to the plaintiff, signed by the defendant, and in the following terms:—

"Theatre Royal Lyceum,
"April 8, 1857.

" My Dear Sir,—I agree to play for you at Sadler's Wells
" Theatre for twelve consecutive nights, commencing Monday,
" April 20, 1857; that, provided I provide Mr. Barrett to
" play the old men in the pieces, you will allow me a clear
" half of the gross receipts, after you have deducted 20*l.* per
" night; provided also, that I play among my pieces the
" characters of William Tell, Rolla, and Ingomar."

The defendant afterwards positively stated to the plaintiff that he would not play at Sadler's Wells Theatre on the evening of the 20th, and that he intended to play at Drury Lane Theatre during the hours of the performance at

---

g) For the important action of *Lumley* v. *Gye*, which arose out of the same facts, see p. 128.

(*h*) 3 Jur. N. S. 432.

Sadler's Wells Theatre. A playbill of Drury Lane Theatre was produced as an exhibit, wherein the defendant was advertised to play in "Macbeth" at that theatre on the evening of the 20th.

Wood, V.-C., on the authority of *Lumley* v. *Wagner*, granted an injunction restraining the defendant from acting at any other place than the plaintiff's theatre during the ordinary hours of performance there for twelve consecutive nights commencing on the 20th of April, on the plaintiff giving the usual undertaking as to damages.

In *Fechter* v. *Montgomery* (i), the plaintiff, the lessee of the Lyceum Theatre, entered into negotiations with the defendant, a leading actor of considerable distinction in the provincial theatres, with a view to engage his services. Interviews took place between them, at which the defendant expressed his earnest desire of acting in London in Shakespeare's plays, and said he was willing to make a pecuniary sacrifice for the attainment of that object. He said, "Mr. Fechter, remember I come to you not to be idle, but to act," to which the plaintiff replied, "Certainly, that is so." The plaintiff promised the defendant an immediate appearance, and stated the parts to be given to the defendant, and he proposed to open with one of such plays.

A day or two afterwards Mr. Barnett, the plaintiff's stage-manager, wrote to the defendant as follows:—

"July 28, 1862.

"Dear Montgomery,—I am directed by Mr. Fechter to "offer you an engagement at the Lyceum Theatre for two "years, commencing January 1st, 1863, at a salary of "7*l*. a week for the first and 10*l*. a week for the second "year; it being thoroughly understood that no advantage

(i) 33 Beav. 22.

" will be taken of the confidence you have reposed in Mr.
" Fechter.

    " Yours truly,
      " H. Barnett,
        " Pro C. Fechter."

The defendant replied by simply accepting the offer on the terms and conditions named in the letter of the 28th of July, 1862. There was no other written agreement. The salary was considerably less than that which the defendant was earning by his country engagements, which was 30*l.* a week.

The plaintiff opened the Lyceum Theatre on the 7th of January, 1863, with a dramatic piece called "The Duke's Motto," in which Mr. Montgomery was not engaged. This piece proved eminently satisfactory to the public and lucrative to the plaintiff, and he had continued the performance of it from day to day down to the date of the suit. Mr. Montgomery had not as yet made his appearance, though he had been willing and anxious so to do, but he had regularly received his salary.

The defendant, being greatly dissatisfied, had an interview with the plaintiff on the 13th of June, 1863, when he complained and stated that he should go, and "that if the plaintiff would not break his engagement in a friendly way, he would break it from the present time." The defendant thereupon entered into an engagement with Mr. Vining to perform at the Princess's Theatre, commencing on the 20th of June. The plaintiff immediately filed this bill to restrain him, and the case now came on upon a motion for an injunction. In support of the motion, the plaintiff's stage-manager made an affidavit, stating as follows:—" It is the custom of actors, and well understood by them in their profession, that when an actor is engaged at a theatre, although the agreement may be silent on the subject of his performing elsewhere, he is bound by the person engaging him to perform only at the theatre at which he is engaged; the object of an engagement by the manager of the theatre being, not merely that it should be at his discretion to avail himself of the present engagement, but should at any time exclude the person from offering his services to any other theatre."

Lord Romilly, M. R.: "I am of opinion that this is not a case in which the Court ought to interfere by way of interlocutory injunction to restrain the defendant from acting.... I am of opinion that it was an agreement entered into by Mr. Fechter to employ Mr. Montgomery during a reasonable time to act at this theatre, and that it was an agreement on the other side that he (Mr. Montgomery) should not perform elsewhere without the consent of Mr. Fechter; that there was a mutuality in the agreement entered into on both sides; on the one side, that he should have an opportunity of displaying what his abilities and talents were before a London audience, and on the other hand, that he should not act elsewhere unless with the permission of the plaintiff.

"That being the state of the case, the only questions are, whether that contract has been really broken between the parties, and who was the person that first broke it, so as to entitle the other to say it is no longer binding upon him. Upon that question it is material to regard the facts that occurred. It is clear that the great object of any gentleman wishing to become a distinguished actor, when he has already established a reputation in the provinces, is to have an opportunity of appearing upon the London stage and before a London audience. That is the object for which a person enters into a contract of this description, and it would be defeated if the effect of the contract is this: that if the gentleman who engaged him is not bound to employ him, and does not in fact do so, so as to give him an opportunity to display his talent and abilities, yet he is not to be at liberty to act elsewhere, unless by the permission of the gentleman who engaged him. I entertain no doubt that it was a mutual contract between the parties, and also that Mr. Fechter so understood it. It is shown by Mr. Barnett's letter, and by the conversation itself, that this was part of the contract entered into between them.

"I now come to the question, whether it can be said that Mr. Montgomery is to blame for saying, on the 13th of June, that he would then put an end to the contract. That there was a binding contract up to the 13th of June cannot be disputed. Mr. Montgomery then said to Mr. Fechter, 'You must employ me to perform on the London stage.' How long was he to go on waiting for the performance of that part of the contract? I am of opinion that the defendant, Mr. Montgomery, waited a reasonable time, and that it was not necessary to give any further notice than to say, 'If you do not comply with the contract, and permit me to appear within a month, I will abandon the contract.' Nay, more, no such specified time was necessary when Mr. Fechter informed him that the piece then running would continue to be played, and would render it impossible for the defendant to appear at the Lyceum. The defendant then enters into a contract to appear elsewhere, and I am of opinion that he was justified in so doing. The letter which has been produced, and which is admitted to be Mr. Montgomery's handwriting, does not vary the case in any way. That was written at a time when he considered the contract to be binding, but finding that state of things was to go on for a longer period, in fact, for an indefinite period, he says, 'I will put an end to the contract; I decline to be any longer bound by it.' I am of opinion that he had a right to do so, and that under the circumstances this is not a case in which this Court can interfere by interlocutory injunction to prevent him from performing at a different theatre."

Mapleson v. *Bentham* (k) was a motion by the plaintiff, lessee of the Royal Italian Opera, to restrain the defendant from singing at a concert at which he was advertised to appear at Brighton on the 30th of November, 1871, or from singing at any other place except in a theatre or concert-room belonging to the plaintiff, without his written permission, during the existence of his agreement with the plaintiff. It appears that in 1870 the plaintiff engaged the defendant to sing for the following season at the Opera, and an agreement was entered into between the parties: it had no date other than the year 1870, and was in the French language. The material clauses are as follows:—

"1. That the defendant shall employ his talents for the "plaintiff as first tenor absolute at theatres and rooms in "Great Britain during the engagement hereinafter men- "tioned with the plaintiff.

"2. That this engagement shall commence at the com- "mencement of the grand season in London in April, and "shall continue during the said season.

"3. That the defendant's salary shall be 3,000 francs "monthly, to be paid each calendar month.

"4. That the defendant shall sing in concerts as well as "operas; and shall sing nowhere else in the Kingdom of "Great Britain except at the theatre of the plaintiff during "the year 1871, nor within twenty miles of London during "the year following the expiration of the said engagement, "without the written permission of the plaintiff.

"10. The plaintiff shall have the right to renew this "engagement for the season of 1872, with a salary of 5,000 "francs monthly, and for the season of 1873 with a salary "of 7,500 francs monthly."

It was alleged by the plaintiff that the defendant had, since the end of the London season, sang at Dover and Gloucester without the plaintiff's consent, and that he was advertised to sing at Brighton on the 30th of November, 1871.

Wickens, V.-C., refused to grant an interlocutory injunction, on the ground that the time was so short, and that a small amount of damage would compensate the plaintiff. The decision was affirmed by the Court of Appeal, it saying there was no evidence of any irreparable injury likely to happen to the plaintiff.

Montague v. *Flockton* (*l*) was a motion on behalf of plaintiff, lessee and manager of the Globe Theatre in London, for an injunction to restrain defendant from acting, except at plaintiff's theatre, for nine months from the 2nd of October, 1872, and in particular from acting at an intended dramatic performance at the Crystal Palace.

In August, 1871, the following agreement was entered into—

"Dear Sir,—

"I accept the engagement for the Globe Theatre, "under the management of H. J. Montague, Esq., at a "weekly salary of 5*l.*, and if required to go into the pro- "vinces, travelling expenses paid and twenty per cent. on "my London salary. Line of business—old men and "character business; to commence about the 2nd of October, "1871. For the season of not less than nine months' dura- "tion. A fortnight's rehearsal to be given prior to the "opening, subject to the rules and regulations of the theatre.
"Signed, C. P. FLOCKTON."

During the pendency of the agreement, namely, on the 2nd of March, 1872, the plaintiff and the defendant entered

(*l*) L. R. 16 Eq. 189.

into another agreement, which was accepted by the defendant, in these terms—

"I hereby accept the renewal of my engagement with "H. J. Montague, Esq., for his next season, on the same "terms as at present existing between us.

"Signed, C. P. FLOCKTON."

It appeared that in May, 1872, a notice was posted in the green-room of the Globe Theatre to the effect that the season would close on the 10th of June, on which day all pending engagements would terminate; and the house was accordingly closed on that day.

A company was then formed by the plaintiff for certain theatrical performances in the provinces, in which the defendant took part, and these performances commenced on the 10th of June and terminated on the 28th of September, 1872. The next London season at the Globe Theatre commenced in October, 1872, and the defendant played at the theatre as he had previously done till the 10th of March, 1873, when he requested the plaintiff to allow him to perform at the Regent's Park Theatre, which was to be opened in May. Upon this occasion, according to the plaintiff's statement, the defendant said, "I only ask you to lend me, and I shall finish my engagement with you afterwards." The plaintiff declined to accede to the defendant's request, on the ground that he should require his services for the next piece that was to be brought out. On the 2nd of April the defendant wrote the following letter to the plaintiff:—

"Dear Sir,—As you are aware that my engagement with "you terminated on the 2nd of December last, pursuant to "our agreement bearing date the 2nd of March, 1872, I am "desirous to close my connection with your theatre, and "therefore now give you four weeks' notice in pursuance of "such my desire."

The defendant refused to perform on being requested.

On the 28th of April, 1873, the plaintiff also discovered that the defendant was advertised as intending to act on the 3rd of May at the Crystal Palace, in the part of Polonius in "Hamlet," and consequently this bill was filed.

It was alleged by the defendant that, according to the prevailing custom, the manager had the right of closing the season by notice, and that he had done so. The plaintiff alleged that notice did not close the season. There was conflicting evidence on that point.

Malins, V.-C., after saying that in his opinion if an actor engages himself for the season he leaves himself at the mercy (within reasonable limits of construction) of the proprietor of the theatre to fix what the season is (*m*). But this case, he said, was different. The duration of the season was fixed; and after proceeding to interpret the contract and the words contained in it as one to continue for nine months from October, 1872, he added: "It appears to me on the plainest ground that an engagement to perform for nine months at Theatre A. is a contract not to perform at Theatre B., or at any other theatre whatever. How is a man to perform his duty to the proprietor of a theatre if, when he has engaged himself to perform for him, he is to go away any night that he may be wanted to another theatre? I must treat Mr. Flockton as if he were the greatest actor in the world, and as if wherever he went the public would run after him; and according to this, if a proprietor engages an actor to perform for him, he is not, because he is only wanted for three nights a week, to be at liberty to go and perform at any other theatre during the other three nights, and thereby take away the advantage of the contract which he has entered into with his employer. That, in my opinion, is utterly inconsistent with

---

(*m*) See *Grant* v. *Maddox*, 15 M. & W. 737, cited later, p. 116.

the proper construction of the contract. There is no doubt whatever that a proper construction of these contracts is, that where a man or woman engages to perform or sing at a particular theatre for a particular period, that involves the necessity of his or her not performing or singing at any other during that time.

"That does not rest on my opinion only, because it was acted upon in *Webster* v. *Dillon* (3 Jur. N. S. 432). The Vice-Chancellor fully adopts there the principle that it is not necessary to have a negative covenant in order to prevent the performance at another theatre."

His lordship next quoted *Fechter* v. *Montgomery* (33 Beav. 22): "There are, therefore, Sir W. Page Wood (when Vice-Chancellor) and the Master of the Rolls (Lord Romilly) taking precisely the same view, that an engagement to act at one theatre is a prohibition against acting at another.

"Under these circumstances I am clearly of opinion that Mr. Montague has established that Mr. Flockton is under an engagement to perform for him, and being under that engagement is not at liberty to perform at any other theatre whatever without his permission. I think it is a matter of very great importance for actors to understand, that entering into a contract to perform at Theatre A. obliges them to perform there alone, and that they cannot be permitted to perform anywhere else so long as the other party performs his part of the agreement. I am therefore of opinion that Mr. Montague is entitled to the injunction."

The following cases are here inserted, which the writer has not been able to include in any of the foregoing classes.

In order to sue a father on his daughter's contract to perform, he must not only consent, but also agree.

Morris v. *Paton* (*n*) was an action by the plaintiffs, lessees

(*n*) 1 C. & P. 189.

of the Haymarket Theatre, against defendant, the father of Miss Paton, an actress, to recover damages for the breach of the following agreement, signed by the defendant :—

"July 29, 1822.
"I hereby agree, on behalf of my daughter, M. A. Paton, "that she shall perform during the remainder of the season "at 8*l.* a week; and I also consent that she shall also enter "into articles with Mr. Morris, if he requires it, to perform "for the three following seasons."

It was proved that Miss Paton performed during the remainder of the season of 1822, and also till the beginning of September, 1823, when she refused to perform any longer, and the house in consequence sustained a serious loss.

Abbott, C. J.: "I am most clearly of opinion that it is not a contract on the part of the defendant that his daughter shall sign, but merely expresses his consent; and if she refuses there is no remedy against him. He has bound himself with respect to the first part, the performance in 1822, but not with respect to the signing of the articles."

Nonsuit.

Fines and rules must be reasonable.

Graddon v. *Price* (*o*) was an action of assumpsit by a singer against Mr. Price, the lessee of Drury Lane Theatre, to recover the balance of salary. All that was due had been paid, with the exception of a sum of 20*l.*, which, it was contended by Mr. Price, he had a right to detain for a fine incurred by the plaintiff under the following circumstances :—It appeared that Mrs. Geesin, who was advertised to play the part of Catharine in the Siege of Belgrade on a particular night, was the day before taken so ill as to render it impossible for her

(*o*) 2 C. & P. 610.

to appear according to her engagement. The plaintiff, who for some time had been in the habit of playing that part, was in consequence sent for by Mr. Wallack, the stage manager, and informed that she would be required to undertake the part. She remained at the theatre, and went through part of the rehearsal, and then asked permission to go home, that she might read over the part, as it was some time since she had played it before. This was assented to by Mr. Wallack, and her name was advertised in the next day's bills to appear in the evening. About two o'clock, after the bills were printed, she sent a message to the theatre, stating that she would not play, and in consequence an apology was made for her non-appearance, and the part was performed by Miss Tree. That part of the rules and regulations on which the defendant relied was as follows:—"Anyone refusing to study, rehearse, or perform at the appointment of the manager, shall forfeit 30*l*." It appeared that 10*l*. of this fine had been remitted.

Best, C. J.: "The services of the plaintiff in this case are admitted; and it is admitted also that they are worth 10*l*. a week, and that 20*l*. is due to her, unless it has been properly deducted for a fine. I think that the proprietors of a theatre are perfectly right in having regulations, and enforcing them by the payment of fines. It is a duty which they owe to themselves and the public; for if performers should refuse to appear on the night for which they were advertised, the property of the house would be in danger of being injured by the audience; and I am sure that performers will find it to their interest to submit to these fines, if they do not appear when the public have a right to expect them. I agree with my brother Wilde, that the regulation relied on in this case must have a qualification. The jurisdiction of a manager is a very arbitrary one, but in this kingdom all arbitrary jurisdictions have a limitation. I allow that in this case there must be reasonable notice. It is said that the plaintiff had sufficient notice for a person who had acted the same character before; and if you think it was so, that will get over the difficulty. But if you think she had not sufficient notice, for a performer is not to destroy her reputation by taking a part in haste, then undoubtedly the defendant had no right to claim this fine, and the plaintiff will be entitled to a verdict for the amount."

Verdict for the plaintiff, damages 20*l.*

Misconduct in a manager is ground for dismissal.

A benefit must be asked for.

In *Lacy* v. *Osbaldiston* (*p*), the defendant was lessee of Covent Garden Theatre, and on 3rd of October, 1835, agreed to give plaintiff a salary of 400*l.* a-year as acting manager; and it was also agreed that the plaintiff should be entitled to a benefit, and all other privileges of his situation.

Plaintiff commenced his duties on 5th of October, 1835, and was dismissed on 1st of September, 1836, as the defendant said, for improper conduct, viz., ridiculing defendant's arrangements and exciting discontent among the actors, and thereby prejudicing the welfare of the theatre. Plaintiff sued for wrongful dismissal, and for losing his benefit and the right and privilege of using a private box and giving free admission, by reason of his dismissal.

Defendant pleaded that he was always ready to permit plaintiff to have the benefit, but plaintiff did not require him to do so.

Vaughan, J., summing up: "There is a precise issue as to whether the plaintiff required a benefit and was refused. You must be satisfied that he did require the benefit, and that the defendant refused to give it. It was for the plaintiff to prove, in the first instance, that he did require his benefit.

(*p*) 8 C. & P. 80.

It seems to me, that the plaintiff's allowing so long a time to elapse without any remonstrance, goes strongly to show that he did not require a benefit. Then as to the dismissal, in my opinion the grounds stated in the plea have not been proved. It is a question of fact whether the plaintiff was so conducting himself as that it would have been injurious to the interests of the theatre to have kept him. If he was, I should have no difficulty in saying that it would be a good ground of dismissal. As to withholding of the privileges, it is not assigned as a breach of the agreement, but only introduced as an aggravation of the damage in consequence of the dismissal. All the witnesses say that it was an act of kindness and courtesy, but not a matter of right, to be claimed as such. It does not seem to me, on the evidence, that they go to the length of supporting any right to the private box or the giving orders."

Incompetence of a performer as defence to an action.

Harley v. *Henderson* (*q*) was an action by a professional singer against the defendant, manager of the Comedy Theatre, to recover damages for a wrongful dismissal. The defendant justified the dismissal on the ground that the plaintiff was not competent to fulfil his engagement, or to sing the music allotted to him.

Mathew, J., in giving judgment, said that the only question in the case was as to whether the defendant had, or had not, in August last, wrongfully determined the agreement into which he had entered with the plaintiff. By the terms of that agreement, the latter was to receive 15*l*. a week for a year, from Easter, 1883, and half salary for matinées; and the defendant had the option of retaining his services for a further period of twelve months at 20*l*. a week. The de-

---

(*q*) The Times, February 18 & 19, 1884.

fendant had set up two defences: (1) that the contract between himself and the plaintiff had been subject to a condition that Mr. Harley should sing in tune any parts that might be allotted to him, and this, as Mr. Henderson alleged, he had failed to do; and (2) that the plaintiff had, in fact, been unable to perform his part of the agreement, having become incompetent properly to perform the parts allotted him. As to such alleged inability on the part of Mr. Harley, it was admitted, on behalf of the defendant, that any temporary inefficiency on the plaintiff's part would not have been a justification for the peremptory determination of his engagement by Mr. Henderson, and that the defendant could only rely upon such inefficiency if it had been of a kind to go to the root of the contract. After reviewing the evidence adduced by either side, the learned judge said that the defendant's manager had treated any inefficiency, of which he had complained in Mr. Harley when acting in Rip Van Winkle, as only temporary. The first formal complaint made by the defendant himself had been in the middle of June, and even then he had only gone so far as to say that he wished Mr. Harley not to sing beyond the termination of the season. On August 5th the agreement had been determined by the defendant, the plaintiff having received an intimation that his salary would be no longer paid. His lordship said that, in his opinion, Mr. Harley had not been shown to have become unable properly to perform the parts allotted to him, and finding this as a fact, he fixed the amount of damages to be paid to him by the defendant at 250*l.*

Judgment accordingly.

If a performer has not actually performed, he should sue for arrears of salary, and not for work and labour. This was held by Lord Abinger, C. B., in *Frazer* v. *Bunn* (*r*).

(*r*) 8 C. & P. 704.

Construction of contract. No salary in vacation.

In *Grant* v. *Maddox* (s), the plaintiff was an actress, and defendant was lessee and manager of the Princess's Theatre. The defendant had engaged the plaintiff to act for three years, on the terms of, as the declaration stated, "paying her 5l. for each week of the first year, 6l. for each week of the second year, and 7l. for each week of the third year." The defendant refused to pay the plaintiff her salary for the space of twelve weeks of the first year, amounting to 60l.; and also for nine weeks of the second year, amounting to 54l.

On the part of the defendant, evidence was tendered to show that, according to the understanding and custom of the theatrical profession, under an engagement to perform for one or more years, actors were never paid during the vacation, when the theatre was closed, but only during what was called the theatrical season.

The reception of this evidence was objected to on the ground that it went to explain and vary the unambiguous written contract between the parties.

The Lord Chief Baron, in summing-up, told the jury that the question for them to decide was, whether the contract was to perform and be paid throughout the three years, or only during the theatrical season in three years, and that in the latter case the defendant was entitled to a verdict. The jury found a verdict for the defendant.

A rule was obtained for a new trial on the ground that the above evidence had been improperly received.

Alderson, B.: "I am of opinion that the evidence was properly admitted, and therefore that this rule ought to be discharged. It is perfectly true that you have no right to qualify or alter the effect of a written contract by parol

---

(s) 15 M. & W. 737.

evidence; but it is perfectly competent to you to qualify or alter by parol evidence the meaning of the words which apparently form the written contract, and to insert the true words which the parties intended to use. This is not to alter the contract, but to show what the contract is. Wherever the words used have, by usage or local custom, a peculiar meaning, that meaning may be shown by parol evidence. Here the contract is that the plaintiff is to be paid for three years a salary of 5*l*., 6*l*., and 7*l*. per week in those years. That means, according to the evidence and the finding of the jury, that she is to be paid so much per week during every week that the theatre is open in those years."

Rolfe, B.: "I am of the same opinion. There has not been in this case any infringement of the rule that parol evidence cannot be received to alter a written contract, for here the evidence is only admitted for the purpose of explaining the words used in the contract. It is clear that this may be done with respect to foreign words or scientific expressions; and I think the same is true of the case where the words of the contract have reference to a particular profession.

On a performer refusing to fulfil his contract of performance, the person hiring him may sue at once for the breach, *Beatty* v. *Mellillo* (*s*).

"Frivolous or vexatious defence" under sect. 28 of the Bankruptcy Act, 1883.

In *Ex parte Ellison* (*t*), the bankrupt, Maria Ellison, was a public singer, and on the 23rd of March, 1861, entered into an agreement with Mr. Charles Morton to sing at two music-halls for the space of one year at a salary of 6*l*. a week, and under a penalty of 5*l*. for each default. She began to sing

(*s*) 10 C. B. 282.
(*t*) 8 L. T. N. S. 407.

on the 27th of March, 1861, but for reasons which she alleged to be the weak state of her health, arising from the severity of her work and the long distances she had to traverse three or four times a night, she repeatedly absented herself from her engagements, and on the 14th of December ceased to fulfil her duties altogether, as she alleged from permanent ill-health. Mr. Morton thereupon brought an action for eleven penalties, which resulted in a verdict for two penalties and costs.

Miss Ellison then petitioned the Court of Bankruptcy, and on the 17th of March came up for her final examination. The assignee asked that a condition might be annexed to the order of discharge, ordering that a portion of the lady's future earnings should be set aside for the benefit of creditors, or that the consideration of the order of discharge might be adjourned. On the other hand, it was argued that no offence within sect. 159 (*u*) of the Act of 1861 (24 & 25 Vict. c. 134), had been proved. There were only three creditors besides Mr. Morton. It was proved by the bankrupt that she had been under medical treatment for sixteen months, and that during that time she had earned no money, but had been living with her parents. The Commissioner refused the order of discharge; the bankrupt appealed.

Lord Westbury, L. C., said that he had examined the paper in the case, and that he had arrived at the conclusion that the appellant was entitled to her discharge. His lordship had inquired into the circumstances of the action, and although her defence to this action had failed, and the petition had since been filed, yet he did not think that the defence was vexatious or frivolous within the terms of the statute. He hoped, however, that the case would not become a precedent for breaking engagements of this nature, but,

---

(*u*) Corresponding to 46 & 47 Vict. c. 52, s. 28, sub-s. 3 (e).

under the circumstances, the appellant might have her discharge.

By Scotch law the salary of a comedian is alimentary, and cannot be attached (x).

By sect. 90 of the Bankruptcy Act of 1869 (to which sect. 53 (2) of the Bankruptcy Act, 1883, corresponds), when the bankrupt is in receipt of a salary or income the Court may appropriate the same for the benefit of the creditors. But in *Ex parte Benwell, In re Hutton* (y), the celebrated bone-setter, the Court of Appeal held that the word "income" in sect. 90 applies only to an income *ejusdem generis* with a salary, and that it does not apply to the prospective and contingent earnings of a professional man in the exercise of his professional skill and knowledge. Perhaps the same might be held with regard to the earnings of a skilled performer.

PRECEDENTS.

AGREEMENT made on the day of Between A. [*manager*], of in the county of of the one part, and B. [*performer*], of in the county of of the other part. The said A. agrees to engage and hire the said B., and the said B. agrees to perform for and serve the said A. for the salary, at the place, and subject to the conditions hereinafter mentioned:

[*Insert here the special terms*]

[*and if necessary,* B.'s engagement and service shall commence on the day of and if the said B. is absent, even from illness, at

---

(x) 1 Bell, 127.
(y) 14 Q. B. D. 301.

the stipulated time the said A. may refuse to proceed further with the agreement (*a*).

or,

and if not then the said A. may postpone the commencement of the said B.'s engagement for as many days as the said B. makes default, and he shall forfeit twice his salary for that time]: And it is further hereby agreed and provided that the said salary shall be payable only during the season or time during which the theatre is open as playhouse pay, unless the said B. shall be performing for the said A. at another place while the said theatre is shut; but if the said theatre is open the said salary shall be payable, whether the said B. performs or not, subject to the following condition: During such time or season of the closing of the theatre, or in case, though the theatre is open, the said A. should not require the said B.'s services, the said B. shall be at liberty to perform at any place distant more than fifty miles from London; but if B. shall so perform elsewhere while the said theatre is open it shall not be obligatory on the said A. to pay to the said B. any salary during such time as the said B. shall be performing elsewhere; but in case the said A. shall make a provincial tour, the said B. shall not be at liberty to perform at any town at which the said A. shall have given a representation within a week before or at which the said A. shall have intimated an intention to give a representation within the week next following.

The said B. shall attend rehearsals and observe and submit to the rules, regulations and fines to be observed by performers at the said theatre; and the said B. hereby recognises and admits the reasonableness of the said rules, regulations and fines, a copy of which was shown and read to the said B. before signing this agreement; and in case the said B. should be so ill as to become unable to perform efficiently he shall not be required or be at liberty to perform, nor shall he receive any salary for such period; but if the said illness is so long, or occurs at such time, or is of such a nature as to go to the root of the matter, the said A. shall be at liberty, at his option, either to engage a substitute at a salary not higher than that paid to B., and either deduct from any money owing from himself to B. or recover from B. such sum as shall be equivalent to the said substitute's salary for one calendar month, or to rescind this agreement:

(*a*) These clauses are alternative, but both might be inserted at the option of the parties; see *Bettini* v. *Gye*, 1 Q. B. D. 183; from the judgment of Blackburn, J., in that case, the above clauses are taken, pp. 187, 188.

'And the said A. shall be at liberty to dismiss B. and to rescind this agreement at one calendar month's notice, or on payment of a month's salary in lieu of notice, if the said B. shall either act or sing or dance inefficiently (it being hereby understood that any temporary inefficiency or hoarseness shall not be a reason for rescinding the contract):

And the said B. shall be at liberty at any time to rescind this contract on payment to A. of the sum of £   :

And it is lastly hereby agreed and provided, that in case any dispute should arise between the parties with reference to this agreement the same shall be referred to an arbitrator, who shall finally determine the same, and in awarding damages for wrongful dismissal he shall take into consideration as well the loss of service as the damage to reputation. The arbitrator shall be an Examiner of the High Court or any other barrister who may be agreed upon between the parties, and it shall not be an objection to the arbitrator that he has no special knowledge of acting, dancing or music, but he shall receive evidence thereon; and he shall be paid his fees in the manner and according to the scale prescribed for Examiners of the High Court by Order XXXVII. of the Rules of the Supreme Court of 1883 as amended (*b*): But as between the parties the costs of the award [and in no case shall the parties be liable to any other costs] shall be borne by the parties, as the arbitrator shall order:

The said award shall be final, and this submission may be made a rule of any of the Divisions of the High Court of Justice on the application of either party.

By the courtesy of Mr. Wilson Barrett and Mr. Augustus Moore, the author has been enabled to insert the following forms now used by Mr. Barrett:—

MEMORANDUM OF AGREEMENT made this   day of One thousand eight hundred and eighty   between WILSON BARRETT, lessee and manager of the Royal Princess's Theatre, London, the Grand Theatre, Leeds, and the Theatre Royal, Hull, of the one part, and   of the other part:

THE SAID   hereby agree   to the best of   skill and ability

(*b*) If this scale is found too low the scale of payment for an Official Referee (Supreme Court Fees Order, 1884, 88 to 91) might be adopted.

to rehearse and perform and also to rehearse and understudy
(or elsewhere   under the management of the said Wilson Barrett, if required, the said Wilson Barrett paying third-class railway fare), in consideration of a weekly salary of   playhouse pay and agree to the rules and regulations annexed to these presents, and which the parties hereto agree to accept as forming part and integral portion of this agreement.

This engagement to be for
Witness

Rules and Regulations of Mr. Barrett's Theatres and Companies.

1. Salaries are not paid for Passion Week (should the theatre be closed), Christmas Day, Ash Wednesday, or when theatrical performances are suspended on account of any Royal demise, calamity, epidemic, &c., nor during a performer's illness, whereby the management is deprived of his or her services, nor for rehearsals, excepting when otherwise agreed upon.

2. Every member of the company must speak the words and sing the music of the play as instructed by the management, and no addition, alteration or omission of any kind is to be made, without the consent of the management, either in the words, songs, dances or the business of the piece. In case of refusal to act or speak or sing a part according to the instructions of the management, to the best of the performer's ability, Mr. Barrett has the option of cancelling this engagement.

3. No member of the establishment is allowed to act, sing or appear publicly at any other theatre or place of entertainment without permission of the management, specially obtained in each separate instance. A breach of this article is a final breach of engagement, and renders the member liable to immediate dismissal.

4. Any member of the company refusing to act a part cast by the management, such part being agreeable to the terms of his or her engagement, incurs a penalty of one week's salary for every such refusal, or, at the option of the management, forfeits the engagement, and may be immediately dismissed from the theatre.

5. No member of the company is permitted to go in front of the house without the permission of the management, the penalty being forfeiture of a week's salary.

6. Addressing the audience, without permission from the management, subjects the offender to immediate dismissal.

7. Smoking in any part of the theatre is most strictly prohibited.

8. Seven minutes (and no more) allowed between the acts and pieces for changes of dress.

9. Any member of the company being intoxicated in the theatre, either before or behind the curtain, incurs a penalty of one week's salary or instant dismissal, at the option of the management.

10. Two weeks' notice of the time fixed for the termination of the season or tour will be posted in the green-room or hall, and at the expiration of such notice all engagements for the season or tour will absolutely end and determine. No notice need be given of short breaks in the tour or season, such as Passion Week, closing the theatre for rehearsals, &c., and no salaries are paid during the time the theatre is closed for rehearsals, except when otherwise specially agreed upon.

11. At rehearsal, ten minutes' grace allowed for the first rehearsal, but not for any subsequent one.

12. Illness not admitted as an excuse for absence, unless a doctor's certificate is sent to the management.

13. Any performer not attending to fulfil his or her duties, except in case of absence from illness, is subject to instant dismissal.

14. Members of the company are not to give any orders to the carpenters, property-men or other *employés* of the theatre, as the latter are strictly prohibited from attending to any directions not received from the management, and are liable to be discharged should they disobey this rule.

15. Members of the company must at all times travel by the train selected by the management—notice of which will be posted in the hall or green-room—or forfeit the full fare, and, at the option of the management, a week's salary.

16. No member of the company is allowed, under any consideration, to receive strangers in the dressing rooms or any other part of the theatre without the special consent of the management, obtained in each separate instance. At any breach of this rule the management shall have the option of cancelling this engagement.

17. Engagements *for London* include the right to Mr. Barrett to use the performer's services at the Crystal and Alexandra Palaces, and at any of the transpontine or East-end theatres, should the regular London company give performances at any of these places of entertainment in the pieces for which the performer has been engaged.

Mr. Wilson Barrett's ——— Company.

AGREEMENT made this   day of   18 , between WILSON BARRETT, of the Royal Princess's Theatre, London, the Grand Opera House, Leeds, and the Theatre Royal, Hull, theatrical manager, of the one part, and   manager of the   of the other part.

1. The said Wilson Barrett agrees to find   company, authors' fees, band parts, wardrobe, picture posters and other pictorials, and to produce   during the term of   nights, commencing   at the above-mentioned theatre.

2. The said   agrees to provide the above-mentioned theatre, and scenery, and properties, suitable and sufficient for the effective production of the above-mentioned   limelight and gas and men for same, stage carpenter and men, property men, stage-doorkeeper, money and check-takers, cleaners, and all workmen and officials necessary for the proper conduct of a theatre; a good and efficient band, and all matters and things pertaining to local publicity—as advance advertisements and posting, advertisements, day bills, posting of bills and posters, delivery of window bills, pictorials and handbills, &c., and also to find   supers and   extra girls for every representation of the said   and for at least   · rehearsals previously.

3. The entire receipts taken at the said theatre during this engagement to be divided nightly, as follows:—The said Wilson Barrett to take   and the said   to take the remaining   .

4. The said Wilson Barrett, or his manager, to have the power, if he choose, at his own expense, to appoint check-takers, or supervisors of check-takers, and to furnish the checks and check boxes to be used by the money and check-takers of the said   .

CHAPTER IV.

TORTS AND CRIMES.

THE following cases deal with wrongful acts not arising from contract or the breach of a statutory duty, and with crimes.

Ashley v. *Harrison* (a) was an action on the case. The declaration stated that the plaintiff had engaged as a performer Madame Mara; that the defendant, intending to injure the plaintiff, and to deprive him of the profits of such performance, published a certain false and scandalous libel of and concerning Madame Mara; in consequence of which she was prevented from singing from an apprehension of being hissed and ill-treated from the impression the public mind received from such libel.

On opening the case for the plaintiff, Lord Kenyon threw it out as his opinion that the action was not maintainable; he said that the injury complained of was too remote, and impossible to be connected with the cause assigned for it, so as to affect the defendant in this form of action. That if the publication was an injury to Madame Mara she might have an action for it, but as her refusing to perform might have proceeded from groundless apprehension of what might never have happened, that the plaintiff should not be at liberty to suggest the libel as the cause of that injury, which might have proceeded from another cause, or perhaps from

(a) 1 Esp. 48.

caprice and insolence. In proving loss of profits his lordship ruled that a question might be asked generally "whether the receipts of the house had not diminished from the time Madame Mara declined to sing," it being stated on the declaration that in consequence of Madame Mara's refusal to perform the plaintiff had lost the benefit of several performances, but that to ask if particular persons had not in consequence given up their boxes, was special damage, and should have been specially laid in the declaration.

His lordship afterwards recurred to his first opinion, that the action was not maintainable, and non-suited the plaintiff.

In *Lumley* v. *Gye*, in commenting on this case, Crompton, J., said (*b*) : "The decision appears to have proceeded on the ground that the damage was too remote to be connected with the defendant's act. This was pointed out as the real reason of the decision by Mr. Erskine in case of *Tarleton* v. *McGawley* (1 Peake, 207)." Later on in the same case (p. 233) Erle, J., said, "it was properly decided that the action did not lie, because the libel upon the contracting party was not shown to be with intent to cause those persons to break their contract, and so the defendant, by his wrongful act, did not procure the breach of contract complained of. If he had so acted for the purpose of procuring those breaches, it seems to me he would have been liable to the plaintiff." Wightman, J., said (p. 243) "that Madame Mara was deterred from singing, not directly in consequence of anything done by the defendant, but in consequence of the fear that what he did might induce some one else to assault or ill-treat her. The injury in that case may well have been held to be too remote."

Taylor v. *Neri* (*c*) was an action on the case. The decla-

(*b*) 2 E. & B. 227.
(*c*) 1 Esp. 386.

ration stated that the plaintiff, being the manager of the Opera House, had engaged one Breda as a public singer during the season at a salary; that the defendant had assaulted and beat the said Breda, *per quod* the plaintiff lost his services as a public performer. Plea of the general issue.

On the circumstances of the case being opened, Eyre, C. J., expressed a doubt whether the action was maintainable or not. His lordship said that he did not think the Court had ever gone further than the case of a menial servant; for that if a daughter had left the service of her father no action *per quod servitum amisit* would lie for debauching her.

The Chief Justice observed that if this present action could be supported every man whose servant, whether domestic or not, was kept away a day from his business could maintain an action. In this case the record stated that Breda was a servant hired to sing, and he was of opinion that he was not a servant at all; and therefore would not leave the case upon the record.

The plaintiff was non-suited.

In *Lumley* v. *Gye* (d), in commenting on this case, Crompton, J., said: "Whatever the law may be as to the class of actions referred to for assaulting or debauching daughters or servants *per quod servitum amisit*, and which differ from actions of the present nature, for the wrongful enticing or harbouring with notice, as pointed out by Lord Kenyon in *Fores* v. *Wilson* (1 Peake, 55), the action for maliciously interfering with persons in the employment of another is not confined to menial servants." And later on (p. 233) in the same case, Erle, J., remarked "that the battery upon the contracting party was not shown to be with intent to cause him to break his contract, and so the defendant, by her wrongful acts, did not procure the breaches

(d) 2 E. & B. 228.

of contract which were complained of. If he had so acted for the purpose of procuring those breaches it seems to me he would have been liable to the plaintiff."

Lumley v. *Gye* (e) arose out of the facts contained in the action of *Lumley* v. *Wagner* (f). It was brought against Gye, who enticed away Wagner, and special damage was alleged.

On demurrer, judgment to the following effect was delivered :—

Crompton, J.: " The effect of the first two counts is, that a person under a binding contract to perform at a theatre is induced by the malicious act of the defendant to refuse to perform, and entirely abandon her contract.

" The third count differs in stating expressly that the performer had agreed to perform as the dramatic artiste of the plaintiff, and had become, and was, the dramatic artiste of the plaintiff, and that the defendant maliciously procured her to depart out of the employment of the plaintiff. It was said in support of the demurrer, that it did not appear in the declaration that the relation of master and servant ever subsisted between the plaintiff and Miss Wagner; then Miss Wagner was not averred, especially in the first two counts, to have entered upon the service of the plaintiff, and that the engagement of a theatrical performer, even if the performer has entered upon his duties, is not of such a nature as to make the performer a servant within the rule of law, which gives an action to the master for the wrongful enticing away of his servant; and that the remedy for enticing away servants was confined to cases where the relations of master and servant in the strict sense subsisted between the parties, and that in all other cases of contract the only remedy was against

(e) 2 E. & B. 216.
(f) 1 De G. M. & G. 604, above cited, p. 97.

the party breaking the contract. Now, it is clear law that a person who wrongfully and maliciously, or, what is the same thing, with notice, interrupts the relations subsisting between master and servant, by procuring the servant to depart from the master's service, whereby the master is injured, commits a wrongful act, for which he is responsible at law. I think that the rule applies wherever the wrongful interruption operates to prevent the service during the time for which the parties have contracted that the service shall continue; and I think that the relation of master and servant subsists sufficiently for the purpose of such action during the time for which there was in existence a binding contract of hiring and service between the parties; and I think that it is a fanciful, and technical and unjust distinction, to say that the not having actually entered on the service, or that the service not actually continuing, can make any difference.

"But it is further said that the engagement, employment, or service in the present case was not of such a nature as to constitute the relation of master and servant so as to warrant the application of the usual rule of law giving a remedy in case of enticing away servants. The nature of the injury and damage being the same, and the supposed right of action being in strict analogy to the ordinary case of master and servant, I see no reason for confining the case to services or engagements under contracts for services of any particular description, and I think that the remedy, in the absence of any legal reason to the contrary, may well apply to all cases where there is an unlawful and malicious enticing away of any person employed to give his personal labour or service; more especially when the party is bound to give such personal services exclusively to the master or employer, though I by no means say that the service need be exclusive."

His lordship referred to two cases cited for the defence; *Ashley* v. *Harrison* (1 Esp. 48), as to which he observed "that

the decision appears to have proceeded on the ground that
the damage was too remote to be connected with the defendant's act, as was pointed out as the real reason of the
decision by Mr. Erskine in *Tarleton* v. *McGawley* (1 Peake,
N. P. C. 207)," and the other case, *Tayler* v. *Neri* (1 Esp.
386), on which he said, "whatever may be the law as to the
class of actions referred to, for assaulting or debauching
daughters or servants *per quod servitium amisit*, and which
differ from actions of the present nature for the wrongful
enticing or harbouring with notice, it is clear that the
action for maliciously interfering with persons in the employment of another is not confined to menial servants, as
suggested in *Tayler* v. *Neri*." His lordship, citing *Blake* v.
Layon (6 T. R. 221), said:—"I think that it was most properly laid down by the Court in that case, that a person who
contracts to do certain work for another, is the servant of
that other (of course with reference to such an action) until
the work be finished. It appears to me that Miss Wagner
had contracted to do work for the plaintiff within the meaning of this rule; and I think that where a party has contracted to give his personal services for a certain time to
another, the parties are in the relation of employer and
employed within the meaning of the rule. I think that we
are justified in applying the principle of the action for
enticing away servants to a case where the defendant
maliciously procures a party who is under a valid contract
to give her exclusive personal services to the plaintiff for a
specified period, to refuse to give such services during the
period for which she had so contracted, whereby the plaintiff
was injured.

"I think that our judgment should be for the plaintiff."

Erle and Wightman, JJ., delivered judgments to the same
effect. Coleridge, J., dissented.

This case was expressly approved by Lord Selborne, L. C.,

and Brett, L. J., Lord Coleridge, C. J., dissenting, in a recent case of *Bowen* v. *Hall* (*g*).

Lewis v. *Arnold* (*h*) was an action for assault and false imprisonment.

Defendant was the owner of the theatre. Plaintiff had paid to go into the pit; it was crowded, and he and two others clambered into a box, whence he was removed. He claimed to return to the pit; an altercation arose, and one of the others struck an official of the theatre, on which the plaintiff and the two others were taken into custody.

Tindal, C. J. (in summing-up): "Even if this plaintiff had been informed there was room in the pit of this theatre when there was not, which on this evidence is matter of doubt, he has still no right to go into this private box. His proper course, if there was not room, was to go out of the theatre and demand the return of his money. If there were to be an idea, that those who had not room in the pit might get into the boxes, the greatest inconvenience would ensue. Mr. Arnold has, therefore, a right to turn the plaintiff out of the private box, using no more force than was necessary. With respect to the imprisonment, if there was a blow given in the lobby, in the presence of the peace officer, it was his duty to interfere and secure the offender. It then becomes material to consider, whether the plaintiff was acting jointly with any other person in committing a breach of the peace in the presence of the constable. It is said that the plaintiff himself did nothing. That no doubt is so; but the question is, did he withdraw himself from the others, or were they all active in one common purpose? It appears that they had all three got into the private box together, and they were all together in the lobby; and I cannot find anything

---

(*g*) 6 Q. B. D. 333.
(*h*) 4 C. & P. 354.

to separate the plaintiff from the other two. If, therefore, you think that these three persons were acting together in a common purpose, the plaintiff was liable to be apprehended, although the blow was not given by him, but by one of the other two persons who were with him."

As to hissing a piece or actor, the law stands thus: It is allowable as the expression of the feelings of the moment, and on the exercise of the judgment, to hiss a piece or an actor; but it is unlawful to go to a theatre with a preconcerted design to hiss a piece or an actor. In the latter case the actor can indict the persons hissing for a conspiracy. It is further doubtful whether it is allowable to hiss an actor on account of disapproval of his private character.

Clifford v. *Brandon* (*i*) was an action for assault and false imprisonment. It appeared in evidence that the plaintiff, a gentleman of great eminence at the bar, on the 31st of October, 1809, between 9 and 10 in the evening, went into the pit of Covent Garden Theatre, which had been lately rebuilt. On this as on every other night from the first opening of the house, great noise and confusion prevailed on account of the prices of admission to the pit and boxes being raised, and the public being excluded from a number of boxes which were let to particular individuals for the season. The performance on the stage was inaudible; the spectators sometimes stood on the benches, and at other times sat down with their backs to the performers. While the play was representing "God Save the King!" and "Rule, Britannia!" were sung in different parts of the theatre; horns were blown, bells were rung, and rattles were sprung; placards were exhibited exhorting the audience to resist the oppression of the managers, and a number of men wore in their hats the letters O. P. or N. P. B., meaning "old prices and no private boxes;" but,

(*i*) 2 Camp. 358.

although there were some sham fights in the pit, no violence was offered to any person, either on the stage or in any other part of the house, and no injury was done to the theatre itself or any of its decorations. When Mr. Clifford entered, there was a cry of "There comes the honest counsellor!" and, a passage being opened for him, he went and seated himself in the centre of the pit. Soon afterwards, a gentleman asked him if there was any harm in wearing the letters O. P. He answered "No." The gentleman then asked him if he had any objection to wear them himself. He said he had not. The letters O. P. were then placed in his hat, and he put it on thus ornamented. He continued, however, to sit without taking any part in the disturbance, and he persuaded a person who was near him to desist from blowing a trumpet. Having conducted himself in this quiet manner while he remained in the theatre, he was retiring from it. Whether the performance was entirely over at the time did, not certainly appear. When he had got about two yards from the pit door, where the money was received, the defendant, who was box-keeper to the theatre, ordered him to be taken into custody. A constable accordingly laid hold of him and carried him to the police-office in Bow Street, before Mr. Read, the magistrate presiding there, but nothing being proved against him, except that he wore O. P. in his hat, after being detained about half-an-hour he was set at liberty. The question was, whether these facts proved the justification. Mansfield, C. J.: "The first great question for the consideration of the jury will be, Whether the plaintiff was instigating a riot at Covent Garden Theatre on the evening in question? and then they must determine whether he was arrested while the riot continued. As to the existence of a riot in the house no doubt can be entertained. It appears that for a great many nights there were riots of such a nature as to put an end altogether to dramatic representation. I cannot tell upon what ground many people conceive they have a right at a theatre to make such a prodigious noise as to prevent others from hearing what is going forward on the stage . . . . These premeditated and systematic tumults have been compared to that noise which has been at all times witnessed at theatres in the immediate expression of the feelings of the audience upon a new piece, or the merits or defects of a particular performer. These cases, however, are widely different. The audience have certainly a right to express by applause or hisses the sensations which naturally present themselves at the moment; and nobody has ever hindered, or would ever question, the exercise of that right. But if any body of men were to go to the theatre with the settled intention of hissing an actor, or even of damning a piece, there can be no doubt that such a deliberate and preconcerted scheme would amount to a conspiracy, and that the persons concerned in it might be brought to punishment.

"If people endeavour to effect an object by tumult and disorder they are guilty of a riot. It is not necessary, to constitute the crime, that personal violence should have been committed, or that a house should have been pulled in pieces. I am clearly of opinion that the scenes which have been described amount to a riot. How can it be said there was no terror? Would any of the jury allow their wives and daughters to go to the theatre during these disturbances? Must not those who entertain a different opinion upon the matters in dispute, and are friendly to the managers, expect to meet violent ill-treatment? The jury will consider, then, whether Mr. Clifford was an instigator of the riot, which one of his witnesses has represented as resembling a quarrel among a thousand drunken sailors. The law is that if any person encourages or promotes, or takes part in riots, whether by words, signs, or gestures, or by wearing the badge or ensign of the rioters, he is himself to be considered a rioter,

and he is liable to be arrested for a breach of the peace . . . .
The rule of law certainly is that a private person cannot arrest
another for a mere breach of the peace, subsequent to the
commission of the offence, without a warrant from a magistrate. But there is some difficulty in determining when this
power to arrest actually ceases. Here, if the riot had been
over for a considerable time, and the plaintiff had taken
O. P. out of his hat hours before, and there appeared no
immediate danger of the riot being renewed, Mr. Brandon
had clearly no right to arrest him, without a warrant, for his
past offence. If, however, at the time of the arrest the riot
which the plaintiff instigated still continued, I 'think he
may fairly be said, under these circumstances, to have been
arrested at the time of committing the offence. There is a
contrariety of evidence as to this point upon which the jury
must determine."

His lordship then requested the jury to state their opinion
separately as to the questions whether the plaintiff had instigated the riot, and whether the riot was over before the
arrest. The jury found a verdict for the plaintiff, with 5*l*.
damages.

Lord Campbell adds, in a note:—

"In the preceding term the Court of King's Bench granted
leave to file a criminal information against Mr. Clifford and
several other gentlemen who were represented as promoting
the disturbances in Covent Garden Theatre for a *conspiracy*,
but before Hilary term the managers agreed, on the new
price of admission to the boxes being allowed, to reduce the
price of admission to the pit to its former standard, to throw
open to the public all the private boxes beyond the number
which had existed in the old theatre, and to drop all the
prosecutions which they had commenced."

And in another note the reporter adds:—

"Macklin, the famous comedian, indicted several persons

for a conspiracy to ruin him in his profession. They were tried before Lord Mansfield, and it being proved that they had entered into a plan to hiss him as often as he appeared on the stage, they were found guilty under his lordship's direction, but the prosecutor declined calling upon them to receive the judgment of the Court."

In a note to *Gregory* v. *Duke of Brunswick* (6 M. & G.), the reporter says (p. 217):—

"The defendants, therefore, had no opportunity, if they had been so advised, of questioning the sufficiency of the indictment by a motion in arrest of judgment."

I have not been able to find any authentic account of the trial.

Shee, Serjeant, in *Gregory* v. *Duke of Brunswick* (6 M. & G.), says (on p. 217): "It is, however, mentioned in the new Annual Register for 1774—1775, and here Lord Mansfield is represented as saying that an action would lie in such a case."

Gregory v. *Duke of Brunswick* (k) was an action on the case for conspiring to prevent the plaintiff from performing in "Hamlet," and in aid of the said conspiracy hiring 200 persons to hiss and hoot, whereby the plaintiff was prevented performing. Special damage was alleged.

Plea, not guilty; and that the plaintiff was proprietor of *The Satirist*, and had been for five years in the habit of libelling her Majesty, and uttering scandalous charges, and was a common libeller and blackmailer, whereby the defendants, in order to compel the plaintiff to desist, and prevent the said scandal, did hiss and hoot.

There was a demurrer to the plea, on which judgment was given for the plaintiff (*l*). On the case coming for trial at

(k) 1 C. & K. 24.
(l) 6 M. & G. 205.

Nisi Prius it was proved that on the 13th of February, 1843, when the plaintiff appeared, there was such hissing and hooting that the plaintiff had to retire. It was proved that the defendants were in the theatre and took an active part. Counsel for the defendants urged that the libels were of such a character and so known to the audience that the hissing arose without any preconcerted design, but from the unanimous feeling and disgust of the audience. Tindal, C. J.: "This action is brought against the defendants for having conspired together in order to prevent the appearance of the plaintiff as an actor at Covent Garden Theatre; and in the declaration two overt acts are stated; the first that the defendants hired a number of other persons to engage in the same design, and by their hissing and hooting produced the effect intended by themselves in the conspiracy; the second that the defendants joined in the hooting themselves.

"The law on the subject lies in a narrow compass. There is no doubt that the public who go to a theatre have the right to express their free and unbiassed opinions of the merits of the performers who appear upon the stage; and I believe that no persons are more anxious that the public should have that right than the actors themselves; for if it were laid down that persons who exercised their free judgment would be subject to actions for damages, not only would it be fatal to the actors on the stage, but it would prevent persons from frequenting the theatre at all. At the same time, parties have no right to go to the theatre by a preconcerted plan to make such a noise that an actor, without any judgment being formed on his performance, should be driven from the stage by such a scheme, probably concocted for an unworthy purpose; and, therefore, it is only if you can see, by the evidence that has been given, that the two defendants had laid a preconcerted plan to deprive Mr. Gregory of the benefits which he expected to result from his appearance on the stage that you ought to find a verdict against them. A distinction has been taken as to the right of the public to express their feelings as to an actor's private character on the stage. It is not necessary that I should give any opinion on that point, as the question here is whether these parties went to the theatre according to a scheme that had been laid to prevent an actor from appearing. I therefore reserve to myself the free exercise of my opinion on the other point, and I will state it whenever it shall become necessary." Verdict for the defendants.

The criminal cases which at all affect the theatre are few and unimportant.

A manager who abets another person in seducing and prostituting his apprentice may be indicted for conspiracy (*m*).

The manager of an indecent exhibition is indictable for a common law nuisance (*n*).

By Scotch law it is not hamesucken to assault a comedian in a playhouse, as it is not sufficiently his dwelling-house (*o*).

(*m*) *R.* v. *Delavel*, 1 W. Bl. 410, 438.
(*n*) *R.* v. *Saunders*, 1 Q. B. D. 15.
(*o*) 1 Hume, 313.

APPENDIX.

STATUTES:—
    25 Geo. II. c. 36.
    6 & 7 Vict. c. 68.
    18 & 19 Vict. c. 122, ss. 22, 30.
    41 & 42 Vict. c. 32, ss. 11, 12, 13, 21, 22.
    42 & 43 Vict. c. 34.

REGULATIONS OF THE METROPOLITAN BOARD OF WORKS.

LOCAL ACTS AND REGULATIONS.

STATUTES.

25 Geo. II. c. 36.

An Act for the better preventing Thefts and Robberies, and for Regulating Places of Public Entertainment, and punishing Persons keeping Disorderly Houses.

* * * * * *

II. And whereas the multitude of places of entertainment for the lower sort of people is another great cause of thefts and robberies as they are thereby tempted to spend their small substance in riotous pleasures, and in consequence are put on unlawful methods of supplying their wants and renewing their pleasures: in order, therefore, to prevent the said temptation to thefts and robberies, and to correct as far as may be the habit of idleness which is become too general over the whole kingdom, and is productive of much mischief and inconvenience: be it enacted by the authority aforesaid, that from and after the 1st day of December, 1752, any house, room, garden, or other place kept for public dancing, music, or other public entertainment of the like kind, in the cities of London and Westminster, or within twenty miles thereof, without a licence had for that purpose from the last preceding Michaelmas quarter sessions of the peace to be holden for the county, city, riding, liberty, or division in which such house, room, garden, or other place, is situate (who are hereby authorized and empowered to grant such licences as they in their discretion shall think proper), signified under the hands and seals of four or more of the justices there assembled, shall be deemed a disorderly house or place; and every such licence shall be signed and sealed by the said justices in open Court, and afterwards be publicly read by the clerk of the peace, together with the names of the justices subscribing the same; and no such licence shall be granted at any adjourned sessions, nor shall any fee or reward be taken for any such licence; and it shall and may be lawful to and for any constable or other person, being thereunto authorized by warrant
 [margin: Unlicensed places of public entertainment deemed disorderly houses.]
 [margin: Constables may enter and]

seize all persons found therein.	under the hand and seal of one or more of his Majesty's justices of the peace of the county, city, riding, division, or liberty where such house or place shall be situate, to enter such house or place, and to seize every person who shall be found therein, in order that they may be dealt with according to law; and every person keeping such house, room, garden, or other place, without such licence as aforesaid, shall forfeit the sum of one hundred pounds to such person as will sue for the same, and be otherwise punishable as the law directs in cases of disorderly houses.
Person keeping the same to forfeit 100*l*.	
Licensed places to have an inscription over them;	III. Provided always, and it is hereby further enacted by the authority aforesaid, that, in order to give public notice what places are licensed pursuant to this Act, there shall be affixed and kept up in some notorious place over the door or entrance of every such house, room, garden, or other place kept for any of the said purposes, and so licensed as aforesaid, an inscription in large capital letters in the words following; videlicet, Licensed pursuant to Act of Parliament of the Twenty-fifth of King George the Second; and that no such house, room, garden, or other place, kept for any of the said purposes, although licensed as aforesaid, shall be open for any of the said purposes before the hour of five in the afternoon; and that the affixing and keeping up of such inscription as aforesaid, and the said limitation or restriction in point of time, shall be inserted and made conditions of every such licence; and in case of any breach of either of the said conditions such licence shall be forfeited, and shall be revoked by the justices of peace in their next general or quarter sessions, and shall not be renewed, nor shall any new licence be granted to the same person or persons, or any other person on his or their or any of their behalf, or for their use or benefit, directly or indirectly, for keeping any such house, room, garden, or other place for any of the purposes aforesaid.
and not be open before five in the evening.	
On breach of either of the said conditions the licence to be revoked.	
The theatres and other places licensed by the Crown or Lord Chamberlain excepted out of this act.	IV. Provided always, that nothing in this Act contained shall extend or be construed to extend to the Theatres Royal in Drury Lane and Covent Garden, or the theatre commonly called the King's Theatre, in the Haymarket, or any of them, nor to such performances and public entertainments as are or shall be lawfully exercised and carried on under or by virtue of letters patents, or licence of the Crown, or the licence of the Lord Chamberlain of his Majesty's household, anything herein contained notwithstanding.
Constable's duty upon	V. And in order to encourage prosecutions against persons keeping bawdy houses, gaming houses, or other disorderly

houses, be it enacted by the authority aforesaid, that if any two inhabitants of any parish or place, paying scot and bearing lot therein, do give notice in writing to any constable (or other peace officer of the like nature, where there is no constable) of such parish or place, of any person keeping a bawdy house, gaming house, or other disorderly house in such parish or place, the constable, or such officer as aforesaid so receiving such notice, shall forthwith go with such inhabitants to one of his Majesty's justices of the peace of the county, city, riding, division, or liberty in which such parish or place does lie, and shall upon such inhabitants making oath before such justice that they do believe the contents of such notice to be true, and entering into a recognizance in the penal sum of twenty pounds each to give or produce material evidence against such person for such offence, enter into a recognizance in the penal sum of thirty pounds to prosecute with effect such person for such offence at the next general or quarter session of the peace, or at the next assizes to be holden for the county in which such parish or place does lie, as to the said justices shall seem meet; and such constable or other officer shall be allowed all the reasonable expenses of such prosecution, to be ascertained by any two justices of the peace of the county, city, riding, division, or liberty where the offence shall have been committed, and shall be paid the same by the overseers of the poor of such parish or place; and in case such person shall be convicted of such offence the overseers of the poor of such parish or place shall forthwith pay the sum of ten pounds to each of such inhabitants; and in case such overseer shall neglect or refuse to pay to such constable or other officer such expenses of the prosecution as aforesaid, or shall neglect or refuse to pay, upon demand, the said sums of ten pounds, and ten pounds, such overseers, and each of them, shall forfeit to the person entitled to the same double the sum so refused or neglected to be paid.

notice given him of persons keeping a bawdy house, gaming house, or other disorderly houses, &c.

The charge of prosecution, and 10l. on conviction, to each of the two inhabitants, to be paid by the overseers, on penalty of forfeiting double the sum.

* * * * * *

XIII. And be it further enacted by the authority aforesaid, that any person entitled to any of the forfeitures by this Act imposed may sue for the same by action of debt in any of his Majesty's Courts of Record at Westminster, in which it shall be sufficient to declare that the defendant is indebted to the plaintiff in the sum of   being forfeited by an Act, intituled "An Act for the better preventing Thefts and Robberies, and for Regulating Places of Public Entertainment, and punishing Persons keeping Disorderly Houses;" and the plaintiff, if he recover in any such action, shall have his full costs.

Recovery of forfeitures.

Full costs.

Limitation of actions.	XIV. Provided, that no action shall be brought by virtue of this Act unless the same shall be commenced within the space of six calendar months after the offence committed.

---

6 & 7 VICT. c. 68.

An Act for Regulating Theatres.
[22nd August, 1843.]

WHEREAS it is expedient that the laws now in force for regulating theatres and theatrical performances be repealed, and other provisions be enacted in their stead:

* * * * * *

All theatres for the performance of plays must be licensed.	II. It shall not be lawful for any person to have or keep any house or other place of public resort in Great Britain, for the public performance of stage plays, without authority by virtue of letters patent from her Majesty, her heirs and successors, or predecessors, or without licence from the Lord Chamberlain of her Majesty's household for the time being, or from the justices of the peace as hereinafter provided; and every person who shall offend against this enactment shall be liable to forfeit such sum as shall be awarded by the Court in which or the justices by whom he shall be convicted, not exceeding twenty pounds for every day on which such house or place shall have been so kept open by him for the purpose aforesaid, without legal authority.
What licences shall be granted by the Lord Chamberlain.	III. And be it enacted, that the authority of the Lord Chamberlain for granting licences shall extend to all theatres (not being patent theatres) within the parliamentary boundaries of the cities of London and Westminster, and of the boroughs of Finsbury and Marylebone, the Tower Hamlets, Lambeth, and Southwark, and also within those places where her Majesty, her heirs and successors, shall, in their royal persons, occasionally reside: Provided always, that, except within the cities and boroughs aforesaid, and the boroughs of New Windsor in the county of Berks, and Brighthelmstone in the county of Sussex, licences for theatres may be granted by the justices as hereinafter provided, in those places in which her Majesty, her heirs and successors shall occasionally reside; but such licences shall not be in force during the

residence there of her Majesty, her heirs and successors; and during such residence it shall not be lawful to open such theatres as last aforesaid (not being patent theatres) without the licence of the Lord Chamberlain.

IV. And be it enacted, that for every such licence granted by the Lord Chamberlain, a fee, not exceeding ten shillings for each calendar month during which the theatre is licensed to be kept open, according to such scale of fees as shall be fixed by the Lord Chamberlain, shall be paid to the Lord Chamberlain. *Fee for Lord Chamberlain's licence.*

V. And be it enacted, that the justices of the peace within every county, riding, division, liberty, cinque port, city, and borough in Great Britain beyond the limits of the authority of the Lord Chamberlain, in which application shall have been made to them for any such licence as is hereinafter mentioned, shall, within twenty-one days next after such application shall have been made to them in writing signed by the party making the same, and countersigned by at least two justices acting in and for the division within which the property proposed to be licensed shall be situate, and delivered to the clerk to the said justices, hold a special session in the division, district, or place for which they usually act, for granting licences to houses for the performance of stage plays, of the holding of which session seven days' notice shall be given by their clerk to each of the justices acting within such division, district, or place; and every such licence shall be given under the hands and seals of four or more of the justices assembled at such special session, and shall be signed and sealed in open Court, and afterwards shall be publicly read by the clerk, with the names of the justices subscribing the same. *Licences may be granted by justices.*

VI. And be it enacted, that for every such licence granted by the justices a fee, not exceeding five shillings for each calendar month during which the theatre is licensed to be kept open, according to such scale of fees as shall be fixed by the justices, shall be paid to the clerk of the said justices. *Fee for justices' licence.*

VII. And be it enacted, that no such licence for a theatre shall be granted by the Lord Chamberlain or justices to any person except the actual and responsible manager for the time being of the theatre in respect of which the licence shall be granted; and the name and place of abode of such manager shall be printed on every play bill announcing any representation at such theatre; and such manager shall become bound himself in such penal sum as the Lord Chamberlain or justices *To whom licences shall be granted.*

T.   L

shall require, being in no case more than five hundred pounds, and two sufficient sureties, to be approved by the said Lord Chamberlain or justices, each in such penal sum as the Lord Chamberlain or justices shall require, being in no case more than one hundred pounds, for the due observance of the rules which shall be in force at any time during the currency of the licence for the regulation of such theatre, and for securing payment of the penalties which such manager may be adjudged to pay for breach of the said rules or any of the provisions of this Act.

Rules for the theatres under the control of the Lord Chamberlain.

VIII. And be it enacted, that in case it shall appear to the Lord Chamberlain that any riot or misbehaviour has taken place in any theatre licensed by him, or in any patent theatre, it shall be lawful for him to suspend such licence or to order such patent theatre to be closed for such time as to him shall seem fit; and it shall also be lawful for the Lord Chamberlain to order that any patent theatre or any theatre licensed by him shall be closed on such public occasions as to the Lord Chamberlain shall seem fit; and while any such licence shall be suspended, or any such order shall be in force, the theatre to which the same applies shall not be entitled to the privilege of any letters patent or licence, but shall be deemed an unlicensed house.

Rules for enforcing order in the theatres licensed by the justices.

IX. And be it enacted, that the said justices of the peace at a special licensing session or at some adjournment thereof, shall make suitable rules for ensuring order and decency at the several theatres licensed by them within their jurisdiction, and for regulating the times during which they shall severally be allowed to be open, and from time to time, at another special session, of which notice shall be given as aforesaid, may rescind or alter such rules; and it shall be lawful for any one of her Majesty's principal secretaries of state to rescind or alter any such rules, and also to make such other rules for the like purpose, as to him shall seem fit; and a copy of all rules which shall be in force for the time being shall be annexed to every such licence; and in case any riot or breach of the said rules in any such theatre shall be proved on oath before any two justices usually acting in the jurisdiction where such theatre is situated, it shall be lawful for them to order that the same be closed for such time as to the said justices shall seem fit; and while such order shall be in force the theatre so ordered to be closed shall be deemed an unlicensed house.

Proviso for the Univer-

X. Provided always, and be it enacted, that no such licence shall be in force within the precincts of either of the Universities of Oxford or Cambridge, or within fourteen miles of the city of Oxford or town of Cambridge, without the consent of the chancellor or vice-chancellor of each of the said universities respectively; and that the rules for the management of any theatre which shall be licensed with such consent within the limits aforesaid shall be subject to the approval of the said chancellor or vice-chancellor respectively; and in case of the breach of any of the said rules, or of any condition on which the consent of the chancellor or vice-chancellor to grant any such licence shall have been given, it shall be lawful for such chancellor or vice-chancellor respectively to annul the licence, and thereupon such licence shall become void. *sities of Oxford and Cambridge.*

XI. And be it enacted, that every person who for hire shall act or present, or cause, permit, or suffer to be acted or presented, any part in any stage play, in any place not being a patent theatre or duly licensed as a theatre, shall forfeit such sum as shall be awarded by the Court in which or the justices by whom he shall be convicted, not exceeding ten pounds for every day on which he shall so offend. *Penalty on persons performing in unlicensed places.*

XII. And be it enacted, that one copy of every new stage play, and of every new act, scene, or other part added to any old stage play, and of every new prologue or epilogue, and of every new part added to an old prologue or epilogue intended to be produced and acted for hire at any theatre in Great Britain, shall be sent to the Lord Chamberlain of her Majesty's household for the time being, seven days at least before the first acting or presenting thereof, with an account of the theatre where and the time when the same is intended to be first acted or presented, signed by the master or manager, or one of the masters or managers, of such theatre; and during the said seven days no person shall for hire act or present the same, or cause the same to be acted or presented; and in case the Lord Chamberlain, either before or after the expiration of the said period of seven days, shall disallow any play, or any act, scene, or part thereof, or any prologue or epilogue, or any part thereof, it shall not be lawful for any person to act or present the same, or cause the same to be acted or presented, contrary to such disallowance. *No new plays or additions to old ones to be acted until submitted to the Lord Chamberlain.*

XIII. And be it enacted, that it shall be lawful for the Lord Chamberlain to charge such fees for the examination of the plays, prologues and epilogues, or parts thereof, which shall be sent to him for examination, as to him from time to time shall seem fit, according to a scale which shall be fixed by him, such fee not being in any case more than two guineas, and such fees shall be paid at the time when such plays, pro- *Fees to be paid for examination of plays, &c.*

L 2

logues and epilogues, or parts thereof, shall be sent to the Lord Chamberlain; and the said period of seven days shall not begin to run in any case until the said fee shall have been paid to the Lord Chamberlain, or to some officer deputed by him to receive the same.

The Lord Chamberlain may forbid any play.

XIV. And be it enacted, that it shall be lawful for the Lord Chamberlain for the time being, whenever he shall be of opinion that it is fitting for the preservation of good manners, decorum or of the public peace so to do, to forbid the acting or presenting any stage play, or any act, scene or part thereof, or any prologue or epilogue or any part thereof, anywhere in Great Britain, or in such theatres as he shall specify, and either absolutely or for such time as he shall think fit.

Penalty for acting plays before they are allowed or after they have been disallowed.

XV. And be it enacted, that every person who for hire shall act or present, or cause to be acted or presented, any new stage play, or any act, scene or part thereof, or any new prologue or epilogue or any part thereof, until the same shall have been allowed by the Lord Chamberlain, or which shall have been disallowed by him, and also every person who for hire shall act or present, or cause to be acted or presented, any stage play, or any act, scene or part thereof, or any prologue or epilogue or any part thereof, contrary to such prohibition as aforesaid, shall for every such offence forfeit such sum as shall be awarded by the Court in which or the justices by whom he shall be convicted, not exceeding the sum of fifty pounds; and every licence (in case there be any such) by or under which the theatre was opened, in which such offence shall have been committed, shall become absolutely void.

What shall be evidence of acting for hire.

XVI. And be it enacted, that in every case in which any money or other reward shall be taken or charged, directly or indirectly, or in which the purchase of any article is made a condition for the admission of any person into any theatre to see any stage play, and also in every case in which any stage play shall be acted or presented in any house, room or place in which distilled or fermented exciseable liquor shall be sold, every actor therein shall be deemed to be acting for hire.

Proof of licence in certain cases to lie on the party accused.

XVII. And be it enacted, that in any proceedings to be instituted against any person for having or keeping an unlicensed theatre, or for acting for hire in an unlicensed theatre, if it shall be proved that such theatre is used for the public performance of stage plays, the burden of proof that such theatre is duly licensed or authorized shall lie on the party accused, and until the contrary shall be proved such theatre shall be taken to be unlicensed.

* * * * * *

XIX. And be it enacted, that all the pecuniary penalties imposed by this Act for offences committed in England may be recovered in any of her Majesty's Courts of Record at Westminster, and for offences committed in Scotland by action or summary complaint before the Court of Session or justiciary there, or for offences committed in any part of Great Britain in a summary way before two justices of the peace for any county, riding, division, liberty, city or borough where any such offence shall be committed, by the oath or oaths of one or more credible witness or witnesses, or by the confession of the offender, and in default of payment of such penalty together with the costs, the same may be levied by distress and sale of the offender's goods and chattels, rendering the overplus to such offender, if any there be above the penalty, costs, and charge of distress; and for want of sufficient distress the offender may be imprisoned in the common gaol or house of correction of any such county, riding, division, liberty, city or borough for any time not exceeding six calendar months. *Penalties how to be recoverable.*

XX. And be it enacted, that it shall be lawful for any person who shall think himself aggrieved by any order of such justices of the peace to appeal therefrom to the next general or quarter session of the peace to be holden for the said county, riding, division, liberty, city or borough, whose order therein shall be final. *Appeal.*

XXI. And be it enacted, that the said penalties for any offence against this Act shall be paid and applied in the first instance toward defraying the expenses incurred by the prosecutor, and the residue thereof (if any) shall be paid to the use of her Majesty, her heirs and successors. *Appropriation of penalties.*

XXII. Provided always, and be it enacted, that no person shall be liable to be prosecuted for any offence against this Act unless such prosecution shall be commenced within six calendar months after the offence committed. *Limitation of actions.*

XXIII. And be it enacted, that in this Act the word "stage play" shall be taken to include every tragedy, comedy, farce, opera, burletta, interlude, melodrama, pantomime or other entertainment of the stage or any part thereof: Provided always, that nothing herein contained shall be construed to apply to any theatrical representation in any booth or show which by the justices of the peace, or other persons having authority in that behalf, shall be allowed in any lawful fair, feast or customary meeting of the like kind. *Interpretation of Act.*

Limits of the Act.

XXIV. And be it enacted, that this Act shall extend only to Great Britain.

* * * * * *

METROPOLITAN BUILDING ACT.

18 & 19 Vict. c. 122.

* * * * * *

Rules as to accesses and stairs in certain buildings.

22. The following rules shall be observed with respect to accesses and stairs:—

In every public building, and in every other building containing more than one hundred and twenty-five thousand cubic feet, and used as a dwelling-house for separate families, the floors of the lobbies, corridors, passages, and landings, and also the flights of stairs, shall be of stone or other fire-proof material, and carried by supports of a fire-proof material.

* * * * * *

Construction of public buildings.

30. Notwithstanding anything herein contained, every public building, including the walls, roofs, floors, galleries, and staircases, shall be constructed in such manner as may be approved by the district surveyor, or, in the event of disagreement, may be determined by the Metropolitan Board; and, save in so far as respects the rules of construction, every public building shall throughout this Act be deemed to be included in the term "building," and be subject to all the provisions of this Act, in the same manner as if it were a building erected for a purpose other than a public purpose.

* * * * * *

METROPOLIS MANAGEMENT AND BUILDING ACTS AMENDMENT ACT, 1878.

41 & 42 Vict. c. 32.

* * * * * *

11. Whenever it appears to the board that any house or other place of public resort within the metropolis which was at the time of the passing of this Act authorized to be kept open for the public performance of stage plays, and which is kept open for such purpose, under the authority of letters patent from her Majesty, her heirs and successors or predecessors, or of a licence granted by the Lord Chamberlain of her Majesty's household for the time being or by justices of the peace, or that any house, room, or other place of public resort within the metropolis, containing a superficial area for the accommodation of the public of not less than five hundred square feet, which was at the time of the passing of this Act authorized to be kept open, and which is kept open, for dancing, music, or other public entertainment of the like kind, under the authority of a licence granted by any court of quarter sessions, is so defective in its structure, that special danger from fire may result to the public frequenting the same, then and in every such case the board may, with the consent of the Lord Chamberlain in the case of theatres under his jurisdiction, and of her Majesty's principal Secretary of State, in all other cases, if in the opinion of the board such structural defects can be remedied at a moderate expenditure, by notice in writing require the owner of such house, room, or other place kept open for any of the purposes aforesaid, under such authority as aforesaid, to make such alterations therein or thereto as may be necessary to remedy such defects, within a reasonable time to be specified in such notice; and in case such owner fails to comply with the requirements of such notice within such reasonable time as aforesaid, he shall be liable to a penalty not exceeding fifty pounds for such default, and to a further penalty of five pounds for every day after the first day after the expiration of such reasonable time as aforesaid during which such default continues: provided always, that any such owner may, within fourteen days after the receipt of any such notice as aforesaid, serve notice of appeal against the same upon the board, and thereupon such appeal shall be referred to an arbitrator to be appointed by her Majesty's First Commissioner of Works at the request of either party, who shall hear and determine the same, and may, on such evidence as he may think satisfactory, *Power to board in certain cases to require proprietors of theatres and certain music halls in use at the time of the passing of this Act to remedy structural defects.*

either confirm the notice served by the board, or may confirm the same with such modifications as he may think proper, or refuse to confirm the same, and the decision of such arbitrator with respect to the requirements contained in any such notice, and the reasonableness of the same, and the persons by whom and the proportions in which the costs of such arbitration are to be paid, shall be final and conclusive and binding upon all parties.

In case of an appeal against any such notice, compliance with the requirements of the same may be postponed until after the day upon which such appeal shall be so decided as aforesaid, and the same, if confirmed in whole or in part, shall only take effect as and from such day.

<small>Power to board to make regulations with respect to new theatres and certain new music halls for protection from fire.</small>

12. The board may from time to time make, alter, vary, and amend such regulations as they may think expedient with respect to the requirements for the protection from fire of houses or other places of public resort within the metropolis to be kept open for the public performance of stage plays, and of houses, rooms, or other places of public resort within the metropolis containing a superficial area for the accommodation of the public of not less than five hundred square feet, to be kept open for public dancing, music, or other public entertainment of the like kind, under the authority of letters patent from her Majesty, her heirs or successors, or of licences by the Lord Chamberlain of her Majesty's household, or by any justices of the peace, or by any court of quarter sessions, which may be granted for the first time after the passing of this Act; and may by such regulations prescribe the requirements as to position and structure of such houses, rooms, or places of public resort which may, in the opinion of the board, be necessary for the protection of all persons who may frequent the same against dangers from fires which may arise therein or in the neighbourhood thereof; provided that the board may from time to time in any special case dispense with or modify such regulations, or may annex thereto conditions if they think it necessary or expedient so to do.

The board shall, after the making, altering, varying or amending of any such regulations, cause the same to be printed, with the date thereof, and a printed copy thereof shall be kept at the office of the board, and all persons may at all reasonable times inspect such copy without payment, and the board shall cause to be delivered a printed copy, authenticated by their seal, of all regulations for the time being in force to every person applying for the same, on payment by such person of any sum not exceeding five shillings for every such copy.

A printed copy of such regulations, dated and authenticated

by the seal of the board, shall be conclusive evidence of the existence and of the due making of the same in all proceedings under the same, without adducing proof of such seal or of the fact of such making.

From and after the making of any such regulations it shall not be lawful for any person to have or keep open any such house, room or other place of public resort for any of the purposes aforesaid, unless and until the board grant to such person a certificate in writing under their seal, to the effect that such house, room or other place was on its completion in accordance with the regulations made by the board in pursuance of the provisions of this Act for the time being in force, and in so far as the same are applicable to such house or other place, and to the conditions (if any) annexed thereto by the board.

In case any such house, room or place of public resort is opened or kept open by any person for any of the purposes aforesaid, contrary to the provisions of this enactment, such person shall be liable to a penalty not exceeding fifty pounds for every day on which such house or place of public resort is so kept open as aforesaid.

13. A person interested in any premises about to be constructed, or in course of construction, which are designed to be licensed and used within the metropolis for the public performance of stage plays, or for public dancing, music or other public entertainment of the like kind, may apply to the licensing authority for the grant of a provisional licence in respect of such premises. The grant of such provisional licence shall, in respect of the discretion of the licensing authority and procedure, be subject to the same conditions as those applicable to the grant of a like licence which is not provisional. A provisional licence so granted shall not be of any force until it has been confirmed by the licensing authority; but the licensing authority shall confirm the same on the production by the applicant of a certificate by the board that the construction of the premises has been completed in accordance with the regulations and conditions made by the board as hereinbefore provided, and on being satisfied that no objection can be made to the character of the holder of such provisional licence. *Provisional licence for new premises.*

* * * * * *

21. The architect of the board, and any other person authorized by the board in writing under their seal, may, at all reasonable times after completion or during construction, enter and inspect any house, room or other place kept open, or intended to be kept open for the public performance of *Power for architect and persons authorised by board, and district* *surveyor, to enter and inspect theatres, music halls, buildings, and works.*

stage plays, or for public dancing, music or other public entertainment of the like kind affected by any of the provisions of this Act, or of any regulations made in pursuance thereof; and the district surveyor of any district may at all reasonable times during the progress and the three months next after the completion of any house, building, erection or work in such district affected by and not exempted from any of the provisions of this Act, or by any bye-law made in pursuance of this Act, or by any terms or conditions upon which the observance of any such provisions or any of such bye-laws may have been dispensed with, enter and inspect such house, building, erection or work; and if any person refuses to admit such architect, person or surveyor, or to afford him all reasonable assistance in such inspection, in every such case the person so refusing shall incur for each offence a penalty not exceeding twenty pounds.

Power to owners, &c. to enter houses, &c. to comply with notices or order.

22. For the purpose of complying with the requirements of any notice or order served or made under the provisions of this Act on any owner, builder or person in respect of any house, building or other erection, room or place, such owner, builder or person, his servants, workmen and agents, may, after giving seven days' notice in writing to the occupier of such house, building or other erection, room or place, and on production of such notice or order, enter such house, building or other erection, room or place, and do all such works, matters and things therein or thereto, or in connexion therewith, as may be necessary; and if any person refuses to admit such owner, builder or person, or his servants or workmen or agents, or to afford them all reasonable assistance, such person shall incur for each offence a penalty not exceeding twenty pounds.

---

42 & 43 VICT. c. 34.

An Act to regulate the Employment of Children in places of public amusement in certain cases.

[24th July, 1879.]

WHEREAS it is expedient to regulate the employment of children in places of public amusement in certain cases:

Be it therefore enacted by the Queen's most excellent Majesty, by and with the advice and consent of the Lords

Spiritual and Temporal, and Commons, in this present Parliament assembled, and by the authority of the same, as follows:

1. This Act may be cited as the Children's Dangerous Performances Act, 1879. *Short title.*

2. This Act shall not come into operation until the 1st day of January, 1880, which date is hereinafter referred to as the commencement of this Act. *Commencement of Act.*

3. From and after the commencement of this Act, any person who shall cause any child under the age of fourteen years to take part in any public exhibition or performance whereby, in the opinion of a court of summary jurisdiction, the life or limbs of such child shall be endangered, and the parent or guardian, or any person having the custody, of such child, who shall aid or abet the same, shall severally be guilty of an offence against this Act, and shall on summary conviction be liable for each offence to a penalty not exceeding ten pounds. *Penalty for employment of any child in dangerous performances.*

And where in the course of a public exhibition or performance, which in its nature is dangerous to the life or limb of a child under such age as aforesaid taking part therein, any accident causing actual bodily harm occurs to any such child, the employer of such child shall be liable to be indicted as having committed an assault; and the Court before whom such employer is convicted on indictment shall have the power of awarding compensation not exceeding twenty pounds, to be paid by such employer to the child, or to some person named by the Court on behalf of the child, for the bodily harm so occasioned; provided that no person shall be punished twice for the same offence. *Compensation for accident to any child.*

4. Whenever any person is charged with an offence against this Act in respect of a child who in the opinion of the Court trying the case is apparently of the age alleged by the informant, it shall lie on the person charged to prove that the child is not of that age. *Evidence of age.*

5. Every offence against this Act in respect of which the person committing it is liable as above mentioned to a penalty not exceeding ten pounds shall be prosecuted and the penalty recovered with costs in a summary manner, as follows:— *Recovery of penalties.*
>In England, in accordance with the provisions of the Act eleventh and twelfth Victoria, chapter forty-three, intituled "An Act to facilitate the performance of the duties of justices of the peace out of sessions within England and Wales with respect to summary convictions

and orders," and of any Act or Acts amending the same; and the Court of summary jurisdiction when hearing and determining an information in respect of any offence under this Act shall be constituted either of two or more justices of the peace in petty sessions, sitting at a place appointed for the holding of petty sessions, or some magistrate or officer sitting alone or with others at some Court or other place appointed for the administration of justice for the time being empowered by law to do alone any act authorized to be done by more than one justice of the peace;

<small>27 & 28 Vict. c. 53.</small> In Scotland, in accordance with the provisions of the Summary Procedure Act, 1864, and of any Act or Acts amending the same; and

In Ireland, within the police district of Dublin metropolis in accordance with the provisions of the Acts regulating the powers and duties of justices of the peace for such district, or of the police of such district, and elsewhere in <small>14 & 15 Vict. c. 93.</small> Ireland in accordance with the provisions of the Petty Sessions (Ireland) Act, 1851, and any Act amending or affecting the same.

THE METROPOLITAN BOARD OF WORKS.

THE METROPOLIS MANAGEMENT AND BUILDING ACTS AMENDMENT ACT, 1878.

REGULATIONS *made by the Metropolitan Board of Works at a Meeting held at the Offices of the Board, Spring Gardens, on Friday, the 2nd day of May, 1879, under the provisions of the above-mentioned Act.*

I.—These regulations shall apply to all theatres, houses, or places of public resort within the metropolis, to be kept open for the public performance of stage plays, and to all houses, rooms, or other places of public resort within the metropolis, containing a superficial area for the accommodation of the public, of not less than 500 square feet, to be opened or kept open for public dancing, music, or other public entertainment of the like kind under the authority of letters patent from Her Majesty the Queen, her heirs or successors, or of licences by the Lord Chamberlain of Her Majesty's household, or by any justices of the peace, or by any Court of Quarter Sessions which may be granted for the first time after the 22nd day of July, 1878.

II.—Every person who, for the first time after the making of these regulations, may be either desirous of obtaining authority to open any house, or other place of public resort, within the metropolis for the public performance of stage plays, or to open any house, room, or other place of public resort within the metropolis containing a superficial area for the accommodation of the public of not less than 500 square feet for public dancing, music, or other public entertainment of the like kind, shall give notice of such desire to the Metropolitan Board of Works. The notice must contain a statement as to the nature of the interest of such person in the premises so proposed to be opened, and be accompanied by plans, elevations, and sections of such house, room, or place of public resort, or of the premises of which such house, room, or place of public resort may form part, drawn to a scale of not less than ⅛th of an inch to a foot, and by a block plan showing its position in relation to the premises adjacent, drawn to a scale of not less than 1 inch to 20 feet, and in the case of new buildings, or of buildings to be adapted as a

_{Drawings of theatres, music halls, &c., to be submitted to Metropolitan Board of Works.}

place of public resort, must be also accompanied by a specification of the works to be executed, describing the materials to be employed and the mode of construction to be adopted, together with such other particulars as may be necessary to enable the board and its officers to judge whether the requirements of these regulations will, when the building has been completed, have been complied with.

The notice must be also accompanied by a detailed statement of the respective numbers of persons proposed to be accommodated in the various portions of such house, room or place of public resort, and of the area to be assigned to each person, which shall not be less than 1 foot 8 inches by 1 foot 6 inches in the gallery, nor less than 2 feet 4 inches by 1 foot 8 inches in the other parts of the house, room or other place of public resort.

Walls.

III.—Every such house, room or place of public resort shall be enclosed with external walls of brick or stone, or partly of brick and partly of stone. The thickness of such walls shall not be less than the thickness prescribed by the Metropolitan Building Act, 1855, for walls of similar height and length in buildings of the warehouse class.

Proscenium wall.

IV.—In any house or other place of public resort, for the public performance of stage plays, or where a proscenium shall be erected, the proscenium wall shall be of brick, not less than 13 inches in thickness, and shall be carried up to a height of 3 feet above the roof, and be carried down below the stage, to the level of the foundation of the external walls.

No openings shall be formed in the proscenium wall, with the exception of a doorway into the orchestra, and one doorway on each side of the stage for communication with the auditorium. These doorways shall not be more than 3 feet 6 inches wide, and shall be closed with iron doors, fixed without woodwork.

The decorations round the proscenium shall be constructed of fire-resisting materials.

Public staircases, corridors, &c.

V.—The staircases and the floors of the passages, lobbies, corridors and landings, shall be of fire-resisting materials. Every staircase for the use of the audience shall be supported and enclosed by brick walls. The treads of each flight of stairs shall be of uniform width.

No staircase, internal corridor or passage-way, for the use of the audience, shall be less than 4 feet 6 inches wide. Every staircase, corridor or passage-way for the use of the audience, and which communicates with any portion of the house, intended for the accommodation of a larger number of the audience than 400, shall be increased in width by 6 inches for every additional 100 persons, until a maximum width of 9 feet be obtained. Provided always that in every case where the staircases are 6 feet wide and upwards a dividing handrail shall be provided.

A clear passage or gangway, of not less than 3 feet wide, shall be reserved round every part appropriated to the audience, except that next the proscenium or place of performance.

VI.—All ironwork used in construction shall be protected against the action of fire in such manner as may be required by the board. Ironwork.

VII.—In all cases where a portion of the audience is to be accommodated over or at a higher level than others of the audience, a separate means of exit, of the width above prescribed for staircases, internal corridors or passage-ways, and communicating directly with the street, shall be provided from each floor or level. Separate tiers of boxes shall for this purpose be reckoned together as forming one floor or level. One additional exit, at the least, communicating with the different levels, and opening directly into the street, must also be provided. Means of exit.

VIII.—All doors and barriers shall be made to open outwards. Doors.

IX.—In theatres and places where the auditorium and stage shall be warmed artificially, hot water only, and that at low pressure, shall be used, and the warming apparatus shall be placed in a position to be approved by the board. Warming.

X.—All openings for ventilation shall be shown on the plans, and properly described in the specifications. The openings shall be made in such places and in such manner as may be approved by the board. Ventilation.

XI.—No workshop, painting-room or dressing-room shall be formed or constructed over the auditorium, or in the space under the same. Workshops.

XII.—No scene-dock, property-room or store-room shall be permitted within any house, room or other place of public resort, unless such scene-dock, property-room or store-room be separated from the house, room or other place of public resort, by brick and fire-proof construction. Scene-docks, &c.

XIII.—In any case where there are not fire mains on con- Water supply.

stant supply there shall be provided on the top of the proscenium wall or at some other place to be approved by the board, two cisterns, each capable of containing at least 250 gallons of water for every 100 persons of the audience to be accommodated in the building. Fire mains shall be connected with these cisterns and extend round the whole circuit of the building, and be fitted with hydrants in such places and manner as may be approved by the board.

Gas.

XIV.—All gaspipes shall be made of iron or brass. No white metal pipes shall be used in any part of the building.

Separation of buildings.

XV.—In cases in which a house, room or other place of public resort, forms a part only of a building, such house, room or other place of public resort, shall be separated from the other parts of the building by proper party walls or party structures.

Alterations and additions.

XVI.—Notice shall be given to the board of any intended addition to or structural alteration of any house, room or other place of public resort, in respect of which the board may have granted a certificate to the effect that such house, room or other place of public resort, was on its original completion in accordance with the foregoing regulations, or otherwise in compliance with the said Act, and the conditions required by the board applicable thereto. Such notice shall be accompanied by plans, elevations and sections, showing such additions or alterations, and also by a specification of the works to be executed in the same manner as in the case of a new building to be certified for the first time by the board; and the board will if necessary cause a fresh survey of the building to be made.

XVII.—Inasmuch as by sect. 12 of the said Act, the board may from time to time, in any special case dispense with or modify its regulations, all applications for dispensation or modification must be in writing, addressed to the board, and contain a statement of the facts of the particular case, and the reasons why it is desired to modify or dispense with these regulations as applicable thereto.

LOCAL ACTS AND REGULATIONS.

REGULATION *of Theatres, Music-Halls, and Places of Public Entertainment in the Provinces.*

[The Author has to thank the town clerks and clerks to the justices of the more important provincial towns for the information kindly afforded him, the results of which are appended. Application has been made, it is believed, to every town of importance in Great Britain. Where the name of a town of any size or importance does not appear in the following pages, it is because either there are no special regulations or no answer has been returned to the inquiries made by the Author.]

ABERDEEN

Has no special legislation, but the form of the theatre licences and the justices' rules endorsed thereon are as follows:—

CITY OF ABERDEEN.

HER MAJESTY'S THEATRE AND OPERA-HOUSE.

Licence under the Act 6 & 7 Victoria, cap. 68.

From ——— to ———.

At a special session held by the ——— magistrates of the City of Aberdeen, as justices of the peace within the said city, for granting licences to houses for the performance of stage plays, in terms of the Act 6 & 7 Victoria, cap. 68, intituled "An Act for regulating Theatres," and holden within the town-house of the said city on the ——— day of ———, 18—.

The said ——— magistrates, justices of the peace within the said city, assembled at the said session, did, and do hereby license, authorize, and empower ——— at and within the theatre and opera-house, called Her Majesty's Theatre and Opera-House, belonging to the Aberdeen Theatre and Opera-House Company, Limited, and situated in Guild Street and Trinity Street of Aberdeen (but not elsewhere), to perform stage plays, and all and every tragedy, comedy, farce, opera, burletta, interlude, melodrama, pantomime, or other entertainment of the stage, under and in virtue of the said Act 6 & 7 Victoria, cap. 68, in such case made and provided: but that only on the conditions and terms specified in the rules established by the Lord Provost and magistrates of the said city hereto annexed, and not otherwise.

This licence to continue in force upon the conditions and terms aforesaid from the ——— day of ———, 18—, for the ——— calendar months next following, and no longer.

HER MAJESTY'S THEATRE AND OPERA-HOUSE, ABERDEEN.

RULES established under the Act 6 & 7 Victoria, cap. 68, intituled "An Act for regulating Theatres," by the Lord Provost and Baillies of the City of Aberdeen, Justices of the Peace for the said City.

First.—That ———, before designed, shall affix, and keep exposed in the front and some conspicuous place over the doors or entrances of the theatre and opera-house mentioned in the within licence, an inscription in large Roman letters, painted either of a dark colour upon a light ground, or of a light colour on a dark ground, in the words following:—"Licensed pursuant to Act of Parliament of 6th & 7th Victoria, cap. 68," and he shall in like manner paint ——— Christian name and surname immediately above the said inscription.

Second.—That such theatre, although licensed as aforesaid, shall not be open for the performance of any stage plays, dancing, music, or other public entertainment of the like kind on Sabbath or any other day set apart for public worship by lawful authority, nor on any lawful day before eleven o'clock forenoon, nor continue open later than half-past eleven o'clock at night.

Third.—That the said ——— shall not permit any breach of the peace, or riotous, indecent, or disorderly conduct within the said theatre.

Fourth.—That he shall not permit or suffer men or women of notoriously bad fame, or dissolute girls and boys to assemble therein.

Fifth.—That he shall not permit or suffer any unlawful games therein whereby the lieges may be cozened and cheated.

Sixth.—That he shall maintain good order, rule, and decency therein; and that at no period of the performance shall the admission prices to any part of the theatre be under sixpence sterling for each person.

Seventh.—That the name and place of abode of the said ———, as the actual and responsible manager of the theatre, for the time being, to whom the licence is granted, shall be printed on every playbill announcing any representation at the said theatre.

Eighth.—That the said ——— shall observe and conform to all the rules and regulations which the Lord Chamberlain of her Majesty's household, for the time being, or any one of her Majesty's principal secretaries of state, or the said lord provost and baillies, justices of the peace for the said city of Aberdeen, may from time to time make, and to all the provisions of the said statute, notwithstanding the same are not herein specially inserted.

Ninth.—That the said ——— shall become bound by bond ———self in the penal sum of fifty pounds and two sufficient sureties to be approved of by the said justices, in the penal sum of twenty-five pounds each for the due observance of the rules which shall be in force at any time during the currency of the licence for the regulation of said theatre, and for securing payment of the penalties which the said ——— may be adjudged to have incurred for breach of any of the said rules or any of the provisions of the said Act; with power to the convicting justices to modify the said penalties to such sum or sums as they shall think fit.

Tenth.—That in case of any breach of any of the rules and regulations aforesaid the licence shall be forfeited and become void.

Eleventh.—That before any licence shall be issued to any person, a report or certificate, at the applicant's expense, by two tradesmen of skill, shall be produced as to the sufficiency and ventilation of the theatre, and proper egress therefrom.

Twelfth.—That all actions for recovery of such penalties or having the said licence forfeited, shall be raised at the instance of the Procurator-Fiscal of the City of Aberdeen for the time being, in the form provided in the said statute.

Thirteenth.—That the said justices may from time to time alter or rescind all or any of the foregoing rules.

Fourteenth.—That the said ——— and ———, cautioners in the said bond, shall sist as their domicile the registered office, in Aberdeen, of the Aberdeen Theatre and Opera-House Company, Limited, where all citations, summonses, notices or intimations necessary for the effectual enforcement of the provisions of the said statute and bond, or of any rules made or to be made as aforesaid, and for payment of the respective penalties aforesaid, may be left, and be legally effectual to all intents and purposes, as if delivered personally or left at the usual domicile of the said ―――― and ―――― cautioners respectively or any of them.

A true copy—Certified by

―――――, *Town Clerk of Aberdeen.*

―――♦―――

BIRKENHEAD.

The BIRKENHEAD CORPORATION ACT, 1881 (44 & 45 Vict. c. cliii), provides:—

Regulations as to places for public dancing.

111. For the regulation of places for public dancing or other public entertainments of the like kind the following provisions shall take effect, namely:

(1.) A house, room, garden or other place, whether or not licensed for the sale of wine, spirits, beer or other fermented or distilled liquors, shall not be kept or used for public dancing, music or other public entertainment of the like kind without a licence for all or some of those purposes first being obtained from a majority of the justices assembled at any special session, convened by at least fourteen days' previous notice.

(2.) Licences to keep or use houses, rooms, gardens or places for all or some of the purposes aforesaid may be granted on such terms and conditions and subject to such restrictions as may be specified in the respective licences, and every licence shall be in force for one year, unless previously revoked.

(3.) A majority of the justices may from time to time, at any such special session aforesaid, transfer any such licence to such person as they think fit.

(4.) Any person intending to apply for any such licence, or for the transfer of any such licence, shall give not less than seven days' notice of his intention to the clerk to the justices.

(5.) If any house, room, garden or place be kept and used for public dancing, music, or other public entertainment of the like kind without such licence, the occupier of the same shall be liable to a penalty not exceeding five pounds for every day on which the same is kept and used for any of the purposes aforesaid.

(6.) There shall be affixed and kept up in some conspicuous

place on the door or entrance of every house, room, garden or place so kept or used and so licensed as aforesaid the words following in large capital letters :—" Licensed for music " (or as the case may be) " in pursuance of Act of Parliament."

(7.) Any house, room, garden or place so kept or used, although so licensed as aforesaid, shall not be opened for any of the said purposes except between the hours stated in the licence.

(8.) The affixing and keeping up such words as aforesaid, and the limitation of the hours of opening, and regulations for the maintenance of good order, shall be inserted in and made conditions of every such licence, and in case of any breach of those conditions such licence shall be liable to be revoked by the order of any two justices.

The following is a FORM of, and the CONDITIONS contained in, the MUSIC LICENCE :—

At a special session of her Majesty's justices of the peace of the borough of Birkenhead, holden at the petty-sessional court-house of the said borough, on the ———— day of ————, 188—.

Borough of Birkenhead, } We, being the majority of her
to wit. } Majesty's justices of the peace assembled at the said special session Do HEREBY GRANT (in pursuance of section 111 of the Birkenhead Corporation Act, 1881, unto ————, being the occupier of a hall ———— called the ———— Hall, situate No. ——— in ———— Street, in Birkenhead ———— in the said borough, this licence to keep and use the said hall ———— for public dancing, music, *and other public entertainment of the like kind*, for the period of one year from the date hereof.

PROVIDED that such hall ———— shall only be used for the purpose aforesaid between the hours of six o'clock in the morning and [*two, as a rule*] o'clock in the *following morning*.

AND ALSO that the said ———— shall affix and keep up in some conspicuous place on the door or entrance of the said hall ———— in large capital letters the words " Licensed for public dancing and music, &c., in pursuance of Act of Parliament.

THAT such hall ———— shall be closed every Sunday, Christmas Day, Good Friday, and during Passion Week, and on days appointed for public fasts or thanksgivings,

THAT police constables when in uniform, and other constables when not in uniform, if known as such to the said ―――― or his servants, shall be permitted to have free access to the said hall ―――― at all times when the same shall be open.

THAT the said ―――― shall maintain and keep good order in the said hall ―――― and prevent anything which is licentious or indecent from being performed or sung there.

GIVEN under our hands and seals in open Court the ―――― day of ――――, 188—.

The JUSTICES' RULES (a) are:—

At a special licensing session of her Majesty's justices of the peace of, and acting in and for the borough of Birkenhead, holden in the police court, Hamilton Street, Birkenhead, in the borough aforesaid, on the 21st day of August, in the year of our Lord 1879, for the purpose of making suitable Rules for ensuring order and decency at the several theatres licensed by the justices within the said borough, and for regulating the times during which they shall severally be allowed to be open.

Borough of Birkenhead, } WHEREAS, by an Act of Parliament, to wit. } made and passed in the session of Parliament holden in the sixth and seventh years of the reign of her present Majesty, intituled 'An Act for regulating theatres,' it is enacted, 'That the said justices of the peace, at a special licensing session, or at some adjournment thereof, shall make suitable rules for ensuring order and decency at the several theatres licensed by them within their jurisdiction, and for regulating the times during which they shall severally be allowed to be open, and from time to time, at another special session, of which notice shall be given as aforesaid, may rescind or alter such rules; and it shall be lawful for any one of her Majesty's principal secretaries of state to rescind or alter such rules, and also to make such other rules for the like purpose as to him shall seem fit, and a copy of all rules which shall be in force for the time being shall be annexed to every such licence; and in case any riot or breach

---

(a) The justices rely on the report of the head constable as to the means of egress, and any structural alterations desired are always made before the licence is granted. But there is no bye-law or local Act to this effect.

of the said rules in any such theatre shall be proved on oath before any two justices usually acting in the jurisdiction where such theatre is situated, it shall be lawful for them to order that the same be closed for such time as to the said justices shall seem fit; and while such order shall be in force the theatre so ordered to be closed shall be deemed an unlicensed house.'

Now WE, the justices assembled at such adjourned special session as aforesaid, do hereby make the following rules, for the purpose mentioned in the said recited Act, that is to say—

- That the theatre shall be closed every Sunday, Christmas Day, Good Friday, and days appointed for a public fast and thanksgiving, and on any occasion, when the magistrates, for the preservation of the peace, shall signify their desire, in writing, to the manager or other person having at the time the care and management of the theatre, that the same shall not be opened.
- That the theatre shall be closed not later than twelve o'clock every night during the week, except on Saturday, when the same shall be closed at the hour of eleven o'clock at night.
- That police constables when dressed in uniform, or other constables when not so dressed, if known as such to the manager or his servants, shall be permitted to have free access to the theatre at all times during the hours of public performances; and in case any disorder shall take place, the proprietor and manager or his servants shall and will assist the police to their utmost, in the capture or expulsion of the offending parties.
- That the proprietor and manager shall, to the best of their ability, maintain and keep good order and decent behaviour in the theatre, during the hours of public performance; and nothing shall be acted, represented, recited, or sung, which is licentious or indecent, or likely to produce riot, tumult, or breach of the peace.
- That no children under twelve years of age shall be admitted into the theatre unless with parents or guardians, or under other proper control.
- For every breach of the above rules, the proprietor or manager shall forfeit and pay a penalty of five pounds.

BIRMINGHAM.

By The BIRMINGHAM CORPORATION (CONSOLIDATION) ACT, 1883 (46 & 47 Vict. c. lxx), it is provided:—

Sufficient means of ingress and egress to be provided for hotels and other public buildings.

40.—(1.) Every building, permanent or not, which is used or intended to be used as an hotel, refreshment room, church, chapel, school or theatre, or other place of public amusement or entertainment, or for holding a large number of persons for any purpose, shall be provided with ample and convenient means of ingress and egress, regard being had to the purposes for which such building is used or intended to be used, and the number of persons likely to be assembled at the same time therein.

(2.) If the owner or occupier of any such building, after the expiration of three months from the receipt of a notice from the surveyor to the effect that the corporation are not satisfied with the sufficiency of the means of ingress and egress provided for such building, and specifying the alterations and additions which the corporation think necessary, shall allow such building to be used for any such purpose as aforesaid without his having first complied with the terms of the notice, he shall for every such offence be liable to a penalty not exceeding fifty pounds.

Regulation of places for public dancing.

133. For the regulation of places for public dancing, music or other public entertainments of the like kind, the following provisions shall take effect (namely):—

(1.) A house, room or other place within the borough, licensed for the sale of wine, spirits, beer or other fermented or distilled liquors, and any room, gardens or place connected or occupied therewith, shall not be kept or used for public dancing, music or other public entertainment of the like kind without a licence for all or some of these purposes first being obtained from a majority of the justices of the borough assembled at their general annual licensing meeting or any adjournment thereof:

(2.) Licences to keep or use houses, rooms, gardens or places for all or some of the purposes aforesaid may be granted on such terms and conditions and subject to such restrictions as may be specified in the respective licences, and every licence shall be in force for one year, unless previously revoked:

(3.) Any house, room, garden or place kept or used for public dancing, music or other public entertainment of the like kind without such licence shall be deemed a disorderly house, and the occupier of the same shall be liable to a penalty not exceeding five pounds for every day on which the same is kept and used for any of the purposes aforesaid:

(4.) There shall be affixed and kept up in some conspicuous place on the door or entrance of every house, room, garden or place so kept or used and so licensed as aforesaid the words following in large capital letters: "Licensed for music" (or as the case may be) "in pursuance of Act of Parliament:"

(5.) Any house, room, garden or place so kept or used, although so licensed as aforesaid, shall not be opened for any of the said purposes, except between the hours stated in the licence:

(6.) The affixing and keeping up such words as aforesaid and the limitation of the hours of opening and regulations for the maintenance of good order shall be inserted in and made conditions of every such licence; and in case of any breach of those conditions such licence shall be liable to be revoked by the order of a court of summary jurisdiction.

There are no bye-laws.

BLACKBURN

Has no special legislation; but the Blackburn Improvement Act of 1882 (45 & 46 Vict. c. ccxliii), by sect. 19, imposes certain structural conditions on all buildings in the town.

BOLTON.

The BOLTON CORPORATION ACT, 1872 (35 & 36 Vict. c. lxxviii), provides:—

108. For the regulation of places for public dancing or music, or other public entertainment of the like kind, the following provisions shall have effect (namely):

(1.) After the expiration of six months from the passing of this Act, a house, room, or other place licensed for the sale of wine, spirits, beer, or other fermented or distilled liquors, or a room, garden, or place, shall not be kept or used for public dancing, music, or other public entertainment of the like kind, or for billiards, bowls, skittles, or other game, without a licence for all or some of those purposes first obtained from the justices acting for the borough, for which licence the fee of five shillings shall be paid by the person applying for the same.

(2.) Such justices may, under the hands of a majority of them assembled at any special session convened by fourteen days' previous notice, grant licences to such persons as they think fit to keep or use houses, rooms, gardens, or places for all or some of the purposes aforesaid, upon such terms and conditions and subject to such restrictions as they by the respective licences determine; and every licence shall be in force for one year, unless the same shall have been previously revoked as hereinafter provided.

(3.) Such justices may from time to time at any such special session aforesaid, transfer any such licence to such person as they think fit.

(4.) Each person shall in each case give seven days' notice to the clerk of the justices and to the chief constable of the borough, of his intention to apply for any such licence, or for the transfer of any such licence.

(5.) Any house, room, garden, or place kept and used for public dancing, music, or other public entertainment of the like kind, without such licence first obtained, shall be deemed a disorderly house, and the person occupying or rated as occupier of the same shall be liable to a penalty not exceeding five pounds for every day on which the same is kept and used for any of the purposes last aforesaid.

(6.) There shall be affixed and kept up in some conspicuous place on the door or entrance of every house, room, garden, or place so kept or used, and so licensed as aforesaid, an inscription in large capital letters in the words following: "Licensed in pursuance of Act of Parliament for ———," with the addition of words showing the purpose or purposes for which the same is licensed.

(7.) Any house, room, garden or place so kept or used, although so licensed as aforesaid, shall not be opened for any of the said purposes, except between the hours stated in the licence.

(8.) The affixing and keeping up of such inscription as aforesaid, and the limitation of the hours of opening, shall be inserted in and made conditions of every such licence.

(9.) In case of any breach or disregard of any of the terms, conditions, or restrictions upon or subject to which the licence was granted, such licence shall be liable to be revoked by the order of any two justices.

The CONDITIONS of the MUSIC LICENCE are:—

That he put and keep up an inscription in large capital letters in the words following: 'Licensed in pursuance of Act of Parliament for "music," "dancing," "billiards," or "skittles,"' as the case may be, in some conspicuous place on the door or entrance of the said house, and do not wilfully or knowingly permit drunkenness or other disorderly conduct in the said house, and do not knowingly suffer any unlawful games therein, and do not knowingly suffer persons of notoriously bad character to assemble and meet together therein, and do not open the said house for music, dancing, or play, or allow the same therein, after eleven o'clock in the evening or before six o'clock in the morning (unless he have a special licence enabling h to keep open h said house, and only during the time to which such special licence extends), or keep it open or allow any play therein on Sundays, Christmas Day, or Good Friday, or on any day appointed for a public fast or thanksgiving, and do not employ any paid or professional musicians or singers or allow them gratuitously to perform upon the premises, but do maintain good order and rule therein. And this licence shall continue in force from the day of the date hereof for one year then next ensuing, and no longer, unless the same shall be revoked in manner provided by the 'Bolton Corporation Act, 1872.' The future grant of a similar licence is in the discretion of the justices.

Given under our hands and seals, on the day and at the place first written.

The justices have lately passed a resolution, after considering the report of the borough surveyor on public buildings, "That any future application for a licence to any of the premises therein condemned be not entertained by the justices until it is first proved to their satisfaction that ample accommodation for access or egress is provided."

BRIGHTON.

The following is the only provision in a local Act on this subject:—

THE BRIGHTON IMPROVEMENT ACT, 1884.

Sect. 76.—Every public building shall be provided with ample and convenient means of ventilation and ingress and egress to be approved by the corporation: Provided always, that this section shall not apply to any barracks, public lunatic asylum, workhouse, prison or hospital.

Sect. 5 provides (*inter alia*) as follows:—
"Public building" means any building used or intended, constructed or adapted to be used either regularly or occasionally as a church, chapel or other place of public worship, or as college, school (not being merely a dwelling-house so used), theatre, public hall, public concert-room, public ball-room, public lecture-room, public exhibition room or public place of assembly, or used or intended, constructed or adapted to be used, either regularly or occasionally, for any other public purpose.

There are no bye-laws on this subject.

The JUSTICES' (*a*) RULES are as follows:—

1.—The theatre shall be closed every Sunday, Christmas Day, Good Friday and days appointed for a public fast and thanksgiving.

2.—The theatre shall be closed every Saturday night at the hour of half-past eleven.

3.—Police-constables when dressed in uniform, or other constables when not dressed, if known as such to the manager or his servants, shall be permitted to have free ingress to the theatre at all times of public performance.

4.—The manager shall, to the best of his ability, maintain and keep good order and decent behaviour in the theatre during the hours of public performance.

5.—For every breach of the above rules the manager shall forfeit and pay a penalty not exceeding five pounds.

It may be added that the Hove Town Hall is licensed as a theatre.

(*a*) According to the words of the Act, it is the Lord Chamberlain and not the justices who has jurisdiction in Brighton under 6 & 7 Vict. c. 68. See p. 29.

CAMBRIDGE.

The CAMBRIDGE AWARD ACT, 1856 (19 Vict. c. xvii), provides:—

Sect. 17.—No occasional public exhibition or performance, whether strictly theatrical or not, other than performances in theatres, which are regulated by the Act sixth and seventh Victoria, chapter sixty-eight, shall take place within the borough (except during the period of Midsummer fair, or in the Long Vacation), unless with the consent in writing of the Vice-Chancellor and the Mayor, and every person who shall offend against this enactment shall be liable to forfeit a sum not exceeding twenty pounds, recoverable in like manner as penalties imposed by the said Act.

The justices have not made any regulations.

CARDIFF

Has a local Act requiring music-halls to be licensed; see a case arising under this Act, p. 54.

The following are the bye-laws:—

BYE-LAWS UNDER THE CARDIFF BOROUGH ACT, 1862 (25 & 26 Vict. c. ccxxiii).

At a special meeting of the council of the borough of Cardiff, held at the town hall, in the said borough, on Wednesday, the 3rd day of September, in the year of our Lord 1862.

Present—Richard Lewis Reece, William Alexander, Aldermen; Charles Redwood Vachell, Henry Clements, John Winstone, Edward Mason, Daniel Jones, William Nell, John Bird, Edward Whiffen, Hugh Bird, and Thomas Evans, Councillors; Alderman Richard Lewis Reece in the chair.

Resolved—That the following bye-laws for regulating places for public dancing, music, or other entertainment within this borough, be made and adopted under the provisions of "The Cardiff Borough Act, 1862."

No person, without having first obtained a licence for that purpose, shall allow any exciseable liquor to be consumed in any house, room, garden, or place licensed for public dancing, music, or other entertainment.

Every person who shall intend to apply for a licence for any house, room, garden, or place for public dancing, music, or other entertainment, shall give fourteen days' notice before the hearing of such intended application, stating therein his residence and description, with the name and situation of every such house, room, garden, or place; such notice to be delivered to the superintendent of the Cardiff police, who shall cause a list of the applicants, with the particulars given by them, to be affixed on the front door of the town hall seven days before the day appointed for the hearing.

No person shall allow gaming, drunkenness, prostitution, or other disorderly or indecent conduct, or permit persons of notoriously bad characters to assemble and meet in any house, room, garden, or place for which a licence, as aforesaid, shall have been granted.

The police of the said borough of Cardiff shall be permitted to have free ingress and egress at all hours to and from any such house, room, garden, or place, for which a licence, as aforesaid, shall have been granted.

The sum of twenty shillings shall be paid for each licence, in addition to the fees authorized to be taken by the clerk to the justices, on the granting of spirit licences.

Any person who shall commit a breach of, or shall not observe either of the above bye-laws, shall be liable to a penalty not exceeding five pounds for every breach for non-observance, at the discretion of the justices before whom he may be summoned.

Sealed with the seal of the said borough, the day and year above mentioned.

CHESTER

Has no special legislation.

The justices have made the following rules, which provide for structural efficiency :—

THEATRE RULES.

(1.) The theatre shall be closed every Sunday, Christmas Day, Good Friday, Ash Wednesday, and on days appointed for public fast.

(2.) The theatre shall be closed every Saturday night at the hour of eleven, and on other nights at half-an-hour past eleven o'clock.

(3.) That no wine, beer or spirits shall be sold or consumed in the theatre save in refreshment-rooms provided for the purpose, and previously approved by the mayor for the time being and two justices of the city, and save only during the time when such theatre is open for performance therein.

(4.) That no person be allowed to enter the theatre in a state of intoxication.

(5.) That no prostitutes or known thieves be allowed to enter or remain in the theatre.

(6.) That nothing be acted, recited, or sung, tending to bring into contempt the Christian religion; nor anything which shall be in any shape offensive to public decency, nor anything calculated to produce tumult or riot or other breach of the peace.

(7.) Police constables when dressed in uniform (or when not dressed in uniform), if known as such to the manager or his servants, shall be permitted to have free ingress and egress to and from the theatre at all times during the time of public performance.

(8.) The manager shall maintain and keep good order and decent behaviour in the theatre during the hours of public performance.

(9.) That all doors and barriers shall open outwards, and never be fastened during the time when the public are in the theatre.

(10.) That during the time when the theatre is opened to the public all the approaches, staircases and passages within the building shall be kept entirely free from obstructions, and that no seats, whether movable or otherwise, shall be permitted in any of the alleys, gangways, or passages within that portion of the building set apart for the spectators.

(11.) That the auditorium shall be lighted by one meter supply and the stage by another, and that such meters and all gas taps shall be guarded and out of the reach of the public, and if any other means of lighting be adopted the same shall be to the satisfaction of the borough surveyor.

(12.) That all the means of exit shall be indicated in the several parts of the theatre in plain characters and in conspicuous places.

(13.) That no smoking shall be permitted within those portions of the theatre set apart for spectators.

(14.) That a man shall be kept in attendance at all times during the performance to attend to the exits and gas meters and water supply.

(15.) That a hose shall be kept in readiness at all times during the performance to connect with the water-plug inside the building, and to the satisfaction of the chief of the fire brigade; and buckets shall always be kept ready filled with water behind the scenes.

(16.) That no structural alterations shall be made without the sanction in writing of two justices in a petty sessional court assembled.

(17.) That the borough surveyor, and any other person appointed by two of her Majesty's justices of the peace for the said borough, shall at all times have access to the theatre to inspect the same, and the foregoing rules for the safety of the theatre shall be carried out to his satisfaction.

(18.) That these rules be printed, placed and kept in view in a conspicuous part of each of the several stories within the theatre.

(19.) For every breach of the above rules the manager shall pay a penalty not exceeding five pounds.

DERBY.

The DERBY IMPROVEMENT ACT, 1879 (42 & 43 Vict. c. ccxv), provides:—

102. From and after the 1st day of September, 1880, no house, room, garden or place within the borough shall be kept or used for public dancing or music without a licence first had and obtained from the justices of the peace for the borough in petty sessions assembled (which licence such justices are hereby authorized and empowered at their discretion to grant) on their general annual licensing day or on any transfer day, and under the hand and seals of a majority of the justices there assembled, and any house, room, garden or place kept and used for any such purposes as aforesaid without such licence first had and obtained shall be deemed a disorderly house, and the person occupying or rated as the occupier of the same shall, on conviction before any two of such justices, be liable to a penalty not exceeding five pounds for every day on which he shall so offend: Provided always, that in order to give public notice what places are licensed pursuant to this Act, there shall be affixed and kept up in some conspicuous place on the door or entrance of every house, room, garden or place kept or used for any of the said purposes, and so licensed as aforesaid, an inscription in large capital letters of such dimensions as shall be prescribed in such licence in the words following: "Licensed for music" (or dancing, or both, as the case may be) "pursuant to Act of Parliament," and no such house, room, garden or place kept or used for any of the said purposes, except between the hours stated in the licence, and the affixing and keeping up

such inscription as aforesaid, and the said limitation in point of time shall be inserted in and made a condition of every such licence; and in case of any breach of any of the conditions of any such licence, such licence shall be liable to be forfeited and revoked by the justices of the peace for the borough in petty sessions assembled on any general licensing day, or on any transfer day or adjournment thereof, or to be suspended and temporarily revoked until the next general annual licensing day by two justices in any case in which it shall be proved to the satisfaction of such justices that more than one breach of such condition has occurred since the granting of such licence: Provided also, that it shall be lawful for any person who shall think himself aggrieved by any order of any such justices to appeal therefrom to the quarter sessions for the borough of Derby (which Court shall have power to hear and determine the same), whose order therein shall be final.

DOVER.

The TOWN HALL is licensed under 6 & 7 Vict. c. 68.

RULES *made on the 21st day of April*, 1882, *by her Majesty's Justices of the Peace of and for the Borough of Dover, for insuring order and decency at the several theatres, houses and places within the said borough, and also for regulating the times during which they shall severally be allowed to be open.*

1st.—That no theatre, house or place licensed within the said borough shall be opened upon any Sunday, Christmas Day, Good Friday, or on any day appointed for a public fast or thanksgiving, neither shall any performance be allowed therein on any such days.

2nd.—That no theatre, house or place duly licensed as aforesaid shall be left open after twelve o'clock on Saturday nights.

3rd.—That all theatres, houses and places duly licensed as aforesaid shall be kept open only during such time or times of the year for which they shall be so respectively licensed, the aforesaid days always excepted.

4th.—Police-constables when in uniform, or when not in uniform, if known as such to the manager or his servants, shall be permitted to have free ingress to the building at all times during the hours of public performance.

5th.—That the managers of all theatres, houses and places

so licensed as aforesaid shall cause good order and rule to be kept therein.

Lastly.—That such manager as aforesaid shall enter into a recognizance, himself in 50*l.* and two sureties of 25*l.* each, for the due observance of these rules.

FOLKESTONE

Has no special legislation.

Under the Public Health Act of 1875, the corporation have made bye-laws imposing structural conditions on all buildings. Bye-law 16 prescribes that the walls of public buildings shall be of a certain thickness proportional to their height, according to a scale laid down in the bye-law.

There is no proper theatre in the town, but theatrical entertainments, &c., are performed in the town-hall, which is licensed under 6 & 7 Vict. c. 68.

GLASGOW

Has no special legislation, nor are music-halls licensed; but the plans of all buildings to be erected or altered must pass the Dean of Guild Court, whose statutory powers are contained in the Glasgow Police Act, 1866.

Rules and Regulations *enacted by her Majesty's Justices of the Peace, acting in and for the Lower Ward of Lanarkshire, for insuring order and decency at the —— Theatre.*

First.—The responsible manager shall affix and keep exposed upon the front and on some conspicuous place over the doors of or entrance to the said theatre, an inscription in large Roman letters, painted either of a light colour upon a dark ground, or of a dark colour upon a light ground, in the words following:—" Licensed pursuant to Act of Parliament, 6 & 7 Victoria, chapter 68," and shall in like manner paint his christian and surname, and the words "responsible manager," immediately above the said inscription.

Second.—The said theatre shall not be opened for the performance of any stage play, or for dancing, music, or for any other public entertainment on the Sabbath, or on any other day in the week set apart for public worship by lawful authority.

Third.—The charge for the admission of any person to any part of the foresaid theatre, as a spectator of the performance, shall not be less than sixpence for each person, either for first, or second, or half-price.

Fourth.—The entertainment shall not be continued later than half-past eleven o'clock at night, at which hour the public shall be excluded, and the theatre closed.

Fifth.—The responsible manager shall maintain good order and decency, and shall not permit or suffer men or women of bad fame, or dissolute boys or girls, to enter the said theatre as spectators, or in any other character, and shall not permit any promenade of the spectators or audience to take place within the buildings or premises attached thereto.

Sixth.—At each representation the responsible manager shall provide two constables, one of whom shall be a practical fireman, to be paid by him, who shall be approved, and be under the directions of the chief constable of the city of Glasgow, to attend at the said theatre, to insure that good order and decency shall be maintained therein.

Seventh.—There shall be a separate and independent exit to the street from the several parts of the theatre, which shall be available at all times; all angles in the lobbies, passages, and staircases shall be rounded, and all the doors of egress shall be kept open—that is, unlocked and unbarred—throughout the whole representation.

Eighth.—The gas supply pipe for the stage shall be quite independent of the supply pipe to the auditorium, and the gas lights in the lobbies and stairs shall likewise be supplied by means of an independent supply pipe; that oil lamps shall be placed throughout the whole building, including auditorium, stage, lobbies, and staircases, and continually kept burning during the whole representation; that the drop scene or screen shall be composed of non-inflammable material, and the partitions between the proscenium and auditorium shall be fireproof.

Ninth.—Before opening the outer doors for any representation the responsible manager shall himself, or by a competent person appointed by him, inspect the whole theatre, and ascertain especially that the gas and oil lamps, and the water appliances for extinguishing fire, are in proper order. This inspection shall be entered in a log-book, and signed by the person making the inspection, which log-book shall lie in the office of the pit cash-taker, and may be examined by any of the public at entering, or at any time during the representation.

Tenth.—A printed copy of these rules and regulations, signed by the clerk of the peace, shall be posted and kept exposed on the walls of the various parts of the lobbies and staircases of the theatre by the responsible manager; and that a copy be transmitted to the lord provost of the city for the information of the magistrates.

Lastly.—The said responsible manager shall become bound to the extent of two hundred pounds, and find security by two cautioners to the extent of one hundred pounds each, for the due performance by him of the foresaid regulations, and for payment of any penalty or penalties he may be adjudged to pay for any act of contravention thereof; and in case he shall violate or contravene any of the rules and regulations, or any part thereof, the licence shall be forfeited and shall become void and null in addition to such penalty.

———, *Clerk of the Peace.*

HASTINGS

Has no special legislation.

The JUSTICES' RULES are:—

1. The theatre shall be closed every Sunday, Christmas Day, Good Friday, and days appointed for a public fast and thanksgiving.

2. The theatre shall be closed every Saturday night at the hour of half-past eleven.

3. No spirituous liquors, wine, ale, beer, porter, cider, perry, or tobacco, shall be sold or disposed of in the theatre, or upon the premises.

4. Police constables when dressed in uniform, or other constables when not so dressed, if known as such to the manager or his servants, shall be permitted to have free ingress to the theatre at all times during the time of public performance.

5. The manager shall to the best of his ability maintain and keep good order and decent behaviour in the theatre during the hours of public performance.

6. For every breach of the above rules the manager shall forfeit and pay a penalty not exceeding 5*l.*

LEEDS.

The LEEDS IMPROVEMENT ACT, 1842 (5 & 6 Vict. c. civ.), provides:—

CCXL.—And be it enacted, that it shall be lawful for any justice, by order in writing, to authorize the head constable or any superintendent or inspector belonging to the police force in the borough, with such constables as he may think necessary, to enter into any house or room kept or used within the borough for stage plays or dramatic entertainment, or for any public show or exhibition, into which admission is obtained by payment of money, and which is not a licensed theatre, or a room or place authorized by the mayor to be used for that purpose, at any time when the same shall be open for the reception of persons resorting thereto, and to take into custody all persons who shall be found therein without lawful excuse; and every person keeping, using or knowingly letting any house or other tenement for the purposes aforesaid, or any of them, shall be liable to a penalty not more than twenty pounds, recoverable before any two justices, and in default of payment of the penalty awarded, and costs, may be committed to the house of correction, with or without hard labour, for a term not more than two months, and every person performing or being therein without lawful excuse shall be liable to a penalty not more than forty shillings; and a conviction under this Act for this offence shall not exempt the owner, keeper or manager of any such house, room or tenement from any penalty or penal consequences to which he may be liable for keeping a disorderly house or for the nuisance thereby occasioned; provided that the onus of proving that such place is a licensed theatre shall be upon the person keeping the same. *Power to enter unlicensed theatres, and to take away persons found there.*

[NOTE.—The mayor occasionally exercises the power given to him by this section in favour of special dramatic performances in unlicensed rooms, and also occasionally in favour of travelling theatres in booths.]

The LEEDS IMPROVEMENT ACT, 1866 (29 & 30 Vict. c. clvii.), provides:—

101. After the expiration of six months after the passing of this Act no house, room or other place licensed for the sale of wine, spirits, beer or other fermented or distilled liquors, and no room, gardens or place shall be kept or used for *Power to licence places for music and dancing.*

public dancing, music or other public entertainment of the like kind without a licence for all or some of those purposes first obtained from two justices; and such justices may at any special sessions, convened by fourteen days' previous notice, grant licences to such persons as they shall think fit to keep or use such rooms, gardens or places for public dancing, music or other public entertainment of the like kind upon such terms and conditions and subject to such restrictions as they shall by such licence determine, and such licence shall be in force for one year; and such justices may from time to time, at any such special session as aforesaid, transfer any such licence to such person as they shall think fit, and such person shall in each case give seven days' notice to the town clerk of his intention to apply for such licence or for the transfer of such licence.

Penalty for keeping unlicensed places for music or dancing.

102. The person occupying or rated as the occupier of any house, room, garden or place which after the expiration of six months after the passing of this Act shall be kept and used for public dancing, music or other public entertainment of the like kind without such licence first had and obtained, shall forfeit not exceeding five pounds for every day on which the same shall be kept and used for any of the purposes last aforesaid: Provided always, that in order to give public notice what places are licensed pursuant to this Act there shall be affixed and kept up in some conspicuous place on the door or entrance of such house, room, garden or place kept or used for any of the said purposes, and so licensed as aforesaid, an inscription in large capital letters in the words following: "Licensed pursuant to Act of Parliament;" and no such house, room, garden or place kept or used for any of the said purposes, although licensed as aforesaid, shall be opened or kept opened for any of the said purposes except between the hours stated in the licence; and the affixing and keeping up of such inscription as aforesaid, and the said limitation in point of time, shall be inserted in and made conditions of every such licence; and in case of any breach of either of the said conditions such licence shall be liable to be forfeited and revoked by any two justices: Provided also, that it shall be lawful for every person who shall think himself aggrieved by any order of such justices to appeal therefrom to the quarter sessions in the manner and subject to the provisions hereinafter contained relative to appeals to quarter sessions from any order of justices.

The following is the FORM of the LICENCE for PUBLIC MUSIC, &c.:—

Borough of Leeds, ⎫ At a special sessions of her Majesty's
   in the   ⎬ justices of the peace in and for the
County of York. ⎭ borough of Leeds, duly convened and
held in the Town Hall in Leeds, in and for the said borough, on the ——— day of ———, 188—.

WHEREAS, in and by the Leeds Improvement Act, 1866, it is enacted that after the expiration of six months after the passing of that Act, no house, room, or other place licensed for the sale of wine, spirits, beer, or other fermented or distilled liquors, and no house, room, garden or place shall be kept or used for public dancing, music, or other public entertainment of the like kind without a licence for all or some of those purposes first obtained from two justices; and such justices may at any special sessions, convened as therein mentioned, grant licences to such persons as they shall think fit to keep or use such house, room, garden or place for public dancing, music or other public entertainment of the like kind upon such terms and conditions, and subject to such restrictions as they shall by such licence determine, and such licence shall be in force for one year, and such justices may from time to time at any such special sessions as aforesaid, transfer any such licence to such person as they shall think fit.

Now, we the said justices being assembled in special sessions as aforesaid, and being a majority of such justices, upon application duly made to us, do hereby grant a licence to and authorize ——— to keep and use one room called the ——— in a certain house and premises, occupied by h situate in ——— in the said borough, called or known as the ——— for public *music*, ——— therein from the day of the date hereof until the 1st day of January next, upon and subject to the following terms, conditions and restrictions, that is to say, ———.

THAT the said room so licensed as aforesaid shall not for any purpose for which the same is licensed be open before eight o'clock in the forenoon, nor continue open after eleven o'clock at night on any day, nor shall any such *music*, ——— be permitted therein at any hour or time whatsoever on Sunday, Good Friday, or any day appointed by authority for a public fast or thanksgiving.

(*a.*)
THAT whilst such room shall be opened for any of the purposes aforesaid, no drunken or disorderly person, and no

---

(*a.*) If the licence be for dancing, insert here "That on Christmas Day no public dancing be permitted."

common prostitute, shall be permitted to enter or remain therein, no drunkenness or other disorderly conduct or proceedings, no unlawful games or gaming whatever, and no obscenity or profanity shall be permitted therein, but good rule and order shall be kept and maintained.

THAT the chief constable of the borough of Leeds and any police officers shall be permitted at all times to enter and remain in and upon the room so licensed for all or any of the hours or times during which this licence shall be in force.

THAT the words "Licensed pursuant to Act of Parliament," in large capital letters, shall, whilst this licence continues in force, be affixed and kept up in some conspicuous place on the door or entrance of the said room hereby licensed.

> GIVEN under our hands at Leeds in the said borough, in special sessions aforesaid, on the day and year first hereinbefore mentioned.

The justices have also (in 1876) passed a resolution, "That no new licence for music or dancing be granted in respect of any room which has a less superficial area than four hundred feet and a less height than ten feet; and that the justices at future licensing meetings be requested to take into their consideration whether certain of the existing licences should be continued by way of renewal or transfer, having regard to the size and suitability of the room in respect of which such renewal or transfer may be applied for."

Under various local Acts the following BYE-LAWS have been made by the Corporation:—

2. "Public building" means a building used or constructed or adapted to be used either ordinarily or occasionally as a .... theatre, public hall, public concert-room, public ball-room, public lecture-room, or public exhibition-room, or as a public place of assembly for persons admitted thereto by tickets or otherwise, or used or constructed or adapted to be used either ordinarily or occasionally for any other public purpose.

30. The person erecting any building of public entertainment or resort, or any church, chapel, or place for holding religious meetings, shall cause such building to be provided with ample means of ingress and egress. Such person shall cause all doors to such building used by the public to be made to open outwards, but so that they shall not extend over the footway of any street.

31. The person erecting any building of public entertainment or resort, or any church, chapel or place for holding religious meetings, shall cause such building, church, chapel, or place to be provided with adequate means of ventilation.

See, too, bye-law 62.

RULES *made by her Majesty's Justices of the Peace for the Borough of Leeds, assembled at a special licensing sessions on the 24th day of October,* 1878, *for insuring order and decency in licensed theatres within the said borough, and for regulating the times during which such theatres shall be allowed to be open, pursuant to the Act 6th and 7th Vict. chap.* 68.

1. That there shall be no performance in any theatre on Sundays, Christmas Days, Good Fridays, or any days appointed by authority for public fast or humiliation.

2. That each theatre be closed not later than half-past eleven o'clock each night, except Saturday nights, when the same shall be closed not later than eleven o'clock.

3. That no exciseable liquors, wine, ale or porter be sold or consumed, or tobacco smoked within that part of a theatre set apart for spectators.

4. That no person be permitted to enter or continue within a theatre in a state of intoxication.

5. That all persons who may be guilty within a theatre of any breach of the peace, tumult, or disorder, or of any violent language or demeanour, calculated or having a tendency to excite any breach of the peace, tumult, or disorder, or of any indecent, obscene, or blasphemous language, be forthwith removed therefrom.

6. That nothing be acted, recited, sung, or exhibited in a theatre, of a seditious, obscene, or indecent nature, or calculated to bring the Christian religion into contempt, or to excite any breach of the peace, tumult, or disorder.

7. That no common prostitute be permitted to enter or continue within a theatre.

8. That good rule and order be preserved within each theatre to the utmost of the power of the manager and his servants and others having any charge or superintendence thereof.

9. That any number of police officers for this borough be permitted while on police duty to enter and continue within each theatre.

10. That two copies of every play bill and advertisement of every theatrical entertainment be left at the head police office, in Leeds, not later than eleven o'clock in the morning

of the day on which the entertainments therein respectively mentioned shall take place.

11. That each theatre be closed, and all entertainments therein cease at any time when any riot or tumult happens, or is expected to happen, upon notice in writing, under the hand of any two justices of the peace for this borough, either given to the manager, or left at the theatre with any of the officers or servants there; and the theatre shall not be re-opened, nor any entertainment therein resumed during the time specified in such notice.

12. That during the time when a theatre is open to the public all the approaches, staircases and passages within the building be kept entirely free from obstructions; and that no seats, whether moveable or otherwise, be permitted in any of the alleys, gangways, or passages within that portion of the building set apart for spectators.

13. That these rules be published and continued in a conspicuous place within each theatre.

LEICESTER.

The LEICESTER CORPORATION ACT, 1884 (47 & 48 Vict. c. xxxii.), provides:—

Places for Dancing, Singing, Music, and other Entertainments to be Licensed.

7. For the regulation of places for public dancing or music, or other public entertainment of the like kind, the following provisions shall have effect (namely):—

(1.) After the expiration of six months from the passing of this Act, a house, room, garden, or other place, whether or not licensed for the sale of wine, spirits, beer, or other fermented or distilled liquors, shall not be kept or used for public dancing, singing, music, or other public entertainment of the like kind, without a licence for the purpose or purposes for which the same respectively is to be used first obtained from the justices acting for the borough, for which licence and for the registration thereof a fee of one shilling shall be paid by the person applying therefor;

(2.) Such justices may under the hands of a majority of them assembled at any annual licensing meeting, or at any special session convened with fourteen days' previous notice, grant licences to such persons as they think fit to keep or use houses, rooms, gardens, or places for all or any of the purposes aforesaid, upon such terms and conditions, and subject to such restrictions as they by the respective licences determine, and every licence shall be in force for one year, or for such shorter period as the justices in the grant of the licence shall determine, unless the same shall have been previously revoked as hereinafter provided;

(3.) Such justices may from time to time at any such special session aforesaid, or at any special session appointed for the transfer of ale-house licences, transfer any such licence to such person as they think fit;

(4.) Each person shall in each case give fourteen days' notice in writing to the clerk of the justices, and to the head constable of the borough, of his intention to apply for any such licence, or for the transfer of any such licence;

(5.) Any house, room, garden, or place kept or used for any of the purposes aforesaid without such licence first obtained, shall be deemed a disorderly house, and the person occupying or rated as occupier of the same shall be liable to a penalty not exceeding five pounds for every day on which the same is kept or used for any of the purposes last aforesaid;

(6.) There shall be affixed and kept up in some conspicuous place on the door or entrance of every house, room, garden, or place so kept or used, and so licensed as aforesaid, an inscription in large capital letters in the words following, "Licensed in pursuance of Act of Parliament for ———," with the addition of words showing the purpose or purposes for which the same is licensed;

(7.) Any house, room, garden, or place so kept or used, although so licensed as aforesaid, shall not be opened for any of the said purposes, except on the days and between the hours stated in the licence;

(8.) The affixing and keeping up of such inscription as aforesaid, and the observance of the days and hours of opening, shall be inserted in and made conditions of every such licence;

(9.) In case of any breach or disregard of any of the terms or conditions upon or subject to which the licence was granted, the holder thereof shall be liable to a penalty not exceeding ten pounds, and to a daily penalty not exceeding five pounds, and such licence shall be liable to be revoked by the order of any two justices;

(10.) No notice need be given under sub-section (4) of this section when the application is for a renewal of an existing licence held by the applicant for the same premises;

(11.) The justices in any petty sessions may, if and as they think fit, grant to any person applying for the same, a licence to keep or use any house, room, garden, or place for any purpose within the meaning of this section for any period less than seven days, which they shall specify in such licence, notwithstanding that no notices shall have been given under subsection (4) of this section.

Premises Licensed for Sale of Intoxicating Liquors not to be altered without the consent of the Justices.

8. No person who has obtained any licence to sell any intoxicating liquor at any place in the borough for consumption on the premises shall, after the passing of this Act, alter (externally), or shall extend, add to, or take from the premises to which such licence applies, except with the previous consent in writing of the majority of justices assembled at a special session held for the purpose of transferring ale-house licences under their hands; and any person who shall offend against this enactment shall be liable to a penalty not exceeding ten pounds, and to a further penalty not exceeding forty shillings for every day during which such offence shall continue after conviction therefor. Provided that penalties under this section and any other enactment for the same offence shall not be cumulative.

───◆───

LIVERPOOL

Has no special legislation. The JUSTICES' RULES are—

1. That no theatre shall be open for the performance of stage plays on any occasion when the magistrates, for the preservation of the peace, may signify their desire, in writing, to the manager or other person having at the time the care and management of such theatre, that the same should not be opened.

2. That there shall be no performance of any stage plays in any theatre on Sunday, Christmas Day, Good Friday, or any day appointed for a national fast.

3. That the several theatres shall be closed not later than twelve o'clock every night during the week except on Saturday night, when the same shall be closed at eleven o'clock.

4. That nothing shall be acted, represented, recited or sung, which is licentious or indecent or likely to produce riot, tumult or breach of the peace.

5. That no person be permitted to enter or continue within a theatre in a state of intoxication.

6. That during the time when a theatre is open to the public, all the approaches, staircases and passages within the building shall be kept entirely free from obstructions, and that no seats, whether moveable or otherwise, shall be permitted in any of the alleys, gangways or passages, within that portion of the building set apart for spectators.

7. That all doors and barriers shall open outwards, and never be fastened during the time when the public are within the theatre.

8. That all gas taps shall be guarded and out of the reach of the public in all passages, staircases and other parts of the theatre to which the public are admitted.

9. That all the means of exit shall be indicated in the several parts of the theatre by printed placards, in plain characters, in conspicuous places.

10. That no smoking shall be permitted within those portions of a theatre set apart for spectators.

11. That no exciseable liquors, wine, ale or porter, be sold or consumed in any theatre, except in the refreshment rooms thereof, and only to the audience and company engaged in the theatre, when the theatre is open for performance therein.

12. That the police shall have free access to any licensed theatre, and in case any disorder shall take place the proprietors shall, by themselves and their servants, assist to the utmost in the capture or expulsion of the offenders.

13. That these rules be printed, placed and kept in view in a conspicuous part of each of the several storeys within each theatre."

MANCHESTER.

At a special session of the justices of the peace, acting in and for the borough of Manchester, in the county of Lancaster, holden at the Court House, in Brown Street, Manchester, in the said borough, on the 25th day of October, in the year of our Lord 1843, for granting licences to houses within the said borough for the performance of stage plays.

That no theatre, within the said borough, shall be open

for the performance of stage plays, or for any purpose whatsoever, during Passion week, nor on any occasion when the magistrates for the preservation of the peace may signify their desire in writing to the manager, or other person having at the time the care and management of such theatre, that the same should not be open.

That the several theatres shall be closed not later than twelve o'clock every night during the week, except on Saturday night, when the same shall be closed at eleven o'clock.

That no common prostitutes or known thieves shall be admitted into, or permitted to remain in, any of the said theatres.

And any manager or other person having the care and management of any theatre, who shall make default in compliance with these rules or either of them, shall forfeit and pay for such offence a sum not exceeding twenty pounds.

NOTE.—At a meeting of the justices held the 2nd day of October, 1866, it was resolved—"That such portions of the rules as restrict the opening of a theatre during Passion week be rescinded."

At a meeting of the justices held on the 4th day of November, 1870, it was resolved—"That no wine, beer or spirits shall be sold or consumed in any theatre save in refreshment-rooms provided for the purpose and previously approved by the mayor for the time being, and two justices of the city, and save only during the time when such theatre is open for performance therein."

NORWICH.

The Justices have made the following RULES, which are annexed to the licence. A form of application for a licence is also given.

The following is a copy of LICENCE:—

City of Norwich and County of the same City, to wit. } At a special session of her Majesty's justices of the peace acting in and for the said city and county at the petty sessional court house in the Guildhall in and for the said city and county, on Thursday, the 15th day of March, in the year of our Lord 1883, for the purposes of granting licences to houses for the performance of stage plays in pursuance of the sixth and seventh years of her present Majesty, intituled "An Act for Regulating Theatres."

We the undersigned, being four of her Majesty's justices of the peace acting in and for the said city and county present at this special sessions, do hereby license, authorize and empower one W. H., he being the actual and responsible manager of a certain company of theatrical players, to have and keep open a certain building called the ——— situate at ——— in the said city and county as and for a place of public resort for the public performance of stage plays under the provisions of the statute aforesaid for the space of twelve calendar months from the 26th day of March instant, provided that the said W. H. do observe and keep the rules for insuring order and decency at and in the said theatre so licensed by us, the said justices, and for regulating the times during which the said theatre shall be allowed to be open, a copy of which rules is on the back of this licence, pursuant to the statute in that case made and provided.

Given under our hands and seals at the special sessions above mentioned.

(L.S.)

This licence was immediately after the signing thereof publicly read in open Court by me, the undersigned, together with the names of the justices subscribing the same.

——— *Clerk to the justices of the said city and county.*

Rules *in force during the currency of the within Licence :* —

1. The theatre shall be closed every Sunday.
2. The theatre shall be closed every night at the hour of eleven o'clock.
3. No spirituous liquors, wine, ale, beer, porter, cider or perry shall be sold or disposed of in the theatre or upon the premises.
4. No tobacco shall be consumed, sold or disposed of in the theatre or upon the premises during the time of public performance.
5. Police constables when dressed in uniform, or other constables when not so dressed, if known as such to the manager or his servants, shall be permitted to have free access to the theatre at all times during the times of public performance.
6. The manager shall, to the best of his ability, maintain and keep good order and decent behaviour in the theatre during the hours of public performance.
7. For every breach of the above rules the manager shall forfeit and pay a penalty not exceeding five pounds.

Form of Application for a Licence.

To ———— Clerk to the Justices of the City and County of the City of Norwich.

I, the undersigned W. H. of ———— in the parish of ———— in the city of Norwich ———— being the actual and responsible manager of a certain company of amateur theatrical performers, and also the actual and responsible manager of certain buildings known as ———— situate in the parish of ———— in the city of Norwich, do hereby in pursuance of and by virtue of the Act of Parliament of the sixth and seventh years of the reign of her present Majesty, entitled "An Act for Regulating Theatres," give you notice that I intend to make application at a special session to be holden in and for the said city and county to the justices of the peace assembled thereat for a licence to be granted unto me for the performance of stage plays in the buildings above mentioned and known as ———— in the said parish of ———— in the city of Norwich for the space of twelve months from the twenty-sixth day of March inst., and I respectfully request that you will within twenty-one days after this application appoint a day for holding a special sessions in the said city and county for the purpose of granting unto me such licence, and that you will give notice of the holding of such session to each of the justices within the said city and county pursuant to statute aforesaid.

Witness my hand the ———— day of ————.

Signed by the said W. H., in the presence of us, the undersigned, two of her Majesty's justices of the peace in and for the said city and county } W. H.

NORTHAMPTON

Has no special legislation. The RULES attached to LICENCE are—

1. The theatre shall be closed for theatrical representations every Sunday, Christmas Day, Good Friday, and days appointed for public fast and thanksgiving.

2. That the theatre shall be closed every night at the hour of eleven.

3. Police constables when dressed in uniform, or other constables when not so dressed, if known as such to the manager or his servants, shall be permitted to have free ingress to the theatre at all times during the time of public performance.

4. That the manager shall, to the best of his ability, maintain and keep good order and decent behaviour in the theatre during the hours of public performance.

5. Refreshments to be sold in the theatre only during the hours of performance and only to the audience and company engaged in the house.

6. For every breach of the above rules the manager shall forfeit and pay a penalty not exceeding five pounds.

OLDHAM.

The JUSTICES' RULES are as follows:—

1st.—That each theatre shall close at half-past eleven o'clock in the evening, except on Saturday night, when the theatre shall close at eleven o'clock.

2nd.—That there be no performance on Sundays, Christmas Day, Good Friday, or any day appointed by public authority as a fast day.

3rd.—That no exciseable liquors or tobacco be sold or smoked within the theatre or the precincts thereof.

4th.—Police constables when dressed in uniform, or other constables when not dressed, if known as such to the manager or his servants, shall be permitted to have free ingress to the theatre at all times during the time of public performance.

5th.—The manager shall, to the best of his ability, maintain and keep good order and decent behaviour in the theatre during the hours of public performance.

6th.—For every breach of the above rules, the manager shall forfeit and pay a penalty not exceeding 5l.

OXFORD

Has no special legislation. The justices have adopted word for word the rules laid down in "Oke's Formulist."

PLYMOUTH

Has no special legislation. There is only one theatre, which is the property of the corporation.

The JUSTICES' RULES are :—

1. The theatre shall be closed every Sunday, Christmas Day, Good Friday, and days appointed for a public fast and thanksgiving, and during Passion week.
2. The theatre shall be closed every Saturday night at the hour of half-past eleven.
3. Police constables when dressed in uniform, or other constables when not so dressed, if known as such to the manager or his servants, shall be permitted to have free ingress to and egress from the theatre at all times during the time of public performance.
4. The manager shall not permit or suffer any person in a state of drunkenness to enter the theatre, nor shall the manager permit or suffer any person found drunk or smoking or committing a breach of the peace or otherwise misbehaving or conducting himself or herself contrary to good rule, order, and decency, to remain in the theatre, but the said manager shall (whether upon complaint made to him or not) forthwith cause such person to be removed from the theatre.
5. The manager shall maintain and keep good order and decent and proper behaviour in every part of the theatre (on and off the stage).
6. For every breach of the above rules the manager shall forfeit and pay a penalty not exceeding twenty pounds.

PORTSMOUTH

Has no special legislation, but the plans of all new buildings have to be submitted for approval, and the construction and means of exit from any such building as a theatre are points which are considered.

ST. HELENS.

ST. HELENS IMPROVEMENT ACT, 1869 (32 & 33 Vict. c. cxx), provides:—

305. For the regulation of places for public dancing or music or other public entertainment of the like kind, the following provisions shall take effect, namely:— *Regulation of places for dancing, music, and other public entertainments.*

(1.) Any house or other place licensed for the sale of wine, spirits, beer, or other fermented or distilled liquors, or any room, garden, or place, shall not be kept or used for public dancing, music, or other public entertainment of the like kind without a licence for all or some of those purposes first obtained from the justices acting for the borough:

(2.) Such justices may, under the hands of a majority of them assembled at any special session convened by fourteen days' previous notice, grant licences to such persons as they think fit to keep or use houses, rooms, gardens, or places for all or some of the purposes aforesaid, upon such terms and conditions, and subject to such restrictions as they by the respective licences determine, and every licence shall be in force for one year:

(3.) Such justices may from time to time at any such special session as aforesaid transfer any such licence to such person as they think fit:

(4.) Each person shall in each case give seven days' notice to the clerk of the justices of his intention to apply for any such licence, or for the transfer of any such licence:

(5.) Any house, room, garden, or place kept and used for public dancing, music, or other public entertainment of the like kind without such licence first obtained, shall be deemed a disorderly house, and the person occupying or rated as the occupier of the same shall be liable to a penalty not exceeding five pounds for every day on which the same is kept and used for any of the purposes last aforesaid:

(6.) There shall be affixed and kept up in some conspicuous place on the door or entrance of every house, room, garden, or place so kept or used and so licensed as aforesaid, an inscription in large capital letters in the words following: "Licensed in pursuance of Act of Parliament":

(7.) Any house, room, garden, or place so kept or used, although so licensed as aforesaid, shall not be opened for any of the said purposes except between the hours stated in the licence:

(8.) The affixing and keeping up of such inscription as aforesaid, and the limitation of the hours of opening, shall be inserted in and made conditions of every such licence, and in case of any breach of either of those conditions such licence shall be liable to be revoked by the order of any two justices.

Power to enter upon unlicensed theatres, &c.

306. Any justice may by order in writing authorize any constable to enter into any building or part of a building, or any place kept or used, or suspected to be kept or used, for stage plays or dramatic entertainments into which admission is obtained by payment of money, and which is not a licensed theatre, at any time when the same is open for the reception of persons resorting thereto, and to take into custody any person found therein without lawful excuse; and every person keeping, using, or knowingly letting any building or part of a building, or any place for the purpose aforesaid, or any of them, shall be liable to a penalty not exceeding twenty pounds; and every person performing or being therein without lawful excuse, shall be liable to a penalty not exceeding forty shillings; and the burden of proving that any such place is a licensed theatre shall be upon the person keeping the same.

There are no bye-laws or justices' rules, but the FORM of the MUSIC LICENCE is as follows:—

MUSIC, &c. LICENCE.
In the Borough of Saint Helens:

At a special session of her Majesty's justices of the peace for the said borough of Saint Helens, held at the court room, Town Hall, in Saint Helens, in the same borough, on the ——— day of ——— 188—, for the purpose of granting licences for regulating places for public dancing or music, or other public entertainment of the like kind, under the provisions of sect. 305 of "The St. Helens Improvement Act, 1869."

We, the undersigned, being a majority of her Majesty's justices of the peace acting for the said borough at this special session, do hereby licence, authorize and empower ——— to have and keep open a certain ——— known as the ——— situated in the borough of Saint Helens aforesaid, for the purpose of being used for public dancing, music or other public entertainment of the like kind, upon and subject to the following conditions, viz. :—

The said ———— shall affix and keep up in some conspicuous place on the door or entrance of the said ———— an inscription in large capital letters in the words following: "Licensed in pursuance of Act of Parliament." The said ———— shall not be opened or used for the purposes aforesaid on Sundays, nor during the time on any other day when the premises licensed under the Licensing Acts relating to inns, alehouses and beerhouses, are directed by such Licensing Acts to be closed.

This licence shall be in force for one year from the date hereof.

SALFORD

Has no bye-law or justices' rules, but it is provided by The SALFORD IMPROVEMENT ACT, 1862 (25 & 26 Vict. c. ccv.).

286. No house, room or other place licensed for the sale of wine, spirits, beer or other fermented or distilled liquors, nor any room, gardens or place shall be kept or used for public dancing, music or other public entertainment of the like kind without a licence for all or some of those purposes first obtained from the justices acting for the borough; and such justices may under the hands and seals of a majority of them assembled at any special session convened by fourteen days' previous notice grant licences to such persons as they shall think fit to keep or use such rooms, gardens or places for public dancing, music or other public entertainment of the like kind upon such terms and conditions and subject to such restrictions as they shall by such licence determine, and such licence shall be in force for one year; and such justices may from time to time at any special session as aforesaid transfer any such licence to such person as they shall think fit; and such person shall in each case give seven days' notice to the clerk to the justices of his intention to apply for such licence or for the transfer of such licence. *Places for dancing, music, and other public entertainments to be licensed.*

287. Any house, room, garden or place kept and used for public dancing, music or other public entertainment of the like kind, without such licence first had and obtained, shall be deemed a disorderly house, and the person occupying or rated as the occupier of the same shall be liable to a penalty not exceeding five pounds for every day on which the same shall be kept and used for any of the purposes last aforesaid: *Penalty for keeping unlicensed dancing, &c., rooms.*

Provided always, that in order to give public notice what places are licensed pursuant to this Act there shall be affixed and kept up in some conspicuous place on the door or entrance of such house, room, garden or place kept or used for any of the said purposes, and so licensed as aforesaid, an inscription in large capital letters in the words following: "Licensed pursuant to Act of Parliament," and no such house, room, garden or place kept or used for any of the said purposes, although licensed as aforesaid, shall be opened for any of the said purposes, except between the hours stated in the licence, and the affixing and keeping up of such inscription as aforesaid, and the said limitation in point of time shall be inserted in and made conditions of every such licence; and in case of any breach of either of the said conditions such licence shall be liable to be forfeited and revoked by any two justices: Provided also, that it shall be lawful for every person who shall think himself aggrieved by any order of such justices to appeal therefrom to the quarter sessions in the manner and subject to the provisions hereinafter contained relative to appeals to quarter sessions from any order of justices.

Appeal to Quarter Sessions.

Power to enter upon unlicensed theatres and take away persons found there.

289. Any justice may by order in writing authorize any constable to enter into any building or part of a building or any place kept or used or suspected to be kept or used for stage plays or dramatic entertainments or for any public show or exhibition into which admission is obtained by payment of money, and which is not a licensed theatre, when the same shall be opened for the reception of persons resorting thereto, if any entertainment or exhibition is about to be commenced, or is or has been going on, and to take into custody all persons who shall be found therein without lawful excuse; and every person keeping, using or knowingly letting any building or any part of a building, or any place for the purposes aforesaid or any of them, shall be liable to a penalty not exceeding twenty pounds, and in default of payment of the penalty and costs may be imprisoned with or without hard labour for not exceeding two months; and every person performing or being therein without lawful excuse shall be liable to a penalty not exceeding forty shillings; and a conviction under this Act for this offence shall not exempt the owner, keeper or manager of any such building or part of a building or place from any other penalty or penal consequences to which he may be liable; provided that the onus of proving that such place is a licensed theatre shall be upon the person keeping the same.

SCARBOROUGH

Has no special legislation. The justices have no general rules, but deal with each case on its merits. It may be added that the corporation have lately inspected all the theatres, and have required important alterations, with a view to the public safety. In all cases the requirements of the corporation have been complied with.

SHEFFIELD.

The SHEFFIELD CORPORATION ACT OF 1883 (46 & 47 Vict. c. lvii.) provides:—

87. That, except as hereinafter mentioned, every building which, after the passing of this Act, is intended to be used as an hotel, church, chapel, school or place of public amusement or entertainment, or for holding a large number of persons for any purposes, and which shall not have been in use for those purposes at the time of the passing of this Act, shall be provided with ample and convenient means of ingress and egress, regard being had to the purposes for which such building is intended to be used, and the number of persons likely to be assembled at the same time therein, and it shall not be lawful for the owner or occupier or person in charge of such building to allow the same to be used for any such purpose as aforesaid unless and until he has obtained a certificate, under the hand of the town clerk and the borough surveyor, that the corporation are satisfied with the sufficiency of the means of ingress and egress provided at such building, and any person who, being the owner or occupier or person in charge of such building, shall permit the same to be used for any such purpose as aforesaid without having previously obtained such certificate shall for every such offence be liable to a penalty not exceeding fifty pounds.

Provided always, that any person who may be aggrieved by the withholding of the certificate of the town clerk and borough surveyor, or by an adverse decision of the corporation under this section, may appeal to the Court of quarter sessions for the borough as if the refusal were an order of a Court of summary jurisdiction, and section thirty-one of the Summary Jurisdiction Act, 1879, shall apply and have effect accordingly.

This section shall not apply in the case of any barracks, lunatic asylum, prison, hospital or railway station.

91. Subject to the provisions of this Act no house, room or other place licensed for the sale of wine, spirits, beer or other fermented or distilled liquors, nor any room, gardens or place shall be kept or used for public dancing, music, singing or other public entertainment of the like kind, without a licence for the respective purposes first obtained from the justices acting in the borough, and such justices may, under the hands and seals of a majority of them assembled at any special session for the granting or transfer of alehouse licences, grant licences to such persons as they shall think fit to keep or use such house, rooms, gardens or places for public dancing, music, singing or other entertainment of the like kind, upon such terms and conditions and subject to such restrictions as they shall by such licence determine, and such licence shall be in force for one year; and such justices may from time to time, at any such special session as aforesaid, transfer any such licence to such person as they shall think fit, and such person shall in each case give seven days' notice to the clerk to the justices and to the chief constable of his intention to apply for such licence, or for the transfer of such licence, and shall also during such seven days cause notice of his intention to be affixed and kept up on some conspicuous place on the door or entrance of the premises to be licensed. Provided always that, in order to give public notice what places are licensed pursuant to this Act, there shall be affixed and kept up in some conspicuous place on the door or entrance of such house, room, garden or place kept or used for any of the said purposes and so licensed as aforesaid, an inscription in large capital letters in the words following, "Licensed for ——— pursuant to Act of Parliament," and no such house, room, garden or place kept or used for any of the said purposes, although licensed as aforesaid, shall be opened for any of the said purposes except between the hours stated in the licence, and the affixing and keeping up of such inscription as aforesaid, and the observance of the hours of opening, shall be made conditions of every such licence, and provisions to that effect shall be inserted therein, and in case of any breach of either of the said conditions such licence shall be liable to be forfeited and revoked by any two justices (*a*).

92. The justices acting for the borough at any ordinary petty session may, on the application of the occupier of any house, room, or other place licensed for the sale of wine, spirits, beer or other fermented or distilled liquors, or of any room, gardens or place, grant a licence to such occupier to use the same for public dancing, music, singing or other public

---

(*a*) The form of music licence and the conditions are given below.

entertainment of the like kind for any particular day or night or days or nights, and upon such terms and conditions and subject to such restrictions as they shall think fit, and every such licence shall specify the particular day or night, days and nights, and the terms, conditions and restrictions for and upon which it is granted, and shall be signed by two at least of the said justices, and shall be called "an occasional licence," and every such occasional licence shall be in force only during the period for which it is granted.

Twenty-four hours' notice to the clerk to the justices of the intention to apply for such occasional licence shall be sufficient, and no other notice either of the intention to apply for such licence, or of the granting thereof, shall be required, and it shall not be obligatory to place such inscription as aforesaid on the door or entrance of the premises.

An occasional licence shall, while in force, be deemed equivalent to a licence granted under the last preceding section, but in case of any breach of the terms, conditions or restrictions specified therein the occupier of the premises in respect of which it was granted shall be liable to a penalty not exceeding ten pounds, and the licence, if granted for more than one day or night shall be liable to be forfeited and revoked by any two justices.

93. Any house, room, garden or place used for public dancing, music, singing or other public entertainment of the like kind without such licence or occasional licence, as the case may be, first had and obtained, shall be deemed a disorderly house, and the person occupying or rated as the occupier of the same shall be liable to a penalty not exceeding five pounds for every day on which the same shall be used for any of the purposes last aforesaid, and such person may, by order of the Court, be disqualified for obtaining any such licence as aforesaid during the period named in the order, but no proceedings for the recovery of such penalty or otherwise under this section shall be instituted except upon the information upon oath of a police constable.

95. Any justice may, by order in writing, authorize any constable to enter into any building, or part of a building, or any place kept or used, or suspected to be kept or used, for stage plays or dramatic entertainments, into which admission is obtained by payment of money, and which is not a licensed theatre, at any time when the same is opened for the reception of persons resorting thereto, and to take into custody any person found therein without lawful excuse. And every person keeping, using, or knowingly letting any building or part of a building, or any place for the purposes aforesaid, or

any of them, shall be liable to a penalty not exceeding twenty pounds, and every person performing or being therein without lawful excuse shall be liable to a penalty not exceeding forty shillings, and if the person charged alleges that the building, part of a building, or place is a licensed theatre the burden of proving that it is a licensed theatre shall be upon the person keeping the same.

96. Any constable shall have power by virtue of his office at any time to enter any premises or other place of the following description, viz.:— . . . .
   (2) Any place to which the public are admitted by payment, and used for the purpose of stage plays or dramatic, musical or other entertainments, or for any show, circus or exhibition :
   (3) Any music, singing or dancing saloon, hall or room, eating-house, coffee-house or other such place . . . .
and therein aid in the preservation of order and in the restoration of order, in case of disturbance, and in carrying into effect the provisions of this Act, and every occupier or keeper of any such premises or other place, or other person having charge thereof who shall not admit such constable when required shall be liable to a penalty not exceeding ten pounds.

Licence for Public Music, Public Singing, or for other Public Entertainment of the like kind to the above.

THE SHEFFIELD CORPORATION ACT, 1883.

At a special sessions for the transfer of alehouse licences, holden at the Town Hall, Sheffield, on the ———— day of ————, 188—, for the borough of Sheffield:

We, the undersigned, ————, of her Majesty's justices of the peace acting for the said borough, and being the majority of those at the said special sessions assembled,

Do hereby, pursuant to section 91 of "The Sheffield Corporation Act, 1883," grant to ————, of ————, in the said borough, ————, this licence to keep for public music and public singing, a room called the ————, in a house situate at ————, in the said borough, and known by the name or sign of the ————, and licensed for the sale of wine, spirits, and beer.

This licence shall be in force for one year from the date thereof, and is granted upon the terms and conditions, and subject to the restrictions following, that is to say :—

I.—That there shall be affixed and kept up on some

conspicuous place on the door or entrance of the said house, room, or place hereby licensed, and kept and used for any of the purposes aforesaid, an inscription in large capital letters in the words following: "Licensed for public music and public singing, pursuant to Act of Parliament."

II.—That the said house, room, or place shall not be opened for any of the said purposes, except between the hours of twelve at noon and eleven at night, ———, unless otherwise specially allowed by an occasional licence under the said Act.

III.—That the said house, room, or place hereby licensed shall not be opened for any of the purposes aforesaid on Sunday or Good Friday.

IV.—That drunkenness or other disorderly conduct shall not be permitted therein, nor shall any person be allowed to enter or continue therein when in a state of intoxication, nor shall prostitutes, reputed thieves, or persons of notoriously bad character be allowed to enter or continue therein.

V.—That there be no exhibition, recitation, acting, singing, or dancing which is of an obscene character, or is in any way offensive to public decency, or calculated to excite any breach of the peace, tumult, or disorder.

VI.—That no lottery, unlawful game, or gaming of any kind whatever shall be permitted therein.

VII.—That any police officer being on duty be allowed to enter and remain in the room during the time of public performance.

VIII.—That no young person under fourteen shall be admitted to any performance, unless accompanied by his or her parent or guardian, or some adult person in charge of such young person, and *bonâ fide* believed by the person hereby licensed to have the sanction of such parent or guardian.

IX.—That two justices of the said borough may at any time on complaint by a police officer of a breach of any of the foregoing terms, conditions, and restrictions, after summons to the person hereby licensed, by their order forfeit and revoke this licence, subject to such power of appeal as may be given by the said Act.

Given under our hands and seals, at the sessions aforesaid.

The Justices have made the following RULES :—

Borough of Sheffield, in the West Riding of Yorkshire. At a special session of the justices of the peace, in and for the borough of Sheffield, in the West Riding of Yorkshire, holden at the town-hall, in Sheffield, in the said borough, on the 21st day of September, in the year of our Lord 1849, for the purpose of making suitable rules for insuring order and decency at the several theatres licensed by the justices within the said borough, and for regulating the times during which they shall severally be allowed to be open.

Now we, the justices assembled at such special session as aforesaid, do hereby make the following rules for the purposes mentioned in the said recited Act, that is to say :—

    1st.—That the name and place of abode of the manager of every theatre shall be printed on every playbill announcing any representation at such theatre.

    2nd.—That every theatre shall be closed not later than twelve o'clock every night during the week, except on Saturday night, when the same shall be closed at half-past eleven o'clock.

    3rd.—That no theatre, within the said borough, shall be opened for the performance of stage plays, or for any purpose whatsoever, on any occasion when the magistrates, in petty sessions assembled, may signify their desire, in writing, to the manager, or other person having at the time the care and management of such theatre, that the same should not be opened ; nor shall any theatre be so opened during Passion week, or on Christmas Day or Good Friday, or any fast day, or day appointed for a public thanksgiving.

    4th.—That two policemen, to be approved of by two magistrates, in writing, shall be kept on duty at every theatre during all the time for which the same shall on any evening or night be open, and the expense thereof shall be paid and borne by the manager of the theatre.

    5th.—That no play, prologue, epilogue, or interlude, or any act, scene, or part thereof, shall be acted or represented in any theatre, after the manager, for the time being, shall have been served with notice, in writing, signed by two of her Majesty's justices of the peace, acting for the said borough, requiring the same to be again submitted to the Lord Chamberlain for his opinion, whether it is fitting for the preservation of good manners, decorum, or of the public peace, to forbid the acting or representing thereof.

6th.—That no common prostitute, reputed thief, or other notoriously disorderly person shall be knowingly admitted into, or permitted to remain in any theatre.

7th.—That the manager of every theatre shall, as far as in him lies, preserve the peace, and maintain good and decent order and behaviour therein at all times.

Given under our hands at the special session aforesaid.

SHREWSBURY.

The JUSTICES' RULES are as follows :—

1. The theatre shall be closed every Saturday night at the hour of half-past eleven.

2. No spirituous liquors, wine, ale, beer, porter, cider, perry or tobacco shall be sold or disposed of in the theatre or upon the premises.

3. Police constables when dressed in uniform, or other constables when not so dressed, if known as such to the manager or his servants, shall be permitted to have free ingress and egress to and from the theatre at all times during the time of public performance.

4. The manager shall, to the best of his ability, manage and keep good order and decent behaviour in the theatre during the hours of public performance.

5. For every breach of the above rules the manager shall forfeit and pay a penalty not exceeding five pounds.

STOKE-UPON-TRENT.

The following RULES have been made by the Justices for Staffordshire acting in the Petty Sessional Division of Pirehill North, in which Stoke-upon-Trent is situated. There is no theatre in the town, but the Town Hall is licensed under 6 & 7 Vict. c. 68 :—

RULES.

1. The theatre shall be closed every Sunday, Christmas Day, Good Friday, and days appointed for a public fast and thanksgiving.

2. The theatre shall be closed every Saturday night at the hour of half-past eleven.

3. No spirituous liquors, wine, ale, beer, porter, cider, perry or tobacco shall be sold or disposed in the theatre or upon the premises.

4. Police constables when dressed in uniform, or other constables when not so dressed, if known as such to the manager or his servants, shall be permitted to have ingress to the theatre at all times during the time of public performance.

5. The manager shall to the best of his ability maintain and keep good order and decent behaviour in the theatre during the hours of public performance.

6. For every breach of the above rules the manager shall forfeit and pay a penalty not exceeding five pounds.

SWANSEA.

SWANSEA MUNICIPAL CORPORATION ACT, 1863 (26 Vict. c. xiii.), provides—

52. No house, room, booth or other place within the borough shall be kept or used for public dancing, music, dramatic or other public entertainment without a licence first had and obtained from the justices of the peace having jurisdiction within the borough (which said licence such justices are hereby authorized and empowered at their discretion to grant) on their general annual licensing day, and under the hands and seals of a majority of the justices then assembled; and any house, room, garden or place kept and used for such purposes as aforesaid, without such licence first had and obtained, shall be deemed a disorderly house; and the person occupying or rated as the occupier of the same shall, on conviction before any two justices, be liable to a penalty not exceeding ten pounds for every day on which he shall so offend: Provided always, that in order to give public notice what places are licensed pursuant to this Act there shall be affixed and kept up in some conspicuous place on the door or entrance of such house, room, garden or place kept or used for any of the said purposes and so licensed as aforesaid an inscription in large capital letters of such dimensions as shall be prescribed in such licence, in the words following: "Licensed pursuant to Act of Parliament," and no such house, room, garden or place kept or used for any of the said purposes, although licensed as aforesaid, shall be opened for any of the said purposes, except between the hours stated in the licence; and the affixing and keeping up of such inscription

as aforesaid, and the said limitation in point of time shall be inserted in and made conditions of every such licence; and in case of any breach of either of the said conditions such licence shall be liable to be forfeited and revoked by the justices of the peace having jurisdiction within the borough at any subsequent general annual licensing day or some adjournment therefrom: Provided also, that it shall be lawful for every person who shall think himself aggrieved by any order of such justices to appeal therefrom to the general quarter sessions of the peace for the county of Glamorgan, which court shall have power to hear and determine the same, and the order of the said court therein shall be final.

53. The corporation from time to time may make such bye-laws, rules and regulations as they think fit for the good government and management of any house, room, garden or place licensed under this Act for public dancing, music or other entertainment, and for the prevention of disorderly conduct therein, and may impose penalties for the breach or non-observance thereof not exceeding five pounds for each offence.

The power to make bye-laws given to the local authority by sect. 53 has not been exercised by them.

WAKEFIELD.

By the WAKEFIELD IMPROVEMENT ACT (40 & 41 Vict. c. cxcviii.) it is provided:—

77. No house, room, garden or place within the borough shall be kept or used for public dancing or music without a licence first had and obtained from the justices of the peace for the borough (which said licence such justices are hereby authorized and empowered, at their discretion, to grant) on their general annual licensing day, and under the hands and seals of a majority of the justices then assembled, and any house, room, garden or place kept and used for any such purposes as aforesaid without such licence first had and obtained shall be deemed a disorderly house, and the person occupying or rated as the occupier of the same shall on conviction before any two justices be liable to a penalty not exceeding ten pounds for every day on which he shall so offend: Provided always that, in order to give public notice what places are licensed pursuant to this Act, there shall be affixed and kept up in some conspicuous place on the door or entrance of every house, room, garden or place kept or used for any of the said purposes, and so licensed as aforesaid, an inscription in large capital letters, of such dimensions as shall be prescribed in such licence, in the words following: "Licensed pursuant to Act of Parliament;" and no such house, room, garden or place kept or used for any of the said purposes, although licensed as aforesaid, shall be opened for any of the said purposes except between the hours stated in the licence, and the affixing and keeping up of such inscription as aforesaid, and the said limitation in point of time shall be inserted in and made conditions of every such licence; and in case of any breach of any of the said conditions of any such licence, such licence shall be liable to be forfeited and revoked by the justices of the peace for the borough at any general annual licensing day, or some adjournment therefrom, or to be suspended and temporarily revoked until the next general annual licensing day by two justices in petty sessions assembled in any case in which it shall be proved to the satisfaction of such justices that more than one breach of such conditions has occurred since the granting of such licence: Provided also, that it shall be lawful for every person who shall think himself aggrieved by any order of any such justices to appeal therefrom to the High Court of Justice (which Court shall have power to hear and determine the same), whose order thereon shall be final.

Under the same Act the corporation have made the following BYE-LAWS, which, however, have not as yet been approved:—

BOROUGH OF WAKEFIELD.

Suggested Bye-Laws to be made under the Wakefield Improvement Act, 1877, for the Regulation of places Licensed for Public Dancing or Music.

1. No room in any house or building shall be kept or used for public dancing or music which shall contain less than 5,000 cubic feet of space, and which shall be less than 12 feet from the floor of such room to the ceiling thereof.

2. The number of persons admitted into any licensed room whilst the same is being used for public dancing or music shall not be more than will allow in the part of such room not used or occupied by musicians or dancers, less than 9 square feet of floor space for each person so admitted.

3. No house, room, garden or place licensed for public dancing or music shall be used for such purposes on any Sunday, Christmas Day or Good Friday, or on any day

appointed for a public fast or thanksgiving, or on any polling day fixed for the election of a member for the borough, or for the election of any person to any "corporate office" as defined by the Municipal Corporation Act, 1882.

4. No house, room, garden or place licensed for public dancing or music shall be used for such purposes or either of them, before seven, nor after eleven o'clock in the evening.

5. No singing in dress differing from ordinary costume, and no stage performance or representation in character, shall be allowed in any such licensed house, room, garden, or place.

6. No person under sixteen years of age shall be admitted into any room licensed for public dancing or music situate in or adjoining any premises licensed for the sale of wine, spirits, beer, or other fermented or distilled liquors.

7. No person holding a music or dancing licence shall allow any drunken or disorderly person, common prostitute, convicted thief, or person of notoriously bad character to remain in the room or place for which he or she holds the licence.

8. Every person intending to apply to the justices for a licence shall, twenty-one days at the least before he applies, give notice of his intention to the chief constable and also to the borough surveyor, for the time being of the borough; and shall in such notice set forth his name and address, and describe the house, room, garden or place for which the application is made, and shall at the same time furnish a statement showing the size and dimensions of the room for which the licence is about to be applied.

9. No house, room, garden or place shall be licensed for public dancing or music unless the same shall be provided with ample and convenient means of ingress and egress respectively, to be approved by the corporation.

10. The inscription "Licensed pursuant to Act of Parliament" required by the seventy-seventh section of "The Wakefield Improvement Act," to be affixed and kept up in some conspicuous place on the door or entrance of every house, room, garden, or place kept or used for the purpose of dancing or music, and so licensed, shall be in capital letters of not less dimension than 1¼ inch in height, and such inscription shall at all times during the continuance of licence be kept uncovered and unobliterated.

11. The holder of a licence for music or dancing shall at all times freely admit into the house, room, garden, or place for which such licence is held any police constable who shall at the time be on duty, and whether such constable be in uniform or plain clothes.

12. Every person offending against any of the bye-laws hereinbefore set forth, shall forfeit and pay for every such

T. P

offence, such a sum of money, not exceeding five pounds, as shall be imposed by any two or more justices of the peace having jurisdiction in the matter, before whom the person offending shall be summoned for any such offence as aforesaid.

WOLVERHAMPTON.

The Wolverhampton Improvement Act (32 & 33 Vict. c. cxxxi.) provides—

262. For the regulation of places for public dancing and music or other public entertainment of the like kind, the following provisions shall take effect, namely:

(1.) A house, room or other place licensed for the sale of wine, spirits, beer or other fermented or distilled liquors, or a room, garden or place shall not be kept or used for public dancing, music or other place of public entertainment of the like kind without a licence for all or some of those purposes first obtained from the justices acting for the borough:

(2.) Such justices may, under the hands of a majority of them assembled at any special session convened by fourteen days' previous notice, grant licences to such persons as they think fit to keep or use houses, rooms, gardens or places for all or some of the purposes aforesaid, upon such terms and conditions and subject to such restrictions as they by the respective licences determine; and every licence shall be in force for one year:

(3.) Such justices may from time to time, at any such special session aforesaid transfer any such licence to such person as they think fit:

(4.) Each person shall in each case give seven days' notice to the clerk of the justices of his intention to apply for any such licence, or for the transfer of any such licence:

(5.) Any house, room, garden or place kept and used for public dancing, music or other public entertainment of the like kind without such licence first obtained shall be deemed a disorderly house, and the person occupying or rated as the occupier of the same shall be liable to a penalty not exceeding five pounds for every day on which the same is kept and used for any of the purposes last aforesaid:

(6.) There shall be affixed and kept up in some conspicuous place on the door or the entrance of every house, room, garden or place so kept or used, or so licensed as aforesaid, an inscription in large capital letters in the words following: " Licensed in pursuance of Act of Parliament":

(7.) Any house, room, garden or place so kept or used, although so licensed as aforesaid, shall not be opened for any of the said purposes except between the hours stated in the licence :*

(8.) The affixing and keeping up of such inscription as aforesaid and the limitation of the hours of opening shall be inserted in and made conditions of every such licence; and in case of any breach of either of those conditions such licence shall be liable to be revoked by the order of any two justices.

* By conditions imposed under sub-sect. 2, music-halls may be kept open from one o'clock till eleven and four times in the year until two o'clock in the morning, on twenty-four hours' notice being given to the chief constable of the said borough. Boys under sixteen are not to be admitted unless in charge of their parents or guardians.

The justices have no regulations with regard to theatres or music halls, but that the following are the conditions upon which licences are granted :—

The theatre shall be closed every night at eleven, and every Sabbath, Christmas Day and Thanksgiving Day.

Police constables when dressed in uniform, and when not so dressed, if known as such to manager, shall be permitted to have free ingress to the theatre at all times during the hours of public performance. Manager to preserve decent order and behaviour at all times during the performance.

WORCESTER

Has no special legislation.

The JUSTICES' RULES are :—

1. The theatre shall be closed every Sunday, Christmas Day and Good Friday, and days appointed for a public fast and thanksgiving.

2. The theatre shall be closed every Saturday night at not later than the hour of half-past eleven.

3. Police constables when dressed in uniform, or other

constables when not so dressed, if known as such to the manager or his servants, shall be permitted to have free ingress to the theatre at all times during the time of public performance.

4. The manager shall, to the best of his ability, maintain and keep good order and decent behaviour in the theatre during the hours of public performance.

5. For every breach of the above rules the **manager** shall forfeit and pay a penalty of not exceeding five pounds.

INDEX.

ABERDEEN, 161

ACTION, representation of, is a test of stage play, 18
limitation of [*see* LIMITATION]

ADJOURNED SESSION, no music licence to be granted at, 53

ADMISSION,
no charge for, 18, 49, 51
of public indiscriminate, 47, 48
right to give free, 113
right of, must be granted by deed, 65 *et seq.*

AESCHYLUS' drama represented is a stage play, 18

AFFIXING ON DOOR [*see* NOTICE]

AGREEMENT, form of, 119

AIR, fresh, means of supplying, 30

ALIMENTARY, salary of comedian is, 119

AMATEURS, 17, 18

ANCILLARY, music, to purpose [*see* PURPOSE]

APPEAL,
from Lord Chamberlain, 24, 25
justices, 33
Commissioners, 30

APPLICATION for licence, 31
form of, 192

ARBITRATION as to structure, 40
[*see* PRECEDENT, 121]

ARCHITECT of Metropolitan Board, 40, 41

ARREARS of salary, 115

ARREST, right to, 42, 45, 46, 56, 131, 132, 135

ASSAULT, 131, 132, 138

BALL ROOM, public, 41

BALLET D'ACTION
    is stage play, 21, 22
    divertissement is not, 21, 22
        does not require licence, 23

BAND may be a nuisance, 57

BANKRUPTCY of performer, 117

BATH, patent theatre at, 26

BEATING a performer no cause of action for manager, 126

BENEFIT must be asked for, 113

BIRKENHEAD, 164

BIRMINGHAM, 168

BLACKBURN, 169

BLACKFRIARS THEATRE, 4, 6

BOLTON, 169

BOOTH,
    is not a theatre, 15
    police can remove, 42

BOX,
    right of admission must be secured by deed, 67 *et seq.*
    rateable as a tenement, 78

BRANDRAM'S, Mr., recitals are stage plays, 23

BRIGHTHELMSTONE, 9, 10, 29, 172

BRIGHTON, 9, 10, 29, 172
    Aquarium, 37, 38

BRISTOL, patent theatre at, 26

BUILDING,
    public, what is, 41
    structural efficiency of, 29, 33, note (*f*), 38

BURBAGE, 4

BURLETTA is stage play, 18, 22

BURNING in ear [*see* WHIPPING]

BYE-LAWS must be reasonable, 33

CAMBRIDGE, 7, 10, 28, 29, 173

CANTERBURY Theatre of Varieties, 23

CARAVAN,
    illegal to exhibit in, 30, 45
    is not a theatre, 15
    offence to perform in, 35
    police may remove, 42

CARDIFF, 54, 173

CARRIAGE [see TRAFFIC and OBSTRUCTION]

CATHOLIC DRAMA, 7

CAUSING performance, 34, 35

CENSORSHIP [see CHAMBERLAIN and STAGE PLAY]

CHAMBERLAIN, Lord, jurisdiction over theatres, 4, 8, 10, 12, 13, 27, 28, 29
    censorship of plays, 23, 24, 25

CHANCELLOR of Universities, 29

CHANGING SEAT, 74, 75

CHARACTER, inquiry into, 32, note (e), 39
    private, of performer, no ground for hissing, 138

CHARITY, performance for, 17

CHESTER, 174

CHILD under 14 [see DANGEROUS PERFORMANCE]

CHURCH, acting in, 1

CIRCUS, 48 (b)

CLAPPING may be nuisance, 38

CLOSING THEATRE, 28, 32, 33
    on Sunday [see SUNDAY]

COLET DEAN, 1, 3

COLLIER, PAYNE, MR., 25

COMEDIAN, 13

COMEDY is stage play, 18

COMMUNICATION, internal, with theatre, 43

COMPLETION of theatre, 40

CONSECUTIVE train of ideas test of stage play, 21

CONSENT of father to engagement of child, 110

CONSPIRACY,
    to hiss actor is actionable, 135, 136
    to seduce actress is indictable, 138

CONSTABLE [see ARREST—POLICE]

CONVERTING theatre to non-theatrical purposes, 75

COPY,
    of play to be sent to Lord Chamberlain, 23
    of rules to be annexed to licence, 32

COPYRIGHT ACTS, 19

CORRIDORS, 41

COSTS, no jurisdiction of justices to give, 35

COVENT GARDEN,
    a patent theatre, 8, 9, 10, 26, 55
    Promenade Concerts at, 27

CRITERION THEATRE, 43

CROWD assembling and remaining is nuisance, 57

CUSTOM, theatrical, 116

DAGGER DANCE is a stage play, 21

DANCING,
    may be a stage play, 21
    what is, 47, 49, 50
    master holding classes, 47

DANGER, special, from fire, 40

DANGEROUS PERFORMANCE, 38

DAVENANT, 7

DEBENTURE HOLDERS, 71, 72

DECORUM,
    reason for forbidding stage play, 24, 25
    rules for maintaining, 28, 32

DEED under seal, 65

DERBY, 176

DESTRUCTION by fire, 61, 62

DISCRETION,
    as to licensing theatre qualified, 28, 32, *Add.*
        music hall absolute, 53

DISMISSING,
    manager, 113
    performer, 114

DISORDERLY,
    conduct, permitting, 42
    house, 45, 56

DOOR, notice over [*see* NOTICE]

DOVER, 177

DRAMATIC,
    piece, 19, 20
    entertainment, place of, 18

DRESS, regulating, 24

DRUNKENNESS,
    permitting, 42
    as self-imposed illness, 84

DRURY LANE THEATRE, 8, 10, 55, 73, 78

DUBLIN, 13, 71

DUOLOGUE is stage play, 20

DURATION,
    of licence, 10, 54
    of season, 109

EAR, burning in, 4

EJECTING spectator, 66, 67, 131

ELSEWHERE, not to perform, 96 *et seq.*

EMOTIONS, excitement of, test of stage play, 20

EMPLOYER, liability of [*see* DANGEROUS PERFORMANCE]

ENTER, power to, 41, 44, 45, 56

218 INDEX.

ENTERTAINMENT,
   of the stage, 19
   other like, 50

ENTICING away performer, 128

ESSENTIAL part of play, 23

EXAMINER of plays, 24, 25

EXCISE LICENCE, 43, 44

EXCITEMENT of emotions, 18

EXHIBITION, 30, 31, 37, 138 [see INDECENT]

EXPENDITURE, moderate, 40

FAIR, lawful, what is, 35, 42
   performing at, 16, 30

FARCE is stage play, 18

FATHER consenting not actionable, 110, 111

FEE for play, 24
   theatre licence, 27

FENCING is not stage play, 19

FIELD, performing in, 16, 35

FIELDING, 9, 12

FINES must be reasonable, 111, 112

FINSBURY, borough of, 27

FIRE, regulations for preventing, 38, 39, 40, 157
   destruction by, 62, 77

FIREPROOF materials, 41 [see FLOORS]

FIREWORKS may be nuisance, 57

FIRST NIGHT, attendance at, material, 94, 95

FLOORS of lobbies, &c., to be of fireproof material, 41

FOLKESTONE, 178

FRANCHISE, licensing of play became, 3

FRIVOLOUS and vexatious defence, 117

GAIETY THEATRE, 43

GALLERIES, 41

GENERAL SESSIONS, 33

GERMAN REED's entertainment is stage play, 23

GLASGOW, 178

GRATUITOUS loan of theatre, 16, 17, 18
    music, 48, 50

HABITUAL music, 48, 49

HAMESUCKEN, 138

HARM, bodily, 38

HASTINGS, 180

HAYMARKET THEATRE, 8, 27, 55, 60

HEYWOOD, JOHN, 2, 5, 6

HIRE, performing for, 16

HISSING, as disapproval of actor, lawful, 132 *et seq.*
    conspiracy for unlawful, 136

HOARSENESS, temporary, 114

HOMERIC DRAMAS are stage play, 18

HORN or noisy instrument, 46

HOURS of opening, 42, 57

ILLNESS of performer, 84, 86, 90, 118

IMPRISONMENT, 45

IMPROVE, covenant to, 60, 61

INCIDENTAL music to performance, 48, note (*b*)

INCOME, appropriation of, 119

INCOMPETENCE of performer, 114

INDECENT REPRESENTATION, 31, 45, 138

INDISCRIMINATE ADMISSION, 47, 48

INFORMER, common, 36, 37, 56

INJUNCTION, 58, 96, 97

INJURIOUS conduct of manager, 113

INJURY very small, 106, 107

INTENTION to make performer break contract, 126, 127

INTERESTED person may apply, 39

INTERLUDE is a stage play, 18

INTERNAL communication, 43

INTRODUCTION to pantomime is dramatic piece, 19

IRELAND, 13, 38

IRON BUILDING, 15

JUSTICES,
    discretion, 32
    jurisdiction, 29
    power of making rules, 33

KILLIGREW, 8

KING'S SERVANTS, 3, 8

KNOWLEDGE of owner of music-hall, 49, 51

LAKE, SIR F., 2

LAMBETH, borough of, 27

LANDINGS, 41

LEASE, covenants in, 60, 61

LECTURE, with scenery and footlights, is stage play, 22

LEEDS, 181

LEGITIMATE DRAMA, 9

LEICESTER, 186

LIBELLING performer, 125

LICENCE,
    excise, 44
    music, 52
    parol, is revocable, 65, 66 *et seq.*
    provisional, 39
    of stage play, 23
    of theatre, 25, 31

LIKE KIND, entertainment of, 50

LIMITATION of action, 37, 57

LINCOLN'S INN THEATRE, 6, note (*u*), 8

LIQUOR, sale of, 16, 17, 33, 42, 43, 44

LIVERPOOL, 26, 188

LOBBIES, 41 [*see* FLOORS]

LONDON,
    city of, 27
    stage, 104, 105

MACKLIN, 135

MANAGER,
    actual responsible, 23, 25, 26, 27, 31, 34
    misconduct of, 113

MANCHESTER, 189

MANDAMUS, 33

MARKET, performing at, 30

MARYLEBONE, borough of, 27

MELODRAMA is a stage play, 18

METROPOLIS, what is, 26

METROPOLITAN BOARD OF WORKS, 39, 157

MICHAELMAS QUARTER SESSIONS, 52

MIRACLE PLAY, 1

MISCONDUCT, dismissing manager for, 113

MODERATE EXPENDITURE, 40

MONEY, taking, 16, 18, 48, 49

MONOPOLY, 11

MUSIC HALL, what is, 47 *et seq.*

NEIGHBOURHOOD may proceed against theatre as a nuisance, 57, 58

NOISE, 46, 57, 58

NOON, music hall may not open before, 55

NORTHAMPTON, 192

NORWICH, 190

NOTICE,
    of illness, 84 *et seq.*
    on door, 50, 51, 55
    to performer, 112

NUISANCE,
    theatre may be, 6, 38, 57
    obscene play may be, 45, 138

O. P. RIOTS, 132

OBSCENE REPRESENTATION, 31, 45

OBSTRUCTION, in streets, 30, 45

OCCASIONAL performance,
    in theatre requires licence, 16
    in music hall does not, 48, 49
    in residence of her Majesty, 27, 29

OLDHAM, 193

ONUS PROBANDI [*see* PROOF]

OPEN-AIR CIRCUS, 57

OPERA is stage play, 18

ORCHESTRA, noise of, 38

ORDINARY HABITS OF LIFE, 38, 58

OSBORNE, 29

OWNER, 40, note (*t*)

OXFORD, 10, 28, 29, 193

PANTOMIME is stage play, 18, 19, 22

PARISH, 27, 29

PARTNERSHIP in unlicensed theatre, 62, 63, 64, 81

PASSAGES, 41

PATENT THEATRES, 8, 11, 26
    performances at, 26, 27, 55, 56

PAYMENT, 16, 49

PENALTY,
    for Sunday performance, 37
    unlicensed music hall, 56
            stage play, 25
            theatre, 24
    who can sue for, 36

PIT FULL, 131

PLACE where her Majesty resides, 27

PLAY,
    bill, name of manager printed on, 26
    house pay, 115, 116, 122
    stage, 18 *et seq.*

PLYMOUTH, 194

POLICE, 30, 31, 42, 44, 45

PORTABLE THEATRE, 15

PORTSMOUTH, 194

POSTPONING PIECE, 95

PRECEDENTS,
    of ordinary performer's agreement, 119
    of Mr. Wilson Barrett's agreement, 121

PRECONCERTED DESIGN TO HISS, 134, 137

PRIVATE HOUSE,
    music in, 49, 51
    performing in, 7, 16, 17
    theatricals, 17

PROFANE SONG, 30, 45

PROFITS, proving loss of, 126

PROMENADE CONCERTS,
    require music licence, 27

PROOF, burden of, 16, 17, 35, 50, 51, 52, 80

PROSTITUTE,
    conspiracy to, 138
    harbouring, 31, 43

PROVISIONAL LICENCE, 39

PRYNNE, 6, 12

PUBLIC, 47, 48
    building, 41
    entertainment, 29, 30
    of like kind, 50
    resort, 30, 42

PURITAN influence, 7, 11

PURPOSE,
    music of house, 48, 49, 50
    illegal, invalidates contract, 62, 63
    converting to untheatrical, 75, 76
    of preventing performance, 126, 127, 128

QUARTER SESSIONS, 33

RATEABILITY of box, 78

REAL BURDEN, 77

REASONABLE fines and regulations, 112
    rules of justices, 33

REFLECTED PLAY, 22

REFUSAL to grant licence, 33
    to perform, 80, 117

REGULATIONS [see RULES]

REHEARSAL, 89

RELIGIOUS DRAMA, 1, 2
    service at theatre, 75

REMOTE DAMAGE, 127

REMOVING spectators, 67, 68

RENTALLERS, 77, 78

RENTER, LIFE, 73, 74, 75

REPRESENTATION, causing, 35
    of action, test of stage play, 18, 20

RETURN PASS, 42

REVELS, master of, 4

REVOCATION of licence, 24, 28, 29, 57, 65

RICHMOND, 9, 10

RINKING to music is dancing, 50

RIOT, 28, 32, 134

ROBIN HOOD, 23

ROOF, 41

RULES,
    of justices, 32, 33, 43
    of theatre, 111, 112
    of Mr. Wilson Barrett, 122
    of Metropolitan Board of Works, 157

ST. HELENS, 195

SALFORD, 197

SCARBOROUGH, 199

SCOTLAND, 3, 12, 13, 35, 119, 138

SEASON fixed by proprietor, 109 [see also 61]

SECRETARY of State, 32, 40

SEDUCE actress, conspiracy to, indictable, 138
    performer from engagement, 128 et seq.

SERVANT, performer is, 128, 129
    responsibility for acts of, 43

SERVANTS, King's, 3, 8

SESSION [see GENERAL, QUARTER, SPECIAL]

SHAKESPEARE's plays, 3

SHEFFIELD, 199

SHOREDITCH THEATRE, 4

SHREWSBURY, 205

SINGING out of tune, 114

SONG may be dramatic piece, 19

SOUTHWARK, borough of, 27

SPECIAL SESSION, 31

STAGE PLAY,
    censorship of, 23, 24, 25
    what is, 18

STAIRS, 41

STATUTES,
    34 & 35 Hen. VIII. c. 1..2
    1 Ed. VI. c. 1..2
    1 Eliz. c. 2..3
    14 Eliz. c. 5..4
    39 Eliz. c. 4..5
    3 Jac. I. c. 21..3
    1 Car. I. c. 1..3, 37
    10 Geo. II. c. 19..10
        c. 28..4, 5, 9, 19, 22, 34, 36, 64, 79, 82
    17 Geo. II. c. 5..5
    25 Geo. II. c. 36..8, 9, 12, 26, note, 27, 32, note, 37, 47,
        50, 53, 56, 141

STATUTES—*continued*
 28 Geo. II. c. 19..47
 8 Geo. III. c. 10..10
 10 Geo. III. c. 75..78
 11 Geo. III. c. 16..10
 18 Geo. III. c. 8..10
 21 Geo. III. c. 49..37, 38
 28 Geo. III. c. 30..5, 10, 82, *Add.*
 1 Geo. IV. c. clx..73, 74
 5 Geo. IV. c. 83..5
 9 Geo. IV. c. 61..32, note
 3 & 4 Will. IV. c. 15..11, 18, 19, 20
 5 & 6 Will. IV. c. 39..43, 44
 2 & 3 Vict. c. 47..15, 42, 43, 44, 45
 5 & 6 Vict. c. 45..19, 20
 6 & 7 Vict. c. 68..11, 15, 144
    s. 2..15, 18, 25, 26, 34
    s. 3..27, 29
    s. 4..27
    s. 5..31
    s. 7..25, 26, 27, 31
    s. 8..28
    s. 9..32, 33
    s. 10..29
    s. 11..15, 16, 26, 34, 35
    s. 12..23
    s. 13..23, 24
    s. 14..24
    s. 15..25
    s. 16..16
    s. 17..35
    s. 19..35
    s. 20..33
    s. 21..35, 37
    s. 22..37
    s. 23..18, 20, 22, 35
 10 & 11 Vict. c. 84..29, 30
    c. 89..30, 31
 11 & 12 Vict. c. 44..33
 18 & 19 Vict. c. 120..20, note, 40, note
    c. 122..40, note, 41, 150
 24 & 25 Vict. c. 134..118
 25 & 26 Vict. c. ccxxiii..54, 173
 31 & 32 Vict. c. 106..42
 32 & 33 Vict. c. 71..119
 35 & 36 Vict. c. 94..44
 37 & 38 Vict. c. 69..44
 38 & 39 Vict. c. 21..55

STATUTES—*continued*
    38 & 39 Vict. c. 55..30
               c. 80..38
    41 & 42 Vict. c. 32..38, 39, 40, 41, 151
    42 & 43 Vict. c. 34..38, 154
    43 & 44 Vict. c. 20..44
    45 Vict. c. 14..42
    46 & 47 Vict. c. 52..118, 119

STOKE-UPON-TRENT, 205

STONE floors and stairs, 41

STORY, dramatic, 21, 22

STREETS, obstructing, 30, 45

STROLLING PLAYER, 4, 5

STRUCTURE, 29, 30, 32, note, 38

SUBSCRIBERS, dance of, 48

SUBSIDIARY purpose, 48

SUBSTITUTE, engaging, 96, 111, 112

SUNDAY, 37

SUPPORTS, 41

SURETY to manager, 27, 28, 31

SURVEYOR, district, 41

SUSPENDING licence, 28, 29

SWANSEA, 206

TEMPLE, performances at, 6, 7

TEMPORARY BOOTH, 15, and note, 16
    crowd at door, 57

THEATRE, what is, 15

THIEVES, harbouring, 31, 43

TICKET,
    for box or stall, 67, 68
    sale of, 17, 18 [*see* SUBSCRIBERS]
    seller of, 37

TIME of opening, 42, 55 [*see* DURATION]

TOWER HAMLETS, borough of, 27

TRAFFIC, 30, 45

TRAGEDY is stage play, 18

TUMBLING is not stage play, 19

UNITED STATES, 13

UNIVERSITIES, 10 [*see* CAMBRIDGE and OXFORD]

UNLICENSED,
    music-hall, 56
    theatre, 34
        contracts as to, 37, 62, 78, 79, 81
        arresting, 44, 45

VACATION, 116 [*see* SEASON]

VAGABONDS, 4, 12, 80

VAUDEVILLE THEATRE, 40, note

VENTILATION, 30

VICE, the, 2

VICTUALLER, 49

WAKEFIELD, 207

WALLS, 41

WARRANT, arrest without, 46, 135

WESTMINSTER, city of, 27

WHIPPING, 4

WINDSOR, 9, 10, 29

WOLVERHAMPTON, 210

Wood, theatre of, 15, 41

Worcester, 211

Writing not essential to constitute stage play, 23

Year, licence for, 54, 55

York's, Duke of, servants, 8

www.ingramcontent.com/pod-product-compliance
Lightning Source LLC
Chambersburg PA
CBHW031738230426
43669CB00007B/398